HOOSIER FOLK LEGENDS

HOOSIER
FOLK LEGENDS

Ronald L. Baker

INDIANA UNIVERSITY PRESS
Bloomington

Library of Congress Cataloging in Publication Data
Main entry under title:

Hoosier folk legends.

　　　1.　Legends—Indiana.　　I. Baker, Ronald L.
GR110.I6H66　　　398.2'09772　　　81–47568
　　　　　　　　　　　　　　　　　　　　　AACR2

ISBN 0-253-32844-6 cloth
ISBN 0-253-20334-1 paper

9 10 00 99

For Cathy, Jill, and Jon

CONTENTS

Death and Burial

Ghosts

Contents

Haunted Houses

Good and Evil

Special Powers

Witches

Contents

Monsters and Snakes

2. PERSONAL LEGENDS

Famous People

Contents

3. PLACE LEGENDS

Bottomless Lakes

Contents

Hoosier: Origin of the State Nickname

Place-Name Legends

Contents

4. MODERN LEGENDS

Legends Nourished by the Automobile

Contents

Contents

Hairdos, Cosmetics, Pills, and Drugs

Occupations

UFO's

HOOSIER FOLK LEGENDS

INTRODUCTION

Legends are among the most fascinating genres of folklore, for they are timeless and universal forms of oral tradition. Legends reach back to antiquity, and they still survive in our highly industrialized modern society. While some legends have disappeared over the years, new legends constantly are being created. The old legends that have survived generally have been changed a great deal, for legends are readily influenced by changes in historical, social, and economic conditions. Since legends are of endless variety in content, length, and form, they virtually defy definition. Following the example of the Grimm Brothers, who introduced legend scholarship in the early nineteenth century, most folklorists continue to define legends by distinguishing them from other kinds of traditional oral prose narratives. In *Teutonic Mythology*, Jacob Grimm writes:

> The folktale [*Märchen*] is with good reason distinguished from the legend, though by turns they play into one another. Looser, less fettered than legend, the folktale lacks that local habitation which hampers legend, but makes it more home-like. The folktale flies, the legend walks, knocks at your door; the one can draw freely out of the fulness of poetry, the other has almost the authority of history. . . . [1]

Jacob Grimm recognized the important qualities of the legend that set it apart from other kinds of folktales. Legends,

1

often short and formless with little narrative quality, generally are not as artistic as *Märchen*, although some storytellers can spin a long well-wrought legend. Also, as Grimm noted, legends are more immediate than other forms of oral prose narratives. Even migratory legends told around the world are localized in their retellings, acquiring new ideas and familiar settings as they pass from one locale to another. Moreover, legends do have the authority of history. Legend formation often begins with an event or alleged fact, and legends frequently serve to instruct or educate.

A workable definition of the legend in modern scholarship is found in William Bascom's article, "The Forms of Folklore: Prose Narratives." According to Bascom, who in the tradition of the Grimm Brothers defines the legend by distinguishing it from other kinds of folktales, the legend is a traditional oral prose narrative that is set in this world in the recent past with humans as main characters. It is regarded as fact by the storyteller and his or her audience, and it may be either sacred or secular, although most American legends are secular.[2] While definitions of this sort have their critics,[3] the most constructive revision of this generally accepted definition has been suggested by Linda Dégh and Andrew Vázsonyi, who demonstrate that storytellers and audiences do not always believe the legends they tell and hear. Rather, it is "the *belief itself* that makes its presence felt in any kind of legend."[4] Thus, as Wayland Hand has observed, "The strong element of belief in the legend as told, or the individual folk beliefs inherent in the legend, constitutes the hallmark which sets the legend apart from the folk tale."[5]

Because of their great variety, legends are no easier to classify than they are to define. Sometimes they are classified according to their distribution as either migratory or local legends; however, migratory legends are almost always localized, and local legends draw upon migratory motifs. Most systems of legend classification are based on subject matter. One example is the tentative International Folk Legend Classification that grew out of a meeting of the International

Society of Folk Narrative Research in Budapest in 1963. A committee of international folklorists proposed four general categories of legends: (1) Aetiological and Eschatological Legends, (2) Historical Legends and Legends of the History of Civilization, (3) Supernatural Beings and Forces / Mythic Legends, and (4) Religious Legends or Mythos of Gods and Heroes.[6] Since many legends are purportedly etiological and historical, including legends with supernatural or religious motifs, the first two categories, while recognizing a function and quality of legends, are not especially useful in organizing collections of American legends. For example, the tentative category of historical legends includes a wide variety of legends dealing with people, places, and events; and many of these, especially the place and place-name legends, are etiological. What's more, it is ethnocentric to place supernatural legends in one category and religious legends in another. As Alexander H. Krappe has suggested, what others believe we call superstition, but what we believe we call religion.[7] Most religious legends have supernatural motifs, so properly they are supernatural legends.

Since a commonly accepted system of legend classification does not exist, I have arranged the legends in this collection under four very general headings: (1) supernatural and religious legends, (2) personal legends, (3) place legends, and (4) modern legends. In more than a few cases, though, a particular legend could fall into two or three of these categories. "Dillinger's Fat Lady" (Tale 180), for example, is included in the general section on personal legends, but since it explains a place name and includes a ghost motif, it could be grouped with either the place legends or supernatural legends. Moreover, if Dillinger is considered a modern hero, the text could be included with the modern legends. Thus, various subheadings are used within each of the four general categories to group the tales more specifically.

Some of the most interesting legends in Indiana deal with premonitions, death and burial, ghosts, haunted houses, good and evil, special powers, witches, and monsters or snakes.

Omen stories are extremely common in Hoosier folklore, as
they are throughout European and American folklore. These
brief tales with folk beliefs inherent in them often relate
first-hand experiences with prenatal influences, death signs,
prophetic dreams, and other premonitions. Strictly speaking,
these first-person accounts of encounters with the supernatural are memorates, or pre-legends; however, as these
personal experience tales are repeated by other storytellers,
they develop into true legends. Some of the most popular
omen stories in Indiana relate warnings which have signaled
the death of a relative or acquaintance. Common death por-
tents are seeing a ball of fire or flaming torch. Generally, any
kind of bird in the house or flying against a window sill is a
sign of impending death. Strange noises, such as three raps
on a house or headboard, with no apparent cause also are
death tokens. Likewise, a fallen portrait, certain kinds of
dreams, and seeing an angel or wraith of a person forecast a
death.
   Death and burial have incited a number of folk beliefs, cus-
toms, and legends, as have other rites of passage. Some interesting legends in this group concern live burials. These tales
once were extremely popular because before embalming it
was not impossible for someone in a cataleptic trance to be
buried alive. This fear gave rise to several legend types. In
one type, an apparently dead person is accidentally buried
alive and is awakened when a grave robber looking for jewels
buried with the body tries to cut a ring off the buried person's finger. In another legend type, the body is exhumed for
some reason, and the corpse has turned over, rubbed off its
hair, or scratched the top of the coffin with its fingernails.
While the legends of live burials deal with the living who are
taken for dead, other stories are just the opposite: the dead
are thought to be alive. Usually the corpse is a hunchback
and has to be wired in the coffin. At the wake or during the
funeral service, the wire breaks and the corpse sits up, usually with comic results. Other death and burial tales are more
somber, though, as in tales when a death occurs through

fright. Sometimes a person loses a limb instead of his or her life, and he or she feels pain when the arm or leg is buried in a crooked position. Ineradicable bloodstains frequently appear at the scene of a tragic death, or grass won't grow where blood has been shed.

People everywhere have believed in ghosts at some time or other, and in Indiana ghost stories can still be collected. Ghosts haunt roads, bridges, cemeteries, hollows, tunnels, mines, colleges, and houses. They do not appear as corporeal revenants, as they do in old European ballads, or in white sheets, as they do in contemporary American popular culture. In Hoosier legends ghosts sometimes appear as ladies in white or black, though. In other tales, they appear as parts of the body, generally as faces, heads, or eyes; or they appear armless or headless. Very frequently, they appear as ghostly lights, somewhat like the elusive will-o'-the-wisp, or they are heard but not seen. Hoosier ghosts sob, moan, scream, jingle chains, and play the organ or other musical instruments. Ghosts return for a number of reasons. Many of the ghosts have died violent or accidental deaths and can't rest in the grave and like ghosts of murdered people haunt the spot of death or burial. Frequently, a person with a missing corporeal member or especially with a missing head returns from the grave to search for the missing part. Other ghosts return to demand proper burial, reenact the sounds of their tragedy, reveal a crime, avenge their murder, or protect treasure. Often ghosts return because their lives have been cut short and they can't rest until their work is finished. High school students play a big role in keeping ghost stories alive in Indiana, for they visit the sites of the legends as a test of courage or to park, make love, drink beer, and watch for headless revenants, ghostly lights, or other spooks.

While haunted houses are found throughout the state, only a few examples can be included in this collection. Some of the houses have glass coffins in which a spouse's corpse is kept after death, and the houses light up strangely. The interior of another house mysteriously changes color. In other houses ghosts appear, sometimes damaging property and other times annoying inhabitants. One interesting haunted house is located in Terre Haute. The oldest dwelling in the city, the Preston House was built in 1823–26 by George Dewees of New Orleans. Dewees, his much younger wife, Matilda, and their small son moved into the house in 1827, and allegedly not long after that the son was killed by Indians. By 1832, the Dewees marriage had problems, and their separation was announced in a local newspaper. Mrs. Dewees, however, failed to appear in court, and her husband reported that she had returned to New Orleans. According to local legend, though, Dewees murdered his wife and bricked her body into one side of a large fireplace on the first floor of the house. Some informants claim that Matilda's ghost rises each night at midnight and stalks the house. In 1843 the house was purchased by Nathaniel Preston and remained in the Preston family until the death of Natalie Preston Smith in May 1973. In August 1968, Mrs. Smith, who spent nights in a local hotel and visited the house only during the day, said:

> Mr. Dewees did have a wife named Matilda. He and Matilda never got along, and he wanted a divorce. Matilda was to go visit relatives one time, and from that time on, no one ever laid eyes on her again. We believe that Dewees killed her and buried her in the wall behind the fireplace in the living room. Since all five of the other fireplaces have cupboards behind them, and this one has cupboards only on one side, it seems a logical place to put her. . . . I can't say for sure if she's in there or not, but it was a good place to put her.

Legends of good and evil in this collection are religious legends, usually dealing with Jesus or the Devil. In some medieval legends and British ballads Jesus appears as a realistic figure who as a child is told to be good when he asks his mother if he may play ball with some other boys. When the other boys insult him because he is " . . . but some poor maid's child / Born'd in an ox's stall," Jesus gets mad and builds a bridge of sunbeams, over which he walks and the other boys follow. When the other boys get to the middle, though, the bridge of sunbeams disappears, and all of them drown. This realistic, vindictive Jesus is not found in Hoosier legends. He appears in more familiar roles to believers, generally saving souls from the Devil and healing the sick. Although rarely mentioned in the Bible, the Devil was fully developed as evil personified in Christianity by the Middle Ages. Apparently influenced by the goat-footed Pan of classical mythology, the Devil became a grotesque figure with horns, hooves, and tail. In Western legends, and consequently in Hoosier folklore, the Devil often is portrayed as a handsome abductor who appears to a girl who wants an escort for a dance. She wants to go to the dance so badly that she says she will even go with the Devil himself. The Devil arrives and packs this unfortunate girl off to hell. In other legends, however, good triumphs over evil, and the Devil is overcome by chasing him with holy water or some other white magic.

The most popular religious legend in Indiana attempts to explain the origin of the dogwood tree's gnarled trunk and striking blossoms. These Hoosier tales actually are variants of a migratory religious legend about a tree that was cursed for serving as the cross on which Jesus was crucified. The legend has been collected in central and western Europe as well as throughout the United States, although naturally the tree varies. For instance, in Great Britain the aspen or elder is the tree cursed for serving as the cross, while in the United States the cursed tree or shrub might be the poplar, cottonwood, or mistletoe. Informants from northern, central, and southern Indiana agree, though, that it was the dogwood that was once a tall, straight tree, but God or Jesus cursed it so it would be unfit for making another cross. Moreover, according to some versions of the legend, the greenish flowering heads of the dogwood represent the Savior's crown of thorns, and the red marks near the notched apex of the white bracts symbolize the nail wounds in his body.

A number of people in Hoosier legends have special pow-

ers to either cause or cure maladies. A person with the evil
eye, for example, can cause illness. Although belief in the
evil eye is not widespread in Indiana, the belief is ancient
and well-nigh universal and has survived in the United
States especially among Americans with Mediterranean ancestry. Apparently the belief arose through fear of the unusual, for persons with crossed, squinted, or other malformed
eyes are thought to have the evil eye. Sometimes even
people with eyes of a color uncommon in a cultural area are
believed to have special powers. While some people thought
to have the evil eye cause illness without malice simply by
staring fixedly at another person, especially a child, usually
the possessor of the evil eye is malicious and can cause illness in animals as well as in people. Through various coun-
tercharms, the evil eye can be averted.

While possessors of the evil eye, sometimes called over-
lookers, make people ill, most people with special powers in
Hoosier legends heal. Some healers specialize in burns.
They can look at the burn, repeat some mysterious words,
and blow the fire out of the burn. Often the name of the Trinity is invoked in fire charms, as it is in the legend of the fire
letter in this collection. Other healers are able to stop bleeding, usually by repeating some silent incantation. Hoosier
bloodstoppers perform a kind of sympathy healing, for some
do not even have to be present to stop hemorrhaging. Other
healers also specialize. A person who has never seen his
father can cure thrush, and the seventh son of a seventh son
can blow off warts. Warts are also cured in various other ways
in Hoosier legends. Some healers rub them, while others
advise the patient not to look at the warts and they will disappear. Warts are also cured by sympathetic magic. Either a
dishcloth or a string is stolen and buried, though the string
must be knotted once for each wart before burying. As the
dishcloth or string decays, the warts will fall off.

Besides the healers, other persons with special powers in
Indiana legends are those who can see future or distant
events in a vision and those who can locate water, buried

treasure, or buried pipes with a divining rod. The seventh daughter of a seventh daughter and a person born with a caul covering the head have second sight and see things an ordinary person can't see. Most water witches are ordinary people who have the one special power to locate water with a divining rod. The methods of Hoosier water witches usually vary only in their choice of wood for the divining rod. Most use a forked stick, often peach, with a fork held in each hand with the palms turned up. The butt end of the rod is pointed upwards at an angle of about 45 degrees. Then the water witch walks over the area where a well is to be dug, and when water is located, the rod rotates or points downward. This method of using a forked stick to find water is widespread in international folklore, and the use of the same kind of stick with metal attached to it, or the use of a metal rod, to find buried treasure is fairly common, too. More recently, bent wires or coat hangers are used to find buried metal pipes.

Although the WPA files, collected during the Depression years, contain a sizable number of witch legends, in recent years only a few witch tales have been reported in Indiana, suggesting witch beliefs are not as popular in Indiana as they were fifty years ago. More intensive field work in the state, though, might prove otherwise. Like other legendary supernatural beings, the witch in Indiana legends is not native to the state but has been imported from Europe; consequently, Indiana witches have more in common with their European parents than with the friendly witches of contemporary American popular culture. In the Euro-American folk tradition, the witch has a compact with the Devil and almost always is feared.

A familiar role of the witch in European and American folklore is meddler in the dairy. In fact, in *Witchcraft in Old and New England* (Cambridge, Mass., 1929), George Lyman Kittredge devotes an entire chapter to "The Witch in the Dairy." Thus, Hoosier witches transfer milk by squeezing a towel, make cows give bloody milk; make cows go dry, and keep butter from coming, unless the witch's spell on the butter is broken by putting hot iron or a piece of silver in the churn. Witches who cause illness also are common in Indiana, as they are in Europe. In some Hoosier legends, people or even animals admired by witches become ill. Often a witch causes her victim to vomit foreign objects, such as pins.

There are several ways to recognize a witch and free oneself from her powers. Often the exorcism is accomplished through sympathetic magic. For instance, sometimes a burning object is used to make a witch reveal herself. In one Hoosier tale, hot irons placed in a churn burns a witch, and the witch is recognized by the burn. If a witch in animal form is wounded, then the witch will show the same injury. Generally, a silver bullet will protect against witches, and in one Indiana legend, shooting a picture of a witch with a silver bullet breaks her spell. When a witch is killed, stones placed on her grave prevent her from returning from the dead. All these motifs from Hoosier witch legends are ubiquitous in European and American folklore, and some of the Indiana legends, such as "The Witch Cat," with versions reported from Asia as well as from Europe and North America, are variants of well-known international migratory legends.

Witches nearly always are women, but another supernatural being, the *loup garou*, is always a man who because of some curse has been transformed into a beast, usually a wolf. These werewolves are not from the 1941 movie, *The Wolf Man*, starring Lon Chaney, Jr., but were brought to the New World from France. Legends of the *loup garou* have been collected from Canucks in both Canada and some parts of the United States, such as upstate New York and the Upper Peninsula of Michigan. While tales of the French werewolf are not common in Indiana, several tales of the *loup garou* in the WPA files were collected from French-Americans in Vincennes. The *loup garou* legend in this collection is a typical one, for such tales often tell of someone being chased by a werewolf and its disenchantment by being cut and shedding blood.

Other monsters in Indiana, such as the Princeton monster, are huge with shaggy hair and resemble the hairy Himalayan Yeti, the Canadian Sasquatch, and the American Bigfoot. The Wampus, also reported in North Carolina, seems to be some kind of spirit in animal form. Often in Hoosier folklore, as in modern American folklore generally, these supernatural beings are rationalized into big cats or other animals and hunted by individuals, groups, or virtually entire communities. One such quest took place in Churubusco in 1949 after the Beast of Busco, a giant turtle, allegedly was seen. The Beast of Busco, weighing 400 to 500 pounds, supposedly is the largest inland snapping turtle ever seen, and its legend inspired a community festival, Turtle Days, in Churubusco.

Since antiquity snakes have been the subject of an enormous amount of folklore, and several widespread snake legends have been collected in Indiana. Hoosier legends tell of whip snakes, hoop snakes, and milk snakes, as well as a strange relationship between a snake and a child. The legendary whip snake is able to crack itself like a whip and often chases or beats people. More common in Indiana is the hoop snake, which supposedly sticks its poisonous tail in its mouth and rolls like a wheel. In legendary accounts, it usually pursues someone down a hill, strikes just as the person ducks behind a tree, and plants its poisonous tail in the tree. Generally the tree dies. In tall tale versions, however, the tree swells to such a size that a whole house is built from the swollen tree. The only problem is that when the house is painted, the wood shrinks to its normal size, and the new house can be used only as a doghouse. Another snake, the milk snake, is said to wrap itself around the leg of a cow and milk it. "The Child and the Snake," an international folktale found over most of Europe and fairly common in Indiana, suggests a sympathetic relationship between a snake and a child, for when a snake that a child has been feeding is killed, the child usually dies, too.

Personal legends are allegedly true stories about people, usually real people, although they do not do all the things attributed to them. In Indiana there are tales about famous

people, local eccentrics, local heroes, folk doctors, and outlaws. An interesting personal legend that still can be collected around Charlestown in southern Indiana concerns
Prince Madoc, a legendary Welsh prince said to have discovered America about 1170. The legend of Madoc was well
known in Wales in the Middle Ages. His story has survived in
two fifteenth-century Welsh poems and in Robert Southey's
long poem, "Madoc," published in 1805, as well as in oral
legends in Wales and the United States. Although there is no
real historical evidence of the existence of Madoc, according
to legend he was one of seventeen sons of Prince Owen
Gwyneth of Wales. At the death of his father in 1167, Madoc
and a band of sailors left Wales and sailed west to either the
gulf coast of Florida or Alabama. Indians forced the Welshmen inland across Georgia, Tennessee, and Kentucky to the
falls of the Ohio near Louisville. Fourteen miles above the
falls they built a large stone fort in southern Indiana, where
they stayed for many years before either being defeated by
Indians or intermarrying with them. John Filson, author of
the first history of Kentucky in 1784, believed the legend of
Madoc and discussed it with several informants when he was
collecting material for his book.

Better known than Prince Madoc is Johnny Appleseed, but
Johnny Appleseed owes his fame largely to children's literature, newspaper features, a Walt Disney film, and poems by
Vachel Lindsay and Carl Sandburg. Frequently he is pictured
as a simple fellow walking barefoot and wearing a gunnysack
for a shirt and a pot for a hat. Born John Chapman in Massa-
chusetts in 1774, he was not a native Hoosier; however, he
roamed the Midwest peddling Swedenborgian tracts, and
there are affidavits attesting that he is buried in Fort Wayne,
although several communities in Ohio claim his grave, too.
Although most Hoosiers know Johnny Appleseed through
print or mass media, not folk culture, there is some evidence,
admittedly slim, that he still lives in oral stories in Indiana.
As in the text in this collection, he is credited with planting
countless apple orchards throughout the Midwest.

Familiar in American ballad studies but neglected in legend scholarship is Pearl Bryan; however, in contemporary Hoosier folklore, oral ballads of Pearl Bryan are extremely hard to find, while legends of Pearl's fate or Pearl's ghost are much easier to collect. A Greencastle girl, Pearl Bryan, was murdered in late January 1896 by her boyfriend and father of her unborn child, Scott Jackson, and his accomplice, Alonzo Walling. Her headless body was found in Fort Thomas, Kentucky, on February 1, 1896, but her head was never found. While ballads stress the murder and occasionally a trial scene in which Pearl's sister pleads with Jackson and Walling to deliver the head, some legends emphasize Pearl's headless ghost in search of the lost head. What is interesting, though, is that Pearl's ghost does not haunt the site of the tragedy in Kentucky but communities closer to home, in Mooresville as well as in Greencastle.

Famous American statesmen like Abraham Lincoln and John F. Kennedy are commemorated in Hoosier legends, too. Lincoln appears in his familiar role of the humble hero, while Kennedy fits the universal pattern of the wounded hero who refuses to die and will one day return to lead his people when his wounds have healed. According to a legend that spread across the United States, Kennedy did not die after the Dallas shooting in 1963. He continues to live, although as a human vegetable, either in the Parkland Memorial Hospital in Dallas or on Aristotle Onassis's private island on the Aegean, a more appropriate Avalon. This story, like so many of the modern legends in the last section of this collection, was taken over by mass media and reported in the July 11, 1971, issue of *The National Tatler*. In that tabloid account, a 46-year-old Greek fisherman reported seeing Kennedy, also described as a "human vegetable," sitting in a wheelchair daily on Onassis's island and staring blankly out into the Aegean. On April 16, 1971, though, the fisherman saw a coffin being lowered into the sea just off the island, and he recognized two of the mourners, Jackie Onassis and Teddy Kennedy. Some versions of the legend apparently attempt to rationalize

Jackie's marriage to the much older Onassis, for informants claim she really didn't marry Onassis. Jackie simply wanted to be close to her husband, and the marriage was only a ruse to explain her presence on the island.

Among the most interesting of personal legends in Indiana are those of local eccentrics, sometimes rich hermits who often bury their money and live in poverty. An example of this kind of miser is Martin Pirtle of Sullivan County. Supposedly, he was an extremely rich peddler with a wife and two or three children. Like other local eccentrics, he was extremely dirty and searched along streets for money or anything he could use. He also stole cookies and candy from barrels in the town store and begged food so he wouldn't have to spend his own money. Allegedly, he attended all the funerals in town because he made a deal with a funeral director that he would get a free funeral if he attended all the funerals. Other local eccentrics in Indiana communities also reputedly are rich but live in complete poverty. They bury their money and beg their food, or sometimes eat garbage.

Although these local outcasts come from all parts of the state, several of their stories share the same pattern. Supposedly they are from respected, wealthy families, are well educated, and once had good jobs; however, something happens to them. Either they experience some tragedy, usually the death or disappearance of a spouse or sweetheart, or they protest some injustice, often unfair taxes or unequal rights. At any rate, they give up their social position and good jobs and become hermits, living in a shack, under a bridge, at a dump, or in the woods. Frequently, they have some talent, although usually it isn't anything that society considers useful. For example, the outsider's talent might be imitating bird calls, writing poetry, painting pictures, tutoring Latin, or repairing toys.

One of these hermits, Martin Piniak, lived under a bridge in East Chicago. According to most informants, he was very rich but quit a good job, left his fine home, and lived in poverty under the Indianapolis Boulevard bridge. Some informants claim Martin dropped out of society because his sweetheart or new bride was killed in an accident, but others say he became a hermit when his sweetheart jilted him. Still other informants maintain that Martin quit his job after the income tax was initiated because he refused to pay taxes on his earnings. Martin's talent was imitating the noises of animals and birds. Like most of these local eccentrics, Martin Piniak, who died in 1976, was a real person.

According to accounts in the WPA files and newspapers, Diana of the Dunes was born in 1881. Her real name was Alice Gray, and she was the daughter of a prominent Chicago physician. After graduating Phi Beta Kappa from the University of Chicago, she stayed at the university as secretary to the president. In 1915, though, she resigned her position because, according to some sources, she protested that men were paid more than women for the same work, and she vanished into the Indiana dunes, where she lived alone and ran naked. The WPA account, however, suggests that disappointment in love motivated Diana to drop out of society: "Why did she deny her social position and the personal comforts that wealth can give? Whether it was for disappointed love or for the quiet, contemplative life unhampered by the restraint of conventions has never been answered." In her seclusion, Diana continued to study, often visiting nearby libraries, and to write poetry. Several years after she went to the dunes, she tied up with Paul Wilson, with whom she lived in a shack until her death in 1925.

Another local character who shares this pattern is Billy Hazard, an Irish nobleman who became a hermit in Salem. According to a newspaper account, Billy majored in Latin and Greek at Oxford and graduated with high honors. After graduation he was commissioned in the British army and served in the Crimean War. When the war ended, Billy returned home, where he fell in love with one of his family's maids, an Irishwoman named Anna. In an attempt to break up the romance, which the family found disgraceful, Billy's father persuaded military officials to send his son to India, where Billy was second in command of a regiment that fought in a conflict over Afghanistan. After this battle, Billy was decorated, honorably discharged, and sent home with a taste for liquor he acquired in India, for officers were allotted one quart of brandy per day as a preventative against disease. Billy's love for the commoner, Anna, did not cool in India, though, and when his father refused to allow him to marry beneath his station, Billy and Anna were secretly married. Disowned by his family, Billy and his new bride sailed to America and arrived in New York in 1863. After unsuccessful attempts to find employment first in New York and later in Louisville, Billy settled in Salem, where he moved from one menial job to another and spent most of his earnings on liquor. Finally, Billy's wife deserted him, leaving him alone in a dilapidated house. In Salem he became well known for his drunkenness and shabbiness. Allegedly, he was an avid reader, though, often spending an entire day reading under a tree. He also read the classics to children and helped them with their high school Latin. Billy died in the county home in 1913.

In virtually every Hoosier community there are anecdotes about local heroes like General Ledgerwood, a hero of the Indian wars, Robert Straight, a high school basketball coach, and the anonymous strong man of Salem. Occasionally one finds stories about a local folk doctor, like Doc Cox of Sullivan County and Dr. Wheat of Pike County. Doc Cox, reputedly part Indian, was a self-taught herb doctor who charged very little or nothing for his services. It is widely held in Sullivan County that he discovered a cure for cancer and large pharmaceutical companies offered him a small fortune for the secret formula. When Doc Cox refused their offers, maintaining that the cure belonged to the people, the drug companies had him arrested for practicing medicine without a license and paid off the judge, jury, and witnesses to get him convicted. According to local legend, he was sentenced to the Indiana State Prison, where he died, taking the secret cure for cancer with him.

Personal legends of outlaws are very popular in Indiana. In fact, one outlaw, John Dillinger, may well be the state hero. The train robber Frank Reno takes on qualities of the noble outlaw who helps the poor and unfortunate, but tales of the Reno Brothers are told mainly around their hometown of Seymour. Thus, like the tales of local eccentrics, the tales of the Reno Brothers are restricted largely to a single community or region in the state. Other outlaws may be well known throughout the state, but they do not have the same appeal that Dillinger has. The train robber Sam Bass was born in Indiana, but at nineteen he left the state and made a name for himself in Texas. Stories of Jesse James and Al Capone are plentiful in Indiana, but neither is a Hoosier. What's more, Capone, unlike Frank Reno and Jesse James, is not a noble robber in Hoosier folklore. For example, one informant refers to Capone's activities as "dirty dealings." In Indiana legends, Capone is portrayed in a familiar role of gambling and providing illegal liquor during the Depression, and when Hoosiers do not reveal Capone's several hideouts to the police, it is not through love, as it is for Dillinger, but through fear.

John Dillinger is different. He was a native Hoosier who stayed close to home, occasionally wandering to nearby states to rob banks or to Wisconsin, Florida, or Arizona to hide out, but always returning to the people who loved and protected him, the residents of his native state. As Hoosier author Jean Shepherd observes in his novel *In God We Trust: All Others Pay Cash* (New York: Doubleday, 1966), Hoosiers are proud of John Dillinger. The narrator, Ralph, returns from New York to the northern Indiana steel town of his youth, runs into an old childhood buddy, Flick, now a bartender, and the two reminisce about the World's Fair in nearby Chicago. Ralph says:

> "You know, Flick, I read somewhere that John Dillinger, the old bankrobber, used to go to that fair and ride the Sky Ride between heists."

"I'll be damned. He was from Indiana, wasn't he?"
Flick's Hoosier pride welled to the surface.
"You're damn right, Flick. ...." (p. 103)

Apparently, though, Hoosier informants have forgotten
that young Dillinger led a gang called "the Dirty Dozen"
who robbed and sold railroad coal, stole liquor, and gang-
raped a girl. Save for a single informant, they don't recall that
when he was twenty he stole a car and joined the Navy to
escape prosecution. Informants don't remember that Dillinger went AWOL several times, spent time in the brig, and
finally deserted, returning to Indiana where he married a
sixteen-year-old girl and played semi-pro baseball in Martinsville. Hoosiers also fail to point out that with Ed Singleton, the umpire for the Martinsville baseball team, driving
the getaway car, Dillinger, armed with a .32 revolver and a
piece of iron, which he bounced off the victim's head, at-
tempted to rob a Mooresville grocer, sixty-five-year-old B.F.
Morgan, of his weekly receipts. Instead, the Hoosier cycle of
Dillinger tales follows familiar patterns of outlaw heroes of
the Robin Hood type.

The "Robinhooding" of three American outlaw heroes —
Jesse James, Billy the Kid, and Sam Bass — has been traced
by Steckmesser, who says, "The similarities between Robin
Hood and the American outlaws are clearly owing to the uni-
formity of folk belief across the centuries."[8] Drawing material
mainly from biographies of Jesse James and Billy the Kid,
Boatright, too, sees Robin Hood's England as the "parent culture" and enumerates six traits of the American outlaw hero:
(1) he must belong to the dominant Anglo-American majority
and come from a respectable but not wealthy family; (2) he
must have an unfortunate childhood; (3) he must commit his
first crime under extreme provocation; (4) he must fight the
enemies of the people; (5) he must perform acts of tenderness

and generosity; and (6) to attain the highest heroic stature, he must pay for his misdeeds by an atoning death through treachery.[9]

While the patterns of Steckmesser and Boatright recognize some typical qualities of the outlaw hero, both writers rely largely on sub-literature or popular biographies rather than on oral traditions; and the outlaw hero of popular culture is not exactly the same as the hero of folk culture. For instance, both writers tend to emphasize the Anglo descent of the American outlaw hero and play down the role of the "noble robber" as super stud and champion of the oppressed. Examining "The 'Good' Outlaw Tradition in the American Southwest," John West has shown that Gregorio Cortez and other outlaw heroes of minority Americans share attributes with frontier outlaw heroes of Anglo-Americans: (1) they are part of a partisan group, which they champion; (2) they display manliness, providing a vital force in a time of social upheaval; (3) they fight an underdog's battle; and (4) they get killed, often treacherously.[10] The image of the "noble robber" as "the righter of wrongs, the bringer of justice and social equity," as Hobsbawm demonstrates, is well-nigh universal.[11]

Biographers generally stress that Dillinger came from a respectable, religious, and rural family. Nash writes, for example, "Unlike the city gangsters of the Thirties, Dillinger sprang from humble rural beginnings. School and work dominated his early life. He was not a 'born' criminal in any sense; only a precocious child who could reasonably be considered as average as any man's offspring."[12] Some informants mention that Dillinger's "family was very nice" and that "John's father was . . . very religious"; however, one oral account relates Dillinger to the orphan hero of tradition: "he was an illegitimate child whose mother was a [Terre Haute] prostitute. She was coarse and vulgar, tough and hard boiled!

She loved food and drink and, uh, being involved in prostitution, she had inclinations towards crime. ...." Although Dillinger was not the bastard child of a whore, his mother, Mollie, died when he was not quite four. Dillinger's father remarried a few years later, and in one oral legend the cruel stepmother motif is suggested: "John was a nice guy until he joined up with hoods like Ed Singleton. Singleton got him into it; he was really bad. He was connected to John's stepmother in some way."

The general notion reflected in Hoosier legends is that young Dillinger was a victim of injustice. As one informant related, John "got a bum deal. When him and Ed Singleton robbed Old Man Morgan's store all they got was apples. So John got sentenced for stealing apples. I heard the judge just made an example of John. ...." A Parke County informant said, "Johnny got a real raw deal when he was real young— you know how the law operates. Well, times were rough and money was tight, real tight, and Dillinger wanted money— fast! But he was real nice. ...." According to another informant, "They told Dillinger to plead guilty and they would give him a light sentence. But they railroaded him. He got into more trouble, but probably wouldn't have if they had done him right."

Like other outlaw heroes, Dillinger rocketed to fame during a time of social upheaval and fought the enemy of the people—the banks, in his case. The attitude of the unfortunate toward the banks during the Depression is reflected in some of Woody Guthrie's songs, like the "Jolly Banker," and in Woody's comments on outlaws and bankers preceding "Pretty Boy Floyd" on his Library of Congress recordings. Woody suggests that many of the Oklahoma bank robberies were inside jobs to give the banks an excuse for going broke, and the bankers blamed the robberies on Pretty Boy Floyd. An informant who claimed her uncle was president of the Greencastle bank told me a similar tale concerning Dillinger.

The Greencastle bank was going broke until Dillinger allegedly robbed it, and after the robbery her uncle prospered. Those who felt cheated by the banks during the Depression saw Dillinger's bankrobbing as about the only way to beat the greedy bankers. When asked if Dillinger was a Robin Hood figure who robbed the rich and gave to the poor, a Parke County informant said, "That's right. He gave me money more than once—ten dollars at a time. And that was when ten dollars was something hard to latch onto. . . ."

The patterns of the outlaw hero agree that his death must result from treachery. Dillinger, of course, was betrayed by Anna Sage, the "Lady in Red," a whorehouse madam who led Dillinger into an F.B.I. trap outside Chicago's Biograph Theater on the night of July 22, 1934. According to most written accounts, she agreed to betray Dillinger for the reward and to stop deportation proceedings facing her. Other motivation is provided in an oral account from Brazil, Indiana, though: " . . . you don't know why she [the "Lady in Red"] turned him in, I bet. Well, I guess old Dillinger had him 16 inches, and he used to just rip that bitch a new asshole every night, so she couldn't take it and turned him in. How's that?" This informant suggests another quality of the American hero overlooked by those basing their patterns strictly on biographic and journalistic accounts. That is, in the oral tradition heroes display manliness not only through courageous deeds but also through sexual prowess. Oral versions of "John Henry" and "Casey Jones" and apparently actual folktales of even Paul Bunyan celebrate the heroes' sexuality. But this quality is not strictly American, as the prototype noble robber, Robin Hood, was a hero of May Day fertility rites in England.

As a matter of fact, the most common tale about Dillinger in Indiana is that he had an enormous penis, from 16 inches in one version to 23 inches in another, and that it is now pickled and on display in the Smithsonian. A male informant claimed that Dillinger used his huge tool "as a weapon by which to flog women and other unfortunate people," while another informant said that even though Dillinger had an enormous penis he wasn't a great lover because he didn't have enough blood to support an erection. In recent years, *Playboy* and *Oui* have featured articles, notes, and letters on Dillinger's penis; however, the oral stories appear to be older, as they date from 1969 to 1971, and the *Oui* article appeared in 1976.

The noble robber, like the good king and John F. Kennedy, generally does not really die in legends, and several Hoosier tales hold that Dillinger was not gunned down in 1934. An informant who said he and a friend visited a funeral home in Mooresville where Dillinger's body was shown claimed, "We got up the casket and looked down, but the man we saw lying there sure didn't look like John Dillinger. I know, 'cause I'd seen him in person before. . . . we had an idea that John got some guy to take his place. . . ." In another memorate, the same informant said he saw Dillinger demonstrating a new type of canning machine at the Indiana State Fair three years after the bankrobber's alleged death: "I'll tell you the truth, I didn't believe what I saw. There, as plain as the nose on my face, was John Dillinger showing the people how to run the machine. . . . there was no doubt in my mind that the man I saw was John Dillinger."

From Dillinger's alleged illegitimate birth, through his youthful sexual prowess, to his death by betrayal and the subsequent claims that he still lives, his cycle of legends parallels patterns of the hero of tradition. Like other outlaw heroes, Dillinger was a champion of the oppressed, a symbol of manliness, a vital force in a time of social turmoil. He was not a social revolutionary who sought to establish a free and equal society; but, like other outlaw heroes, his righting of wrongs took the form of transferring wealth from the bankers to the poor people. As Hobsbawm points out:

The traditional "noble robber" represents an extremely primitive form of social protest, perhaps the most
primitive there is. He is an individual who refuses to bend
his back, that is all. . . . They cannot abolish oppression.
But they do prove that justice is possible, that poor men
need not be humble, helpless and meek.

That is why Robin Hood cannot die, and why he is in-
vented even when he does not really exist. Poor men have
need of him, for he represents justice. . . . [13]

Place legends are closely associated with a specific lo-
cality. Sometimes these stories are called local legends or
historical legends, but some local and historical legends deal
more with people or events than with places. Place legends
frequently are etiological, though, explaining something
about local history or the origin of topographic features and
place names. An interesting group of Hoosier place legends
deals with bottomless lakes, a ubiquitous motif in American
folklore. What may be unusual, however, is that several of the
Hoosier bottomless lakes are named Blue Hole, a descriptive
name suggesting a deep pool of blue water. Since the name
usually is informal and not on maps, only extensive field
work will reveal just how many bottomless lakes named Blue
Hole are in Indiana and if there are other bottomless lakes
named Blue Hole in other states.

Often accompanying the bottomless lake motif in lakes
named Blue Hole near Brazil, Prairieton, and Seymour are
accounts of hidden treasure, enormous fish, giant monsters,
lost buggies or wagons, wrecked automobiles, and especially
derailed trains in the lake. For instance, one informant says,
"In Brazil there was a really odd thing that happened to a
train. This train went across a trestle over a big cavern every
day . . . until one day the trestle collapsed. The train fell in it,
and it was never seen again." An intriguing fact is that on
March 27, 1913, a train moving over a trestle in Washington,
Indiana, actually fell into a pool named Blue Hole when the
trestle collapsed during a flood. Possibly this incident was
localized in stories about Blue Hole in Brazil, Prairieton, and

Seymour and perhaps in other Hoosier communities with
bottomless lakes, too. Of course, not all the alleged bottomless lakes in the state are named Blue Hole, as the tale of
"Half-Moon Springs" in this collection illustrates. What's
more, stories of bottomless rivers in Indiana share motifs
with bottomless lakes. For instance, some informants claim
part of Lost River in Orange County is bottomless and that a
man drove his horses and carriage in there and they were
never found.

Some of the most widely known legends in the state attempt to explain the state nickname, Hoosier. One informant
says that *hoosier* "was at one time a slang word in the South
referring to a 'jay' or 'hayseed,'" and his account might be
partially true. According to atlases and field records of American regional English, *hoosier* is a derogatory epithet suggesting rusticity or uncouthness in some southern states. Evidently, pioneers in Indiana were considered extremely
backward by their relatives and friends in the earlier established Middle Atlantic and South Atlantic states, the home of
many settlers in southern Indiana. Most residents of Indiana
do not recall that a Hoosier is a hayseed, though, and they
have not seen the published atlases or field records of lin-
guistic geographers; consequently, they still pass on numerous legends about the origin of the state nickname. Most of
the legends suggest that the nickname comes from questions
or words that sound like "Hoosier." The most common account is that pioneers in Indiana called "Who's 'ere?"
through the doors of their log cabins when a visitor knocked.
A more amusing legend says that frontiersmen in Indiana
fought constantly in pioneer taverns, and often they bit off
ears and noses. After one of these fights, a customer sometimes found an ear on the sawdust floor of a tavern and asked,
"Whose ear?" Another popular explanation holds that a
Louisville contractor, Samuel Hoosier, liked to hire men from
across the Ohio in Indiana because they were good workers,
and his employees became known as "Hoosier men" or simply "Hoosiers."

Legends explaining the names of geographic features, natural as well as artificial, are very common in Indiana, but only a few examples can be included in this collection. Most Hoosier place names that appear on maps have been borrowed from either names of other places or names of people; however, the historical accounts of place naming are not always known, and legends are created to explain the origin of these unimaginative names, as H. L. Mencken calls them, as well as the origin of Indiana's more colorful map names. Moreover, around every Hoosier community are numerous unofficial names that do not appear on maps, and these folk names that natives know and use daily have inspired legends, too. Although usually historically inaccurate, place-name legends are what the names mean to the people who use them and often serve as a better index of culture — revealing something of the beliefs, values, prejudices, and humor of the natives — than the sober factual explanations.[14]

While it is not uncommon for place names to honor women, there are some unusual place-name legends about women. Examples are the legends about the naming of Noblesville and Hymera in this collection, but there are a number of others. For instance, Galveston probably is a transfer name from Texas, but a local legend gives a more imaginative account. The name was suggested by a girl with a vest on who passed before the founder when he was trying to decide on a name for the town. Bellmore allegedly was named for the beautiful ("belle") daughters of a resident, Thomas Moore, although the name appears to be a combination of a family name, Bell, and a Celtic generic name, "-more." Saratoga probably was named for Saratoga, New York, but a local legend says it was named for Sara Loller, who just happened to walk into Albright's general store when the postmaster and Albright were there trying to think of a name for the town. The postmaster asked Miss Loller, a beautiful redhead, if she would like to have a town named for her, and she said she would. Albright suggested that they add "toga" to her first name, and the town's name became Saratoga.

According to legends, several Hoosier place names were chosen randomly from books. One name, Jasper, allegedly was selected from the Bible, suggesting a form of bibliomancy, or divination from a sacred book. One informant said, for example, "Jasper was named when some ol' lady opened the Bible and put her finger on the word *jasper*. She was the oldest in the community, so she got the honor of naming the town." Throughout Europe, the Bible, often opened with a golden needle, was used for divination or advice. Orland probably is a transfer name, but according to a local legend the postmaster opened a hymn book and selected the name from the title of the first hymn he saw. Geography books also are used in place-name legends to find names. For example, Zulu supposedly was selected from a geography book when a pin stuck in the book fell on the word "Zulu" on a page about Africa.

Various remarks, sayings, or exclamations also inspired a number of place names, according to Hoosier legends. Although Brazil is a transfer name from South America, one informant told me, "In the early days a man named Bray worked in the train station here. Once when a train came in, the conductor asked for Mr. Bray and was told, 'Bray's ill.' That's how Brazil got its name." Daylight supposedly was named for a statement made by a railroad engineer. Each evening when he dropped off a construction crew, the engineer said, "I'll pick you men up at daylight," so eventually Daylight became the name of the village. Allegedly, Rome City, founded in 1837 when Sylvan Lake was being made, received its name from a proverb. Both French and Irish workers were employed on the construction of the dam, and apparently the French had the best quarters. When the Irish demanded equal living conditions, the superintendent of construction led the French against the Irish, telling the Irish to "do as the Romans do." The Irish called their camp Rome, and when the town was platted on the campsite, it was named Rome City. Roann most likely was named for Roanne, France, but a local anecdote says the name comes from an

exclamation. Once during a flood a girl named Ann was trying to row a boat to shore; however, a swift current kept carrying the boat downstream. Watching helplessly, her father
called, "Row, Ann! Row, Ann!"

Sometimes utterances by non-native speakers of English,
drunks, or Indians became place names in Indiana legends.
The text about the naming of Tampico in this collection, for
example, deals with an old German who "got his English
pronunciation fouled up when he got excited or mad."
Eugene sounds like a personal name, but according to legend
the community got its name from the cry of a town drunk,
who often called "Oh, Jane!" for his wife, but because of his
drunkenness it sounded like "Eu, Jene!" The text dealing
with the naming of Tecumseh in this collection is a good
example of a name supposedly coming from a remark made
by an Indian, but there are several others. For instance, a
legend claims that Merom received its name from "Me,
rum!"—an utterance repeated by Indians asking for liquor at
a local tavern. Although Auburn is a transfer name, legends
give another explanation. Several Indians were sitting around
a fire when one Indian stuck his finger in the fire and yelled,
"Ah, burn!"

Indiana legends suggest that a couple of place names were
taken from signs. Pikes Peak, according to a local legend, was
named for a sign on a prairie schooner. When James Ward, an
early settler, heard about the gold rush out west, he put a
sign, "Pikes Peak or Bust," on his prairie schooner and set
out. Arriving in Madison, however, he became homesick,
purchased enough supplies to open a store, and returned
home. When his customers had to visit his store, they said,
"Guess I'll go over to Pikes Peak for supplies," so the village
was named Pikes Peak. Indiana has two communities named
Pumpkin Center, and the names may have been applied
humorously, denoting a rural, isolated place, as in the case of
Pumpkin Center, South Dakota. A local legend dealing with
the naming of Pumpkin Center in Orange County provides
another explanation of the origin, though. A local farmer grew

enormous pumpkins in the largest pumpkin patch in the state. One year he grew a pumpkin that weighed 107 pounds, and he was so proud that he put up a sign that read "Duncan's Pumpkin Center of the World." After that the community was called Pumpkin Center.

While a number of Indiana place names are descriptive, accounts of descriptive naming in legends are not always accurate. For instance, Greencastle was named for Greencastle, Pennsylvania, home of the earliest settler; however, a local legend tells how the first settler built his house on posts that sprouted after his house was built, so he called the house his "green castle." Another legend says that Morocco is descriptive of a stranger's boots, which were trimmed with morocco leather, but the town probably was named for the North African country. Solsberry was named for Solomon Wilkerson, founder and builder of the first house in the community, but informants say Billy Souser sold berries there. Dublin probably was named for the Irish city, although a couple of legends provide other accounts. One story says that stagecoaches and wagons had to double team to get through the mud there in early days, while another tale says the town got its name from the old Huddleston House, which locally was known as the Double Inn, descriptive of its double doors. Cayuga was named for the New York lake, but a legend says the name describes the sound of horns on Model-T Fords.

Other legendary accounts of naming descriptive of incidents concern Hartford City, Oxford, Limberlost Creek, and Sardinia. Hartford City, first called simply Hartford, probably was named for Hartford, Connecticut, home of early settlers; however, some people claim the city was named for the Hart family who forded Licking Creek near the settlement. A similar local legend says Oxford was so named because wagons drawn by oxen forded a nearby stream, but Oxford was named in 1843 for the English town and university. Limberlost Creek takes its name from a nearby swamp, formerly called Loblolly. According to traditional accounts, the name

of the swamp was changed to Limber Lost when an athletic
young man called either "Limber Jim" McDowell or
"Limber Jim" Miller, depending on the version, got lost in
the swamp while hunting. Sardinia probably was named for
the Mediterranean island, but according to a local legend the
community was named Sardinia because old Frank Gaston
gave a free sardine supper to get people to trade at his store.

While many Hoosier place names commemorate people
—especially national or state heroes and local pioneers or
founders—usually they do not honor the kinds of people remembered in legends. For example, Buddha probably was
named for Buda, one of the two Hungarian cities that formed
Budapest, but one legend says, "Buddha was named for a
tramp. Back in the 1880's . . . a tramp named Buddha used to
pass through the town, and it was later named after him. He's
now buried in an old cemetery west of there." Bono apparently was named for early settlers, the Bono brothers; however, a legend says the name comes from a French settler
who was driven out of town. According to a traditional account, Francisco was named for a Spanish laborer who
worked on the Wabash and Erie Canal, but he was fired on
the spot, built a shack, and became the first settler.

In place-name legends, names considered unusual often
are thought to be Indian names. For example, Radnor and
Somerset are said to be names of Indian chiefs; but Radnor is
a transfer name from Wales, perhaps via Pennsylvania, and
Somerset is a transfer name from England. Similarly, Nap-
panee was named for Napanee, Ontario; however, some
legends say the name means either "mud" or "knee-deep-
in-mud," and the community was so named because an Indian maiden was found there knee deep in mud. Another
legend, though, says early settlers found an Indian girl there
napping on her knees, so they named the place "Nap-on-
knee." Modoc, in fact, was named for an Indian tribe, but
according to local tradition it received its name from a picture
of a Modoc chief on a cigar box.

Frequently, legends arise to explain existing place names,

as in the examples already given; however, sometimes local names come from folk legends. That is, the legend, often supernatural, comes first, and the setting of the legend takes its name from the story. A good example is Monsterville, a folk name that has been applied to three different spots in southern Vermillion County. First, high school students gave the name to an old strip mine near Centenary where a giant, shaggy monster allegedly was seen by several people. Students from the area often went there to park and consequently needed a name for the place. When the county bought the strip mine and turned it into a dump, teenagers had to find another place to park, so they moved to an abandoned deep mine with a row of deserted company houses and offices two miles south of Centenary near Universal. The name Monsterville and the legends of a Bigfoot-type monster followed the students to their new parking spot; however, the site of the second Monsterville was purchased by a strip mining company, the buildings were razed, and the area was mined, forcing the students to relocate again, though not spelling the end to the traditional place name and its accompanying legend. At last report, Monsterville now is located between Universal and Centenary near property owned by the Izaak Walton League.

A popular notion is that folklore is something from the past that survives only among illiterate hillbillies or other backward people. Some religious, ethnic, and regional groups do retain old ways of life, and folklorists certainly are interested in these survivals in modern culture. But folklore is a dynamic process of sharing informal culture within close-knit groups, so the old folklore is ever changing, sometimes even disappearing, and new folklore is constantly being created. Ballads, for example, are not as popular as they once were; however, college folksongs, which resemble the old songs in form and function, have arisen and are fairly easy to collect. Legends are especially intriguing, for industrialization and popular culture have not spelled the end of legend telling. Many of the old legends have survived, though usually they are modified, and many new legends have been created over the years.

Modern legends sometimes are called urban legends or urban belief tales, but not all of these newly created stories deal exclusively with the city. Modern legends also flourish in remote communities. But wherever they are found, they are nourished by modern mass culture, which provides the tales with fresh themes and speeds their dissemination through electronic and print media. Science and education have rationalized the folk a bit, too. In the old tales, mysterious lights were interpreted as ghosts or death omens, but in modern legends similarly described lights sometimes are said to be flying saucers. The supernatural has become extraterrestrial. Likewise, agents of evil in the old legends were supernatural, but often they are natural in the new legends. We are no longer wary of the Devil and the *loup garou*, but we had better watch for human assailants in the back seats of our automobiles and in shopping center rest rooms. Science and technology have solved many human problems and alleviated some of our fears; however, uncontrolled, they have indirectly created other problems—including pollution, overpopulation, urban crime, contaminated food, and the bomb—which have contributed to new fears. Thus, the threats in the modern world come from human sources, not from supernatural forces.

In form, modern legends resemble the older legends; however, the products, institutions, recreations, fads, fashions, occupations, and heroes of mass culture have had an enormous impact on the subject matter of recently created legends. A modern invention that has inspired a number of legends is the automobile. Although "The Vanishing Hitchhiker" apparently is older than the automobile, the tale owes its development in the United States to the automobile. The spread and localization of modern forms of this story would be severely limited in cultures without many automobiles and highways. Moreover, American mass culture helped spread this tale through reworkings in popular songs, short stories, and a television play. As early as the Depression this tale was transformed and transmitted in Indiana by radio as well as newspaper, as a journalistic text in the WPA files shows.

Other legends inspired by the automobile include "The Death Car" and "The Assailant in the Back Seat." "The Death Car" is a migratory legend that has been around since at least the 1940s. In 1953 Richard Dorson collected a version that was set in Michigan in 1938 and dealt with a jilted man who committed suicide in a 1929 Model-A Ford.[15] Since then innumerable versions have been reported about new Buicks, Cadillacs, Corvettes, Jaguars, and other models for sale from around $25 to $350 because someone died in them and, as one informant said, "you can never get rid of the death smell." When I mentioned this tale as a good example of a modern legend several years ago in a folklore class, an older student remained after class to tell me this was no legend. He said it happened in North Terre Haute when he was a policeman, and he knew the officers who investigated the incident. According to his account, a man parked his Cadillac in a cornfield, ran a hose from the exhaust pipe through a window, and committed suicide. He said it got so hot in the Cadillac that the man's body melted and ran through the upholstery. I suggested he might investigate the suicide for his term project, but when he interviewed the alleged investigating officers, they didn't know anything about it. What's more, although he said he knew exactly when it happened, he could not find any report of the investigation in police records. Similarly, another informant claimed "The Assailant in the Back Seat" was true. She said, "Why, that's no legend. That really happened to me!" Then she related a long personal experience tale about finding a man in the back seat of her car after stopping at a restaurant on the way home from work one night. The plausibility of modern tales like "The Death Car" and "The Assailant in the Back Seat" suggests why there is such a strong element of belief in them.

The automobile also has contributed to the development of

contemporary parking legends like "Hook Man," "The Boyfriend's Death," and "The Purple Lady." As a matter of fact,
the modern custom of necking and drinking in parked cars
has had a tremendous influence on the development of other
Hoosier stories like "Spook Light Hill" and "Monsterville,"
for as soon as teenagers get their driver's licenses they often
visit the remote sites of Indiana legends, ostensibly to see a
spook or monster but sometimes as an excuse to drive to
some desolate place to park, make love, and drink beer. As
one informant of "Spook Light Hill" said, "Anyway, it is a
real nice spot; there is a small bridge, creek, and the rest of
the things needed for a romantic spot. A lot of us kids used to
park there in my day." In the old days, young people often
laughed at the supernatural and historical legends told by
their elders, but today in Indiana teenagers and young adults
are responsible for keeping many of the local legends and
migratory legends alive. After visiting the sites of supernatural legends, young people often give credence to the
legends by relating personal experience stories of encounters
with the supernatural.

The telephone is another invention that has inspired modern legends. In one popular legend a baby-sitter gets a
number of threatening phone calls from the same person and
finally asks the operator to trace them. The operator calls her
right back and tells her to get out of the house at once because the calls were made from an upstairs extension phone.
A local legend in Terre Haute inspired by the telephone says
that Martin Sheets either was afraid of being buried alive or
believed in a second life and wanted a telephone installed in
his mausoleum so he could call a cab to come after him when
he awoke in the cemetery. Near Terre Haute in Highland
Lawn Cemetery there is actually a mausoleum that was built
in 1910 for Martin Sheets (1853–1926) and his family. When
the mausoleum was completed, Sheets, an eccentric businessman and philanthropist addicted to making wills, placed
a prized chandelier in the vestibule of the tomb, which gave
rise to stories that he planned to have electricity installed in

the mausoleum. In time, the legend was altered to include phone service as well as electrical service, but today informants tell only of the phone in the mausoleum.

Modern legends also have been spread by the telephone. For example, housewives in Brazil phoned one another and passed along a variant of a migratory legend about a vacationing dentist, or in some versions a banker, who left the driving to his wife while he napped in the travel trailer. When his wife stopped abruptly for some reason, he peeked out the rear door of the trailer to see what was going on. At the same time, his wife sped off, and clad only in his boxer shorts, he was thrown out of the trailer onto a busy street. Like so many of the other modern legends, this tale was taken over by popular culture, as it was dramatized in a Doris Day movie, "With Six You Get an Egg Roll" and reported as "A True Story" in an instructional book on weekend camping.

Institutions like department stores, shopping centers, fastfood chains, and colleges are the subjects of modern legends, too. One of the most popular tales dealing with a modern institution is "Department Store Snakes." This tale tells of a woman who was shopping in a large discount store, usually a K-Mart, for yard goods. As she reached into a bolt of imported yard goods, something pricked her finger, and a short time later she died. On investigation, a poisonous snake, or in some versions a nest of poisonous snakes, was found in the imported material. Several K-Mart managers who have been interviewed claim the tale was started by a competitor to ruin the K-Mart's business, but probably the tale warns Americans not to buy cheap foreign products. Fear of health risks associated with modern products is suggested in "Kentucky Fried Rat," which deals with contaminated food in a fast-food chain. Likewise, fear growing out of the negligence of modern institutions is reflected in a tale about a woman embalmed alive. A dress worn by a corpse was returned to a department store after the funeral, and when a woman purchased it, embalming fluid on the dress entered her body through freshly shaven armpits and killed her.

Virtually all of the modern legends circulating in general American folklore are well known on college campuses, too; however, college students also have their own legends that deal exclusively with college life. Students tell tales about famous or popular coaches and about absentminded, eccentric, or incompetent professors. They relate stories about star athletes or other students, such as the Bird Man of I.U., who gave the signal for panty raids during the sixties. But especially popular on college campuses are dormitory legends like "The Roommate's Death," which deals with an ax murder, and tales of fatal or near fatal fraternity or sorority initiations. Probably the oldest and most widespread of the initiation stories is "The Cadaver Arm." In this tale, actives steal an arm from a cadaver in the medical school or anatomy lab and tie it to a chain on a light switch in a closet. Then a pledge is ushered into the dark closet and told not to turn on the light. When the actives return for the pledge, they find the light on. The pledge's hair has turned snow-white, and the pledge has either died of fright or has gone mad and is chewing on the arm. Ghost stories are popular in colleges, too, as "The Ghost of Burford Hall" at Indiana State suggests. "The Faceless Nun" is included with other ghost stories in this collection to illustrate the motif of the faceless ghost, but since it is set on a college campus, it exemplifies a college ghost story, too.

As Richard Dorson demonstrates in *America in Legend*, a lot of American folklore from the nineteenth and early twentieth centuries is occupational.[16] A modern counterpart of the older occupational heroes, especially of the heroes of the early transportation industries, is the truck driver, for the anonymous trucker is the hero of several contemporary legends. The most popular tale about a truck driver in Indiana actually is a migratory American legend about a trucker who ran over several motorcycles in a restaurant parking lot after some bikers had given him a hard time. This tale, too, was taken over by mass media, as it appeared in Norton Mockridge's column in the *New York Times* and was used in a scene in the popular film "Smokey and the Bandit." A Hoosier tale about a Gary steelworker who fell into a furnace and came out in a sheet of steel follows a familiar pattern in American occupational folklore, for countless cowboys, loggers, miners, and railroaders also get killed performing their jobs in ballads and tales. Other heroes of modern legends, like John F. Kennedy and the Beatles, are drawn from politics and entertainment.

Modern legends sometimes are more ephemeral than the older legends, mainly because frequently they are nourished by popular culture, which itself is characterized by ephemeralness. That is, legends sometimes draw upon current fads and fashions for subject matter, and the legends lose their immediacy and die when the fads and fashions become outmoded. A good example is "The Beehive Hairdo," a tale that was extremely popular throughout the United States when the bouffant hairdo was in style. Although the legend still can be collected from informants who recall the bouffant or from those who have adapted it to the Afro, the tale is not nearly as popular now as it was in the 1960s. Moreover, many of the modern legends have been assimilated into mass culture, which saturates the entire country with the tale in a short time and then moves on to another sensational story. Sometimes these popular treatments of legends in films, popular songs, short stories, television programs, and print journalism tend to squelch oral versions, especially when the subject matter is topical, too. But legends are tenacious forms of folklore, and many of the new legends live on alongside the many old legends that have survived in Hoosier tradition.

As this collection suggests, Indiana is rich in legendry. Legends have been reported from all parts of the state, in urban as well as in rural areas. Ideally, legends should be collected professionally with a tape recorder—or, better still, with a video recorder to show something of the performance and social and physical contexts of the stories—and faithful transcriptions of the texts would look more like playscripts than short stories. Moreover, more than a few versions of each text should be published, for many of the tales in this collection are well known throughout the state and are found in hundreds of variants. But such a large area as Indiana cannot be covered by one person who is only a part-time field worker, and printing more than a single version of most texts would make the cost of a legend collection prohibitive.

Consequently, this collection is merely a sample of some of the legends in Indiana, and the texts have been drawn largely from the manuscript files of the Federal Writers' Project of the Works Progress Administration for the State of Indiana and from the Indiana State University Folklore Archives, although a few of the tales are from the Indiana University Folklore Archives. Of course, the collectors of the WPA material during the Depression were not professionally trained folklorists, and the student collectors of most of the material in the archives of the two universities had but a single course in folklore. Still, the WPA files offer the best examples of folklore from the state during the thirties, for no professionals were collecting in the state then, and many folklore students have produced nearly professional collections. Although the professional folklorist will demand more versions and more contextual data than can be given here, the general reader, for whom this collection is intended, should find the texts readable and the notes informative.

NOTES TO THE INTRODUCTION

1. Quoted in William Bascom, "The Forms of Folklore: Prose Narratives," *Journal of American Folklore*, 78 (January-March 1965), 18.

2. Bascom, pp. 4–5.

3. See Robert A. Georges, "The General Concept of Legend: Some Assumptions to be Reexamined and Reassessed," in *American Folk Legend: A Symposium*, ed. Wayland D. Hand (Berkeley: University of California Press, 1971), pp. 1–19.

4. Linda Dégh and Andrew Vázsonyi, "Legend and Belief," *Genre*, 4 (September 1971), 301.

5. Wayland D. Hand, "Status of European and American Legend Study," *Current Anthropology*, 6 (October 1965), 441.

6. Hand, "Status of European and American Legend Study," p. 444.

7. Alexander H. Krappe, *The Science of Folklore* (1930; rpt., New York: Norton, 1964), p. 203.

8. Kent L. Steckmesser, "Robin Hood and the American Outlaw," *Journal of American Folklore*, 79 (April-June 1966), 354.

9. Mody C. Boatright, "The Western Bad Man as Hero," *Mesquite and Willow*, ed. Mody C. Boatright, Wilson M. Hudson, and Allen Maxwell. Publications of the Texas Folklore Society, XXVII (1957), 96–104.

10. John O. West, "To Die Like a Man: The 'Good' Outlaw Tradition in the American Southwest," Diss. The University of Texas, 1964.

11. Eric Hobsbawm, *Bandits* (n.p., 1969).

12. Jay Robert Nash, *Bloodletters and Badmen: A Narrative Encyclopedia of American Criminals from the Pilgrims to the Present* (New York: M. Evans, 1973), p. 160.

13. Hobsbawm, p. 48.

14. Ronald L. Baker, "The Role of Folk Legends in Place-Name Research," *Journal of American Folklore*, 85 (October-December 1972), 372.

15. Richard M. Dorson, *American Folklore* (Chicago: University of Chicago Press, 1959), pp. 250–252.

16. Richard M. Dorson, *America in Legend* (New York: Pantheon, 1973), pp. 127–128, 235–242.

R.L.B.

PART ONE

Supernatural and Religious Legends

PREMONITIONS

1. Prenatal Fear Causes Birthmark

I have heard my grandmother tell this story many times. This happened a long time ago. Well, anyway, in the times when people did their butchering at home, it seems that several members of the family would gather at one house in the early winter and butcher hogs or whatever to last all the winter for everyone. There was a pregnant girl at one of these butcherings. Sometime during the day she left the room, the kitchen, where they were doing a lot of the cutting. One of the guys picked up the hog's head from the table and goes to the doorway where she will reenter the room. Not seeing him, the pregnant girl steps into the room. As she entered the room he shoved the hog's head at her. Terrified, she screamed and put her hands to her face. When her baby was born, it had coarse, hoglike hair on its face in exactly the same place as where the mother touched her own face on the day she was frightened.

2. Ball of Fire as Death Token

When I was nine years old, I lived in the country and attended a country school. It was about a mile from my house. On my way to school I passed the home of Murrell Myers, a girl a little older than I. One Friday afternoon we were walking home from school together, and as we neared her home, she screamed, and when I asked her what was the matter, she told me that she had seen a big ball of fire back of her house. I did not see anything. Her people were superstitious and believed in such things as death tokens.

The next day, about eleven o'clock, her little brother, Tony, who was a little past two years old, was burned to death. The father had put small potatoes in a large iron kettle out of doors over a fire to cook them for the hogs. Before he left for the woods to work for the day, he cautioned the family to keep the little children away from the fire. The mother was just getting up for the first time, as she had a ten-day-old baby, and Murrell was busy helping with the housework. Tony got out of the house and too near the fire. Murrell heard his screams, but Tony had run as far as he could before he fell in the snow with all his clothes burned off but the neck band of his dress and his shoes. He lived for about one hour. Murrell thought that the ball of fire she had seen the evening before was a token of Tony's death.

3. Flaming Torch as Death Token

A friend of mine worked on the railroad near Huron, Indiana. At this time, he had a very sick daughter at home. This particular evening he got off the handcar and had to walk several blocks in the snow to his home in the dark. He was worried about his daughter, and in those days phones were nearly unheard of. So he had to wait till he got home to find out how his daughter was. He was a-hurryin' along in the darkness, and all at once he noticed on the left a flaming torch was following him in the ditch. And it stayed with him all the way home. His wife met him at the door crying and told him that their daughter had just died. He believes to this day that the torch was a warning of his daughter's death.

4. Bird as Death Token

About eighteen years ago, Mrs. Nora Graham's father and mother, Samuel and Betty Kinzer, who lived near Haggon, Virginia, were sitting before the fireplace in the evening after the chores were done. Mr. Kinzer leaned over in his chair and seemed to grab for something, and his wife asked him what he was doing. He told her that he had seen a large white bird fly in front of him and that he had grabbed for it, but that all at once it had disappeared. She laughed and told him he must be seeing things because she hadn't seen anything.

The next morning they went to the barn together to do the work. She went to the part of the barn where the cows were and seated herself by a cow and had just started to milk when she fell over dead from a heart attack. Mr. Kinzer heard the bail of the milk bucket hit the bucket when she dropped it, but of course thought she was just changing her position. After he had finished what he was doing, he came around to where she was and found her lying beside the cow dead. Then he thought of the white bird he had seen the evening before and knew that it was a token of his wife's death.

5. Dream of Coffin as Death Token

My mother, when she was ten years old, lived at the Blocks in Dugger. And one night after she had gone to bed and gone to sleep, she thought she felt someone touch her. But when she awoke all that was there was a candleholder and candle. And, as she watched, this candle and the candleholder went around the room as if someone was searching for something. But there wasn't anyone holding it, just the' candle and the candleholder. When she went back to sleep, she dreamed about a little neighbor boy. She dreamed that he was lying in his casket and that there were people in the room with him. Three days later her mother took her to the neighbor's house. The little boy had died with a fever, and he was lying in his casket just as she had dreamed.

6. Falling Portrait as Death Token

There's this one story I heard at home. They used to tell it all the time. There was this house owned by this old couple. It's a real old run-down place now. We used to go look at it all the time when we were in high school. There used to be a picture of the old man on this certain place on the wall, and it always hung there. It hung there for years and years, always in the same place on the wall, till one day it fell off the wall. He died that same day. It was a picture of him that fell.

7. Broken Dish as Death Token

When my mother was young and was washing dishes with her mother, an odd thing happened. A dish which my great-grandmother had given my grandmother as a wedding gift just fell off the shelf for no reason at all. My grandmother yelled that her mother had died. When they got to my great-grandmother's house they found her dead. She had died moments before.

8. Three Raps on House as Death Token

At two o'clock one morning, a farm family near here was awakened by a knocking sound. They heard three loud raps against the side of the house. Wondering what it could be, they got up to investigate. At first they thought that a tree branch was hitting the house, but there were no trees close enough. Besides, the wind was dead calm. Unable to find the cause, they all went back to bed. The next morning, they received a telegram. Their grandmother had died unexpectedly at two o'clock that morning.

9. Three Raps on Headboard as Death Token

Years ago, when we had neighbors sick, we took turns sitting up with them. My aunt was ill for a long time, and one night my mother was sitting by her bed around 2:00 in the morning. Everyone else was sound asleep in the house. In the still of the night, she heard three knocks on the headboard of my aunt's bed. My mother knew there was no other sound in the house to make the noise. She believes in death knocks and said my aunt would be dead in three days. She died on the third day.

10. Wraith as Death Token

I remember Grandma Newman. She was an old lady who always used to come over to see us kids. Grandma Newman and her daughter didn't get along too well. Well, anyhow, this one afternoon us kids were in the kitchen and Mom was getting dinner ready when she looked out the window and saw Grandma Newman coming up the walk. Well, all us kids ran to the door, and Grandma Newman wasn't there. Mom said she knows she saw Grandma Newman coming up that walk. Anyway, the next day we got word that Grandma Newman had died.

11. Angel as Death Token

Back in the mid-1800s my great-grandmother told a story that she was sitting in her lawn chair. Not very far from her house there was an open pond. She was watching the pond and the surroundings when all of a sudden an angel appeared hovering over the pond, and she watched it for some time. She had a feeling then that soon there was going to be a tragedy. A few days later, her small child was playing by the pond and drowned herself. At every anniversary of the child's death, the angel would appear again and hover over the pond.

12. Clock Stops When Person Dies

My Grandma Kennedy was lying sick one morning with the death rattle several years ago now. All of her relatives

were taking turns sitting up with her. My Aunt Essie had just
gone home, and it was my turn to relieve her. I was really
afraid something would happen to her while I was there, so I
was watching her real close. All of a sudden, this musical
powder box started playing. The lid was shut on it, and it was
only supposed to play when it was open. It just kept on playing. The next day she died. When she did, the clock in her
room stopped. They covered the face of the clock with a cloth
and never used it again.

After this all happened, I heard that one night Grandma
Kennedy was supposed to have woke up, and it felt like
someone was pulling on her arm. She told Aunt Essie that
she thought it was her husband. He had died before her and
she thought he was trying to tell her something. This also
happened shortly before her death. Now I won't sleep with
my hands out from under the covers. I do believe in premonitions like these. My mother had that same kind of thing
happen to her before, too.

13. Watch Stops at Owner's Death

Now, this story isn't any tall tale or lie. I know this to be
a fact. It happened to my great-grandfather. He was a railroad
worker, and he had this small gold railroad pocket watch. On
the night he died . . . he died at midnight . . . the watch
stopped at midnight. Well, my grandfather got that same
watch after great-granddad's death. Well, every night at midnight that watch stops. It still stops at midnight every night to
this day, and great-granddad has been gone for years. It's the
weirdest thing I ever saw.

14. Feather Crowns Found in Pillows of the Dead

This is a fact to me. I know it to be so. When someone dies in bed with their head on a feather pillow, you can open the pillow and inside the feathers there will be a little crown. The crown will range from one inch to four inches of thickness of feathers in the pillow. There has been deaths in my family and there's a feather crown for each one of the people. My mother has saved them all. She keeps them in little thread boxes. A lot of our neighbors would save them also. It never fails.

15. Person Will Die When Feather Crown Forms in Pillow

Another incident happened to a good friend of mine who also as a small child was always ill, and doctors could find nothing seriously wrong with him, either. Someone also told them to examine the child's pillow, which they did and found an almost completed perfect wreath made of the feathers that were in the pillow. They were told that if the wreath had been completely finished, the child would certainly have died. So they took the wreath to the parish priest, who told them to burn it, which they did, and the person who held the spell over the child also [dis]appeared. This person was also well known by me. The child got well immediately and is now past 60 years of age and is in good health and is one of my closest neighbors.

16. Murder Revealed in a Dream

Before the advent of the automobile, horses and mules were used as means of travel as well as for work. During this time horse traders were numerous throughout the country. In the latter part of the eighteenth [nineteenth?] century two traders had traveled over Starke County for several months and had apparently accumulated quite a sum of money. One of the men decided to dispense with the other by shooting him, thereby gaining possession of all the money. After the man was dead, the partner killed the mule they had recently traded for, dug a small hole in the ground, placed the body of the man in it, covered it with dirt, then dug another larger hole directly over the body of the man, and placed the mule in it. The burial place being in the midst of a dense forest, the trader had no fear of either being located.

As time passed, residents of the county who had known both men began to get suspicious, and an investigation began. The burial place of the mule was discovered, but excavation revealed only the mule. Finally, the son of an ignorant family was accused of the crime and placed in jail. The mother, greatly worried and believing her son innocent, had a dream that revealed the body of the man as being buried beneath that of the mule. Being so sure her dream was true, she appealed to the officers of the county to make another investigation, which they did, resulting in the discovery of the man who had been hidden in the small grave beneath the mule, then carefully covered. Upon removal of the mule and dirt covering from the body, a pressure was removed, thus causing the tightly wedged body, placed in feet first, to rise up considerably above the top of the grave, presenting to the onlookers a horrible sight. The innocent boy was released from jail, and the murderer given a long prison term.

DEATH AND BURIAL

17. Buried Alive

Now, I'm not sure that this is what you want. In fact I don't really know that much about it. All I know is that my mother once told me, when we went back to visit her, that her sister, my aunt, had been to this ceremony where they were transferring the casket to a different location and taking out some of the items that really shouldn't have been buried with her. Well, all I know is that when they opened the casket up, it was a lady that had been buried. Her eyes were open, her hair was much longer, and her fingernails had grown. Not only that, but the top of the casket, the lining, had been ripped into a million pieces. I don't know about you, but I get the creeps everytime I think about that.

18. Grave Robbers Awaken Woman Buried Alive

Well, anyway, years ago they didn't embalm people, you know. My girlfriend told me what had happened to her great-grandma. It's supposed to be true, and it is true. Her great-grandmother had a diamond ring that was supposed to have been worth a lot of money. A couple of men had tried to buy it from her husband, but he wouldn't sell it. Anyway, her grandma died, and they buried her. Her husband had her buried with the diamond ring on her finger. That same night these same two men decided, you know, to steal the ring. So they dug her up to take the ring, and it was real dark, and they were in a big hurry. They had trouble getting the ring off her finger, so they decided to cut the finger off. While they were cutting, they hit a nerve in her finger. Her grandmother rose up and scared the two men half to death, and they run off. Her grandmother had been paralyzed, it seems. She could hear things but couldn't say anything or move her body. It was as if she was dead, but she wasn't. She was aware of where she was at and was terrified. So she walked home after she gathered up her senses. My girlfriend's mother was only a very little girl at the time. But she could still remember her grandmother knocking on the door. Everyone was terrified and screaming because they thought she was dead. So they let her in, and everything was all right. She lived several years afterwards.

19. Buried Amputated Arm Causes Pain Until Straightened

One day in the spring of the year when it became warm enough to roll down the car windows, a young man was standing talking to a friend sitting in his car. The young man was standing against the car with his elbows propped up on the door. A car came screeching around the corner out of control. The car hit the young man, tearing off his arm. The boy's family took their son's arm to the cemetery and buried it in a casket. The boy's arm hurt just as though it was still there. Well, the pain continued for some time, and no kind of medication would help. Finally, the boy's grandfather went to the cemetery, dug up the arm, straightened it out, turned it so it would be laying east and west. After this was done the arm no longer bothered the boy.

20. Corpse Sits Up at Wake

A mortician down at Rosedale told this one. Once there was this old man that had a real hunched back. Well, he died, and they took him to the funeral home and got him fixed up, you know. Well, he looked real fine, except because of his hunched back he wouldn't lie down in the casket, so they just strapped him down.

This was in the days that someone always sat up with the body at night. Well, this friend of his was staying there with him. Someway or another, a cat got into the funeral home and was slippin' around. Well, this friend saw it and picked up a broom and started chasin' that old cat around the room. Well, this cat jumped upon the body and the friend came down with the broom. This broke the straps that held the old boy down, and he shot straight up. The friend turned around and said, "Sit down, John; I'll take care of this damned cat."

21. Corpse Sits Up during Funeral Service

There was an old man that died and he had a very hunched back. When they buried him they had to strap him down in the casket because he wouldn't lie flat. When they were having the service at the church the minister got all worked up during the sermon and cried, "This body will rise again!" Suddenly the strap that was holding him broke loose, and he shot up in the casket. The people all ran out of the church.

22. Soul Weighs Four Pounds

Anyway, this lady was dying in the hospital, and somehow they had the bed rigged up so it was on a scale. And the night she died, the next morning she weighed four pounds less. Well, it wasn't the next morning; it was right after she died. They could tell by the hearteogram or something like that. It's supposed to have really happened in the Linton hospital back a few years ago when everyone was debating about whether or not we all had souls. I guess they brought in big specialists from the big cities and everything.

23. Death from Fright

Two men were driving along a country road near here when they had car trouble. As they were going for help a terrible storm blew up, so they decided to take cover in a nearby church. The sky grew darker and darker until it looked more like night than day. The men were just sitting inside the church when one of them got up and walked over to the window. Lightning flashed, but the man could see nothing out the window because the rain was so heavy. The sky grew even darker than before. The man was looking out into the darkness. Suddenly lightning flashed, and there at the window was a horrible face grinning terribly in at the man. As it turned out, the "face" belonged to an escaped inmate of the insane asylum. But the man that had been looking out the window died of fright; his hair had turned completely white.

24. Ineradicable Bloodstain on Church Floor

There is a church in Heltonville that isn't used anymore. A long time ago there was a man that was murdered inside the church. His blood was all over the floor. After several

years they couldn't get the bloodstains off the floor. This
bothered the members of the church so much that they
stopped using the church. The bloodstains are still on the
floor.

25. Ineradicable Bloodstain on Porch Floor

A guy was shot while fleeing a bank, which he had
robbed in Williamsport, Indiana. He was shot by the state
police on the porch of a house. He died, and the white porch
was covered with blood. Everytime it rains, the blood comes
out from the boards of the porch, even though the shooting
happened over fifty years ago.

26. Grass Won't Grow Where Blood Has Been Shed

A few years back, there was a murder committed by a
man a few blocks away from our house; and as the police
chased him, they finally shot him down on the front lawn of
this one house. The blood stained the grass and turned it
brown, and to this day no grass will grow in that area where
the blood had been.

GHOSTS

27. Ghost of Father Searches for Daughter's Head at Spook Light Hill

Well, this girl was drivin' back home in the horse-and-buggy days when the horses ran away with her. She fell out of the buggy, and the wheel ran over her neck and cut her head off. It happened right on top of this big hill. They didn't find the body till the next day, and they didn't find her head at all. I guess some animals drug it off. Her old man went nuts and went out every night lookin' for it with a lantern for years. The only thing is that when he died, the light from the lantern kept comin' out every night.

You can go out there and go down the hill and up the other hill and wait for it to come out. Sometimes it doesn't come out. It's creepy as hell out there, even with houses all around. The only way out is back over that same hill 'cause the floods have washed all the other roads out. The dogs bark and everything when it comes out.

Mickey and a bunch of guys camped out to try to catch it one night. They waited till it came out; then they ran up both sides of the hill shootin' at it with shotguns. They had walkie-talkies and everything, but it just disappeared, so they walked back down the hill and stopped at the bridge. Then they heard something walkin' in the water and then in the grass. They all started runnin', and he fell down and skinned the shit out of his shins. He's still got the scars to prove it. You remember how the car wouldn't start on that bridge the night you were tryin' to scare those two girls. Your goddam eyes weren't so small that night either.

28. Ghosts of Elderly Couple Search for Cow
at Spook Light Hill

You take Highway 40 from Terre Haute to Brazil. At the intersection of 40 and 59 you go north for five or six miles. At this point a road goes off to the right that leads to Carbon, Indiana. It is a gravel road. Soon you come to three hills. You stop and look back down toward the second hill. If you are lucky, for one cannot see it every night, you can see soft lights that resemble a lantern light. The legend is this:

An old man and old lady lived on this land once. One night their herd of cows came in except for one who was supposed to have a calf. The old man and old lady went out to look for the cow. There was a funeral the next day in a nearby cemetery, and the old lady fell in the open grave and died. A few years later the old man died of natural causes. The lights are supposed to be from the lanterns of the old couple as they search for the cow. One reason it seems possible is because the lights have no definite pattern but just generally go back and forth.

29. Ghost of Farmer Searches for His Head
at Spook Light Hill

Do you know about the legend of the Spook Lights? There's a field in Brazil, I think. A long time ago, a farmer was plowing this field. He fell off of the plow, and it somehow cut off his head. Well, they say this man wanders the field with a lantern searching for his head. You can see the light, supposedly from his lantern, almost every night. But you can't see it all of the time.

I can't really believe this legend. But about a year ago, I

heard that some guys from Rose [Rose-Hulman Institute of Technology] went there and investigated it. They couldn't find any scientific explanation for the lights. They checked for gas seepage and for reflection from car lights. But none of these things explain these strange lights. So in view of this, I have to admit I have an open mind about this legend.

30. Father Searches for Daughter's Murderer at Spook Light Hill

Near Brazil on a country road there is a light that seems to come from nowhere. It is said that an old farmer lived on a farm near there and had a young daughter that he was very strict with, and since his wife died he never let her date. During the Civil War a soldier came to see her, and she finally talked her father into letting her go out with him. The father woke up the next morning to find his daughter lying dead on the steps, and since then he has been out searching every night with the lantern for the soldier who killed his daughter.

31. Gas from Elm Stumps at Spook Light Hill

That's where your swamp gas or fox fire comes from. It's real easy to explain. At certain times of the year, usually in the spring or fall, a gas comes out of the elm tree stumps and glows in the dark. Some people say it is just reflected light from the road, or a few of the old-timers say it's the ghost of some dead person from the graveyard on the hill, but I know better. The gas glows brighter the more concentrated it is, and elm tree stumps is where it comes from. I have been in the woods and watched the gas come out of the stumps and float off into the woods. Some people say that they see the gas or light only if they flash a light on it, but this is explained easily. The gas reflects the light like the hands on a clock. When it is exposed to light, like a street light or a car light or a bright moon, the gas just becomes illuminous and glows. So all it is is elm tree gas.

32. Will-o'-the-Wisp (Jack-o'-Lantern) Chases Car

One night about three o'clock in the morning, one of my friends from Salem, who had been over to visit his girl in Shoals, which is about an hour and a half from Salem, was driving back to Salem. He reached a long strip of straight highway, and he was going about 90 miles an hour. He happened to look in his mirror, and there was a big ball of fire following the car. It was off the ground and right behind him. He went faster, and it kept following. He looked at the road for a second, and then the next time he looked it was gone. He was so shook up that when he got home about 45 minutes later, he went in and woke up his dad and told him about it. His dad said it was probably a jack-o'-lantern. He had seen one when he was a boy and lived in the country.

33. Will-o'-the-Wisp (Jack-o'-Lantern) Leads
Person Astray

When I was a boy on the farm, I used to go frog hunting all the time. At times after dark I would see strange lights floating around the swamps. I would always try to catch one of these lights, but never could. Then one night I got one cornered by a steep waterfall. When I put out my hand, I was knocked unconscious. I woke up the next day, and when I reached for my pocket watch to check the time, I found it had melted along with all my change and hunting knife. After that I never tried to catch another will-o'-the-wisp.

34. The Light in the Big Tunnel

This story takes place back in the twenties or thirties, I'm not for sure which, at Tunnelton, Indiana. My grandmother's brother was the first to see the light in the old tunnel.

There's this old B&O Railroad tunnel that's about a mile and three- or four-tenths long that runs under this hill. It has a bend in it. You can stand at one end of it, and you can't see through to the other. Inside the tunnel about one hundred feet or so, there are holes built in the side of the wall so you can get into out of the way of a train if one should come. As the tunnel was being built there was a man killed in the tunnel by a train moving in materials.

Now on a rainy night about twelve o'clock you can see a light moving through the tunnel. They say that if you step back into the hole in the wall that it will go right on past you. The tunnel is so dark that you can't see anything except the light. It's believed that it's the ghost of the man who was killed and the light is his lantern. I have never seen it myself but Grandma's brother and dad has.

35. Ghost Plays the Organ

When I was living at home and I was still in high school, the kids at school used to talk about a place called Tanglewood. They say it's haunted. It's in Shelbyville by the Blue River. An old man named Paul Tindell used to live there. He's dead now, and the house is empty. But when he was alive he used to always play the organ out in the barn. His wife didn't like to hear it, so she made him take it to the barn. Now at night you can still hear the organ play. We went there one night, and all the lights were on in the house. You could see them shining in the river. We didn't stay around very long, let me tell you, 'cause no one's lived there for ages, and we couldn't figure out what was going on. I suppose some other kids could have been there and turned them on, but I don't know. I can't figure out why the electricity would still be turned on, you know.

36. The Crying Ghost

Back in 1890 I knew a man by the name of Elmer Myers. He's telling me a ghost story. On State Road 13 about four miles south of the county seat of Hamilton County is a place then called Ghost Hollow. One night when he was riding through this hollow on horseback, all of a sudden the horse stopped and refused to go another step. On looking down beside the horse's head, he saw the form of a woman clothed in a white robe weeping and drying her eyes with a white handkerchief. He asked her what was wrong—no response. He then reached forward, while still mounted on the horse, to take hold of the woman's arm, but she disappeared in the darkness. He then gave the horse the command to go forward. But before he passed through the hollow, the same thing occurred for the second time. She again disappeared. He then moved on with all the speed his horse possessed and rode out where he felt safe.

37. Ghost Jingles Chains

There was a house that stood for years between Middletown and Anderson, Indiana, that was hainted. And I know this to be the truth. No one could live in it because of all the noises that went on there. Always at midnight every night you could hear the spooks dragging chains across the floor. It was so loud that people used to come and sit in their cars outside and listen. Even long before that when people came in horses and buggies the horses would throw a fit when they drew near the house. There was some people who bought the property, but they refused to live in the old mansion. Instead they built a new house right next to the hainted house and used the hainted house for an old storage area. The reason they left the hainted house standing was that they were afraid if they tore it down the ghosts would come into their new house.

38. Ghost Looks for Arm

This young kid had gotten his driver's license a couple of days ago, and his father had bought him a new convertible. He was speeding down a gravel road when the car overturned and the boy's arm was caught underneath, cutting it off. The boy wasted away and died within a year of his accident. All this happened about thirty years ago. Anyway, now they say that his ghost can be seen, when the moon is full, walking around in the gravel road where he is looking for the stub of his arm. I've never seen it myself, but a couple of times when I was out parked, we've heard a moaning that Jack said was the ghost. I think it was just the wind, though.

39. Vanishing Hitchhiker on Cline Avenue

I think they call this story the White Lady. Well, anyway, there was this lady in white, standing in the highway that goes under Cline Street. There's a lot of woods there. Well, she was standing there, and she had a dog with her. A cab driver came along, and she stopped the cab driver, and he picked her up. He picked up the radio to say that he had a passenger. But then he only saw the dog; the lady had disappeared. He knew that he had seen her get into his cab, but she was gone. My friends and I went out there one night. It was raining real hard, and there were a lot of mud puddles. Our car got stuck. We really started getting scared. There was a big field there, and all the corn was dead. There were no lights around at all. Well, we got out of the car and tried to push it. We had heard that if you heard a dog barking, it was her 'cause nobody lived out there. We heard this dog barking; it kept getting closer and closer. We were so scared that we took off and never found out.

40. Ghost of Murdered Bride on Cline Avenue

About seventy or eighty years ago there was this girl that was raped on her wedding night in Hammond in this woods off Cline Avenue. She was raped and then murdered by the assailant. And every year supposedly around the time of her wedding there is a white figure observed more or less floating across the prairie lands out by Cline Avenue. There is a superhighway that intersects this prairie now, and they hadn't seen her for a few years. But last year around the date of her wedding she was seen again. There was quite a turmoil about it in Hammond, and people were out with flashlights trying to find out what it was. They even had an actual picture of what it was supposed to be.

41. Ghost of Mother with Baby on Cline Avenue

Quite a few years ago, there was this highway that was being built between East Chicago and Griffith and was named Cline Avenue. Now, the road wasn't completed yet, but traffic was permitted on it. It was late in the evening one night, and a car ran off the road near a turn and crashed below in a ditch. When help came, they found no victims in the wreck. Later, it was made known that there was a young woman and baby in the car. No trace as of today has been found of the two.

The story goes that there has been numerous reports made by motorists of seeing a woman dressed in white holding a bundle as if it were a small baby standing by the exact spot where the car went off the road looking down toward the ditch.

42. The Cline Avenue Ghost

In 1954 a man killed his bride at Cline Avenue and Michigan Avenue and buried her in the woods near there. This was in a poor people's graveyard. In 1965 people started to see a lady dressed in white walk around that area. Well, many incidents followed that, such as stories about her disappearing in a cab and many others.

Well, anyway, one day a lady walked into a store and got a bottle of milk and walked out without paying for it. The next day the lady came into the store, got a bottle of milk, and walked out again without paying for it. The following day the same lady came into the store and got a bottle of milk, but this time three men followed her from the store to the grave-yard, where she disappeared from sight into a grave. The men dug up the grave and found the woman. She was dead, and next to her was a baby and three empty bottles of milk. The baby was alive.

43. Victim's Face Pressed into Wall

There is this huge house here in Terre Haute which has a big stone wall going around it. There is an imprint of a face in this wall, and it is supposedly the face of the son of the man who owns this home. When he was sixteen years old his father bought him a new car, and he was out one night and had been drinking and was going rather fast. And he started to turn into his driveway and hit the wall instead, and he was killed. And his body was thrown up against the wall, and this is the imprint of his face on the wall.

44. Face in the Wall Reminds Motorists to Drive Slowly

There is a place out on Fruitridge Avenue where the road turns to cobblestone. There is a brick wall that also runs along the road. It's said that a boy was dragging and smacked up against the wall and died. His face was so smashed that the impression of his face is said to have been imprinted in the brick wall. When people go by there, they see the face on the wall, and it reminds them to slow down.

45. Face in the Wall Serves as Test of Courage

The face in the wall is out on the old Blumberg's stone fence. I've heard that a little boy was out playing near there one day when he was struck by a reckless hit-and-run driver. The driver was never caught. The boy died, and soon afterward a face suddenly appeared in the wall and is supposed to resemble the child. In high school it was a test of courage to go out at night and touch the face. If you touched the face you were supposed to die soon. The face has disappeared in recent years. I don't know what happened to it.

46. Face in the Wall Appears on Day of Victim's Funeral

Many years ago, a young boy was killed by a man in a car while riding his bicycle. This happened in front of his home, and on a brick wall surrounding his home is an image of the boy's face with eyes that glow in the dark when a car drives by. This image began appearing the day of the boy's funeral, and the story goes that anyone who sticks his fingers in the eyes of the image will die within 24 hours.

47. The Negro in Concrete at the Avon Bridge

This railroad bridge is located southwest of Avon on a gravel road. The bridge is made of concrete, and the middle is fixed so people are able to walk through if you can jump the wide gap from land to the bridge. Kids carry flashlights and sometimes stay all night in one end. The reason it's

haunted is that a Negro man working on the bridge accidentally fell into the cement, and the other workers decided just
to go ahead and fill the structure in. It would have taken too
much time to get him out. His pick and an outline of his face
can be seen on the side of the bridge closest to the road.

48. Ghost of Worker Screams at the Danville Bridge

There's this bridge in Danville, and while it was being
made one of the workmen fell into a form. It was one of the
concrete things, you know, to make the bridge. Well, they
were pouring concrete in it, and this guy fell into one of
them, and they figured it was too much trouble to fish him
out. So they just went ahead and poured the concrete in and
covered him up with it. But the only thing the matter was
that his saw was sticking out of the form. So they just cut it
off. So now at night the bridge is supposed to be haunted,
and you can hear screams of this guy that got buried.

49. Mother's Ghost Calls Baby at the Avon Bridge

Well, there was this old woman who was trying to take
her sick baby to Indianapolis to the doctor. She decided to
follow the railroad tracks since it would be shorter. It was
around midnight in the summer. I think it might have been
more toward fall. She was walking along these tracks when
she came to the bridge. She was about half way across when
she heard a train whistle blow. She tried to hurry, but she got
her foot caught in one of the ties. She finally worked the foot
loose and started to run. When she did, the train came up real
fast and blew the horn. She jumped, but her baby flew out of

her arms. She escaped, but the baby was killed. She went crazy and died about a month later. They say that every time the New York Central train comes through there at midnight you can hear the woman calling her baby.

50. Ghost of Boyfriend Screams at the Avon Bridge

Students at my high school were always talking about the lover of the Avon bridge. The high school is in the northeast corner of the city of Indianapolis. The bridge is on the east side of the small town of Avon.

The story goes that a man was going with this girl, and the girl had him over one night, and he stayed too long at the girl's house. He had to rush home so his folks wouldn't get after him and so he could see the girl again. In order to save time, he decided to cross the old train bridge which crossed over a ravine with a stream going through it.

When he got about half way, he heard a train whistle and saw the light of a train coming down the track. In the dark he didn't know exactly where he was, but he decided to jump off the bridge rather than get run over by the train. He jumped, and soon realized that he jumped into the deepest part of the ravine and that he was going to die from the fall, so he screamed just before he hit bottom. It's said that on a dark night that you can hear a train whistle and a few seconds later the scream of the man who jumped.

51. Ghost of Murdered Woman Screams at the Avon Bridge

There's this haunted bridge at Avon, and a lot of kids go there to drink and make out. About twenty years ago, a white woman was murdered there by a colored man. He cut her with a knife at different places all over her body and just enough so the blood would show. The man made her eat her own blood by making her lick her open wounds. Around midnight, a train crossed the bridge, and the colored man threw the woman under the train. A lot of kids say if you go out there at midnight and a train happens to cross the bridge, then you can hear the woman screaming.

52. Ghost of Chinese Man Screams at the Avon Bridge

There's this bridge around Avon. They say that a Chinese man was run over by a train on the bridge and killed. Every night at midnight you can supposedly hear him screaming if you are underneath the bridge. The bridge is really ugly and scary with lots of old dead trees around it.

53. The Mooresville Bridge: Another Worker in Concrete

This is a story that took place in central Indiana some-where outside of Mooresville. There's a concrete bridge that was built a long time ago, and one of the workers, while they were building the bridge, supposedly fell into the concrete. And by the time the rest of the workers knew he was in there, he was at one end of the bridge, and they were at the other. And by the time they realized it, he was in the concrete. The concrete had become solid, and they knew he was dead, so they didn't bother to take him out. One arm was hanging over the edge of the concrete and just dangling there, and so they didn't even bother to do anything about it. They just cut his arm off and put some concrete over it so you couldn't see the stub or something, and if you park there at night sometimes the arm will appear, and it will point. Most of the time it just points at nothing special, but one time it did indicate one of the cars parked there, and the legend with this is if it points at you, you will die within three days later. These kids were driving their car, and the engine just blew up.

54. Ghosts Sob at the Azalia Bridge

The story goes there was a woman who conceived a child out of wedlock. She was a social outcast of Azalia for many years, and she turned to isolating herself. This woman supposedly went insane and threw her baby off the bridge into the water. Well, I guess afterwards she went around mourning the death of her baby. She is always draped in black clothing and veils all the time and walks down to the bridge weeping. On full moonlighted nights, she goes to the edge of the bridge and weeps.

It has been said if you go to the bridge and look over the edge of it you can see an image of a baby wrapped in a white blanket lying in the creek, and it is crying. And also if you look on the bridge you can see the woman draped in black and can hear her weeping.

55. Ghost Rides across the Azalia Bridge with Motorist

There's a bridge called the Azalia Bridge, and if you go there at midnight, stop your car, blink your lights three times, and then start the car and slowly drive across the bridge, a

woman will get in and ride across the bridge with you. In
order to get in she does open the door. She is supposed to be
a ghost. I've never tried it.

56. Headless Ghost of Tramp at the Free Springs Bridge

Southeast of the city limits of Sullivan, Indiana, there is a
place called Free Springs. A small stream runs parallel to a
railroad track, and there is a narrow gravel road that crosses
the railroad tracks and a bridge over the stream. According to
legend, there was a body found under the Free Springs
Bridge sometime in the past. This body was headless, and no
one could identify it. It was generally supposed that it was
the body of a tramp that had met foul play and been dumped
from a train passing through this area. No great effort was
ever made to identify the body, and it was buried without the
head. Ever since the body was buried, there have been many
reports of strange noises and sightings of headless beings
around the Free Springs Bridge. This legend is common
knowledge among the teenagers of Sullivan County. A favorite pastime of many of these is to go to Free Springs in the
dead of night to see or hear the ghost.

57. Ghost of Boyfriend Calls at the Free Springs Bridge

Quite a few years ago near Free Springs, which is near
Sullivan, there was a car accident. A boy and his girlfriend
were coming home from a date when they had their wreck.
The car burst into flames. The girl's body was found, but no
one ever did find the boy. It is said that every year on the

anniversary of the accident, one can hear the boy calling the girl's name if you are close to the place where the accident took place.

58. Ghost Carries Lantern at the Free Springs Bridge

When I was in high school everyone was scared to go out to Free Springs Bridge because of the story about the headless man. I guess this man was the one who always rode in the caboose of a train, and one night he fell off and landed with his head on the tracks, and the train ran right over his neck and cut his head off. If you go out to the bridge and park on it, you can see the man walking down the track swinging a lantern looking for his head.

59. Ghost as Head at the Free Springs Bridge

There is this bridge called Free Springs Bridge. A man was murdered out there, I think. His ghost is still supposed to be out there. I've heard this story for years, but I've never seen the ghost. On certain nights you can see his head floating around, they say.

60. Red Eye Bridge

Well, down at Edwardsport; no, close to Elnora; no, closer to Bicknell; yeah, that's it, Bicknell. Well, anyway, there was this real bad wreck here a while back about 15

years ago, and both boys were killed. It was a rainy drizzly
night, and the wreck was a really bad one, and the boys were
really cut up badly, so bad that the rescue crew couldn't find
all the pieces. There was one boy who had bright red hair,
freckles, and the whole works, and everything was found on
him except his left eye. They searched and searched but
never could find the eye, and it is said that on a warm summer night you can look into the creek where the accident
happened and see a glowing sparkle coming from the creek
bottom, and if you look close enough you can see the image
is in the shape of an eye.

61. Mother of Decapitated Girl Warns Parkers in Stepp Cemetery

This is a legend known by everyone around Martinsville,
Indiana. There was this couple out parked in the Morgan-
Monroe Forestry. They were in the car making out pretty
heavily when they realized that it was a quarter till twelve.
Since the girl had a twelve o'clock curfew and her mother got
upset if she was late, the boy had to get her in on time. There
was a big dance next week, and they wanted to be sure to get
to go to it. Both the girl and boy were still in high school, and
at the time they considered hot-rodding the thing to do. The
road through the forestry is very windy and should be
traveled about 25 miles an hour. They were in a big hurry
and were taking the curves 60 to 70 miles per hour. They
were going this fast on the sharpest curve in the whole forestry. All at once the young man lost control of his car,
smashed into a tree, and both of them were killed. The young
girl was decapitated, but her head was never found.

For some reason, the mother of the girl insisted that the

death of the two kids be kept quiet. The story of their death
was relatively unknown until several years later. Actually it
came out about four years afterwards. Oh, also, it didn't come
out in the papers until the mother had died. Another couple
of the same age was parked in the forestry in the same spot. A
stirring was heard directly in front of the car. This startled the
young girl, causing her to look up and scream. The boy was
also frightened and looked up. They both saw in front of
them a small gnarled woman who was dressed entirely in
black, and she wore around her neck the head of a young girl.
The head was all beaten up and bruised and badly smashed.
After this, several other couples saw the same woman.

Some people say this old woman represents the mother of
the young girl that was killed. They say she reappears to
warn other couples not to park and then have to speed home
through those dangerous curves and be killed. The forestry,
which had been a popular spot for parking in the dark hours
of the night, now became only a daytime picnic area. There's
another version just like the original story except they say the
old woman sits on a tombstone in the forestry. The tombstone
is actually a petrified tree hollowed into a bench, and it can
be found in the Stepp Cemetery.

62. Wife Guards Husband's Grave in Stepp Cemetery

When they were building the Morgan-Monroe County
Forestry a long time ago, a man was killed working construction there, and he was buried in the graveyard in the forestry.
His wife goes out there every night to sit on his grave to keep
people away from it. She has done this for years, before and
even after she had died.

One night a guy and a girl I know parked there because

none of us kids every really believed about the lady. While
they were there they heard a knock on the car window, and
there she was dressed in a black cape, black hat, and a long,
black dress, and she was shaking her finger at them.

63. Chain Appears on Tombstone after
Husband Kills Wife

There's a cemetery in Orleans that has a grave of a man
who killed his wife with a chain. The man was never proven
guilty, but his wife's family swore his guilt would be there
and if so it would be exposed. So when the man died he was
not buried with his wife but was buried alone. The grave
marker was put up, and in a few days this thing which looked
like a flaw in the stone started to appear. Well, it finally
formed a chain link. This was the proof of his guilt that had
been sworn would appear. Well, for every year on the day the
man had killed his young wife a new link would form in the
chain. Soon the word got out, and there was lots of people
coming to see the stone. The church didn't like all this popu-
larity, so they changed the original stone for another one,
hoping or knowing this would take care of the problem. Well,
on the date that the link should have been added on, it was.

Now people started to wonder how the links were getting
there. Some thought that someone was going out there and
carving them, so the day before the link was to appear some
men started to get up enough courage to go out there and
spend the night. Well, two men went, and a little before
midnight they both fell asleep. When they woke up, the new
link was there. But they still did not know how they got
there.

Some young guys were messing around and decided to go

out there. One of them believed the story, but the other one didn't. The guy who didn't believe it touched the chain, and on the way home he got killed in a car wreck. Someone had stretched up a log chain, and the boy driving didn't see it. The other boy was not hurt at all. So now everyone swears that if you touch the chain you will die by the chain. I know it's there because I've seen it. It looks like a chain with a bar across it. I don't know what the bar is supposed to mean. I've touched it, too. It feels like the rest of the smooth part of the tombstone, but it doesn't look like a flaw to me. I'm hoping I can go back next year to see if a new link has formed. Some people say that you can't see it in a picture, but I have one that it showed up good in.

64. Chain Appears on Tombstone after Master Kills Slave

The legend of the chain on the tombstone has puzzled people for a long time. The story goes that a Negro slave was killed by his master. Supposedly, his master struck him with a chain and it killed him. The slave's name was John Pruitt, and he's buried at Bonds Chapel near Orangeville, Indiana. Some people think that even the name of the chapel has some importance.

Well, even today no one knows why or how, but a chain-type of coloration has formed a cross symbol on the side of this slave's gravestone. It is on the north side. What is really strange about it is that they have had all kinds of professional scientists and geologists to try to find an explanation for the formation, and it hasn't been done.

Another thing about the formation is that it is supposed to grow a link every year. There is no possible way that it has been painted on, carved into the stone, or even lacquered on. It's just something that can't be explained why it's there or how it got there.

65. Stiffy Green in Mausoleum

In Highland Lawn Cemetery here in Terre Haute, there's the mausoleum with a dog in it. The dog is called Stiffy Green. It has real weird eyes. They're green. This dog was owned by a real rich man; and when the man died, the dog did, too. So they had the dog stuffed and put it in the mausoleum with the old man's body. The dog is supposed to protect his master. Whenever anybody goes around there at night, the dog's green eyes follow the intruder. When danger is near, like someone trying to break into the mausoleum thinking there might be some money in there, the dog is supposed to howl.

66. Stiffy Green's Head on Tombstone

When I was in high school, all the kids used to talk about this really fantastic cemetery somewhere on the east side of Terre Haute. There was supposedly a headstone there and on top of the headstone a real dog's stuffed head. Rumor had it that this old man had lived alone for years with his little dog. The old man knew that he would soon die and had mentioned to friends that the dog would die soon after that. He wanted his dog to be with him even in death because they were such devoted companions. So when the old man died, his little dog grieved for days, and then one day was found dead. So he was stuffed, and his head was placed on the old man's grave so they could be together eternally.

67. McHarry's Tomb

An interesting reminder of the steamboat era in Indiana is a large and imposing tomb that is built into a Harrison County hillside overlooking the Ohio River. This large stone tomb is located in Posey Township near the little village of Bridgeport, about ten miles southeast of the county seat of Corydon.

The tomb was built by Frank McHarry, a steamboat captain before the Civil War and owner of an immense tract of land around Bridgeport. He selected a very prominent site on one of the bluffs and there constructed an elaborate tomb that offered a commanding view of the river. McHarry selected this solitary location so that after his death, and burial there, he (or his ghost) could shout curses at the steamboats passing on the river below.

Upon his death, his wishes were carried out and his body placed in the prepared tomb. After several years, his relatives in Louisville, Kentucky, finally had the remains moved to the Cave Hill Cemetery at that city.

However, the large tomb remained, and since it is in such an isolated place, it has mainly remained undisturbed. It still stands on the cliff where it can be seen easily by modern boats moving up and down the Ohio River.

68. Heart of Murdered Girl Beats from Grave

There was this other tombstone near French Lick where this girl was killed, and it was said that you could hear her heart beating, and my brother and some of his friends went there, and they got near it, and they actually heard the heartbeat, and they were scared to death, and they kept saying it was Ronnie's heart because he was really scared. But my brother actually got down on his hands and knees and crawled and followed the sound of the heartbeat, and it took him right to the tomb. No one can figure it out.

69. Heart of Giant Beats from Grave

Down in Springs Valley there is this spot where you can hear this giant heartbeat coming out of the ground. They say that a giant was killed there long ago. But I know it is one of those Texas oil well lines that goes underground, and the oil changes levels at that spot, and it drips down in the pipes and sounds like a giant heartbeat.

70. Death in the Graveyard: Fork in Dress

There was this girl once who had long dark hair. This was back in the days when girls wore long dresses. Well, she used to brag about how brave she was, so one day her friends dared her to go into the graveyard at midnight and stick a fork into the grave of this old man. She did, but she never came out again.

The next day they went into the graveyard with her parents, and they found her on the ground, lying by the grave. Her hair had turned a pale white color because she had died of fright. Apparently, when she stuck the fork into the ground she caught her long dress and thought that something was holding on to her.

71. Death in the Graveyard: Knife in Apron

During the early part of the 1880s, five or six teen-age girls visited a nearby farm to attend a corn shelling party. When it became dark, they began telling ghost stories concerning the nearby cemetery. Soon they were daring each other to enter the cemetery. One girl declared that she would not only enter but would plunge a butcher knife into a grave. When she did not return in a reasonable time, the adults were routed to search for her. They found her dead, slumped over a grave. She had placed the knife in a grave, but in so doing had anchored her apron to it and died of fright.

72. The Ghosts of Heady's Hollow

On State Highway 13, between Indianapolis and Noblesville, near the town of Fishers, the road crosses a deep valley. At the bottom of this valley, the road is flanked on each side by heavy woods and is very dark at night. The valley is known as Heady's Hollow, and for many years, prior to 1900, the place was thought to be haunted, and its ghosts were known as "The Ghosts of Heady's Hollow."

Many people traveled that road and dreaded to pass through the valley at night. Some believed they were chased by many horsemen, and many a traveler was known to race his horse at top speed, to get out of the valley before being caught by the unseen horsemen. It has been said by many people that when riding or driving through the valley, when a certain place was reached, there came a sound of many horses following close behind, yet none were ever seen, and when the traveler was nearly out of the valley, the hoofbeats of the pursuing ghost-horses became less noticeable and finally were left far behind.

It was learned later that the cause of the sound, as of many horses, was a reflection of sound waves, or an echo of the hoofbeats of the traveler's horse reflected in all directions by the arrangement of the trees and hills beside the road.

73. Sleepy Hollow

Over at Frankfort, Indiana, there is this lonely road where all the kids go to see how brave they really are . . . to see if they are chicken or not. You see, there is this bridge over some creek, and this old woman a long time ago was supposed to have killed her husband and cut him in small pieces and thrown him over this bridge. If you go down to that bridge and stop . . . you have to wait for a few minutes . . . and then slowly down the road you will see a faint light. The light will get stronger the longer you wait. It is supposed to be the old lady coming down to the bridge. See, she doesn't like anyone to be there. One night a bunch of us guys got a case of beer and decided to go and wait on the bridge to see what would happen. One of the guys got out of the car and stood under the bridge. The rest of us went on down the road. When we came back the guy under the bridge said, "Thought you would scare me by all those funny noises, didn't you?" We all said, "What noises?" I swear we didn't go back to the bridge after we let him out. Now just what those noises were I don't know. We all left in a damn hurry though!

74. Haunted Hollow

Haunted Hollow is located in southern Harrison County about two miles northwest of Mauckport on the Mauckport and New Amsterdam Road. This is a very dreary and lonely

place that travelers hurry past, especially in the dead hours of
night.

It is reported that many years ago a man landed a boat at
this place and built himself a cabin on the banks of the Ohio
River. During his stay there he operated a lime kiln and was
preparing to take his lime down the river when he was
robbed and murdered. His head was cut off, and his body
thrown into the river. At various times since then this headless man has been seen in the vicinity of the scene of the
crime.

75. Ghost of Miner Runs Dragline

Back in the early 1930s there was something happened
that I still don't believe but can't explain either. I worked in
the Old Glory #33 mine that was then east of Clay City, Indiana. Lee, and I can't remember his last name for nothing,
had been a runner [operator of a dragline] for years, and that's
all he ever done. He worked the "hoot owl" ever since he
started with the mine. One morning, about 1:00 A.M., Lee's
neighbor called and said that he had passed away.

Well, I jumped in my truck and headed for the mine 'cause
I was in charge at that time. I wanted to make sure that there
was somebody running the drag 'cause we were loading cars
the next day. I drove up to the mine office and went in. There
were some guys standing around the salamander, and I told
them that old Lee was gone. They said that they had seen
him running the drag not 15 minutes ago. I said that couldn't
be 'cause he died at home. We all jumped in the mine truck
and headed for the pit. When we were close enough, we saw
the lights on the drag and saw the boom swinging like it was
digging okay. We drove on toward the drag and had to pass

around a big spoil pile. When we rounded the last one and saw the drag, we couldn't believe it. All the lights on the drag were out, and the bucket was sitting on the bank just like it hadn't been started. We checked, and the engine was cold. Ol' Lee was at work that night. The funny part was, that was his last night before he was to retire.

76. The Faceless Nun

The legend of the faceless nun has its origin on St. Mary-of-the-Woods campus and dates back to some twenty years ago. It begins like this: There was a nun in this order of sisters who loved to paint. Her speciality was portraits, in which she always did the face last. One day she decided to paint a portrait of herself. However, before she could finish the face, she died. The rest of the nuns put the picture aside and never brought it out again. Well, one day one of the sisters was praying in church and noticed that the only nun with her, who was a couple of pews ahead of her, seemed to be weeping. So she thought she would go up to her and see if she could console her. When she tapped her on the shoulder, the nun had been horrified at the sight she saw. For this nun had no face! She let out a bloody scream, and the other nuns in the convent came running to her and tried to calm her down. But they did not see this faceless nun that she was screaming about. Because of the tremendous shock that this nun experienced, she was put in the hospital and remained there till she died.

Soon other nuns began to encounter the faceless nun, not only in the church but all over the campus. They finally had to have all the buildings on the campus exorcised by the priests, and ever since this was done the faceless nun hasn't reappeared. The older nuns, however, still can recall the visitations of this faceless nun. Some of them even knew her when she was alive. Her tombstone is still here on the campus, but her spirit has left us alone . . . so far!

77. Ghost Laid by Bible

Many years ago, when houses were built the bedroom was built away from the rest of the house. While my grandfather was at home growing up, he lived in a home like this. His father always hung the horses' harness on the outside of the bedroom wall. At night when everything became real still, and there was no wind at all, strange things would begin to happen. The horses' harness would begin to rattle as though the wind was blowing. Then the door would come open. Try as hard as they would, they could not keep the door shut. Then the stairs would begin to creak. My grandfather had a rocking chair, which belonged to his grandmother, that always sat in the living room. After all these strange things happened the rocking chair would rock just as though Grandma was sitting there. No one was ever seen, and the only way the spirits could be stopped was for Grandpa to get his Bible and put it under his pillow and sleep on it. This same thing happened many times, and sleeping on the Bible was the only way to stop it.

HAUNTED HOUSES

78. The House of Blue Lights

There was a rich millionaire in Indianapolis named Tess [sic]. To prove that he was a real person, there's an office building in Indianapolis named after him. He had his wife and loved her and that kind of rot. Unfortunately, for him, his wife died; and so when she died, he had her embalmed and put in a plastic enclosed casket so you could see her. Her favorite color was blue, so in this room in his house where the casket was, he put blue lights everywhere. Legend has it that he had this casket upright with a fan behind it so her hair would look like it was blowing in the wind. The estate covered a square mile and was on top of a hill. He didn't use city electricity; he had a generator which made a loud noise. As the legend grew, kids flocked to the house to see if they could see the woman standing upright in the casket. Visitors became so frequent they purchased big white dogs and put up a high barbed wire fence to keep people out. Police finally had to patrol around it.

This story was told to me by my brother who saw the house with the blue lights, and my aunt also saw it when she was in high school. It was a favorite thing to do in our high school to go to Indianapolis and see the house. You can hear the generator and see the lights, but everyone wanted to try to get up close and look in the windows to see the lady.

I read in the paper when this guy died about how he was crazy. He collected cats and when they died put them in caskets. They found these when he died. During the war he bought railroad cars of non-perishable foods . . . ketchup and stuff like that.

79. The Glass Coffin

There's a house about a mile north of my home—about four miles straight south of Hobart. An old man used to live there. It's just a tiny square house with yellow siding and a bunch of junk in the back. The man killed his wife and put her in a coffin with a glass top right in front of his picture window. He kept a candle burning, sitting right on top of the coffin at night with no other light in the whole house. He used to just sit there and look at her. These kids got suspicious and started peeking in his windows and harassing him with firecrackers and stuff. It finally drove the old man crazy, and he killed himself. The cops didn't find him till a week later. They said the whole house smelled like rotten flesh. They never found the coffin, but they did find a sulphur candle sitting on the ledge of the front picture window.

80. Haunted House at Medora

The story centers around the owners of a house, the remains of which are located at the top of the Knobs west of Medora, Indiana, on [old] U.S. 50. Dr. and Mrs. Creed Wilson built this house in 1848, five years after the birth of their youngest son, Aesop.

Aesop's mother doted on him because he was the youngest. When he was 17, he wanted to enlist in Captain Gordan Tanner's company of Volunteers assembling at Medora in the spring of 1861. But his mother forbade him to go and even ordered Captain Tanner not to take him. Aesop joined anyway on July 11, 1861, and became a drummer boy with Captain Tanner's Company B, 22nd Regiment, Indiana Volunteers. He was sent to Jefferson City, Missouri, and later transferred to Boonville, Missouri, where he died.

In April 1862, Dr. Wilson had his son's body returned to Medora. Not satisfied that it was the body of her son, Mrs. Wilson had the casket opened and gazed once more on her youngest child's features. She still would not consent to the burial of the body; and, at her request, an undertaker placed the body in charcoal and sealed the casket. It was placed in the upstairs hallway in front of the window. For twelve years the mother kept the casket there. Each afternoon she would go upstairs, make herself comfortable in a little wicker chair, and sew and talk to her dead son.

All this time, Dr. Wilson insisted that the body should be buried. Finally, in 1873, he hired a Mr. and Mrs. Kegwin, spiritualists from Louisville, Kentucky, to come to their house and hold a seance. After a long pause, a voice was heard saying, "This is Aesop, Mother." After other conversation, in which Mrs. Wilson was firmly convinced the voice was that of her son, she asked, "Would you like to have your remains buried?" "Yes, Mother," answered the voice. "Where?" she asked. "In the cedars just north of the house," the voice replied. The body was buried the next day.

The "Haunted House" is now crumbling and decaying, but it is a place where ghosts and spirits are said to gather. When a lone rider passes the house at night, he might see the white, wraith-like figures at the windows and hear the moaning before hurrying on his way.

81. Murdered Wife Buried in Wall of the Preston House

It is the oldest house in Terre Haute in which a woman was supposed to be walled up in the dining room after her husband had murdered her. The man came from New Orleans, and so did his wife. When they came to Terre Haute he

had had the house built. They had all kinds of servants, and
the house was located far out of town in what was considered
the country. Now it stands at 14th and Poplar. His wife was
supposed to take a visit back to relatives. All the servants and
townfolk believed she'd gone. However, the relatives soon
wrote and inquired as to her whereabouts. Since she had
never returned it was taken for granted she had been killed
on the way there. The servants had a different explanation.
They believed the husband had killed his wife. They knew
that he had wanted a divorce and she wouldn't give him one.
Shortly after her disappearance a patchwork of cement had
appeared in the dining room. Where a cupboard had always
been, now there was this large cement patch where, the servants believed, the husband had buried his wife.

82. Ghosts of Slaves Haunt the Preston House

You know that legend about the underground railroad,
don't you? Well, on Poplar Street, at about 14th Street, there's
a two-story, white, frame house. It sits way back off the street.
There's a fence that goes all around the place. The house is
real run-down and dark and creepy looking.

Anyway, according to the story, this house was part of the
underground railroad. You know, it was part of that system of
tunnels that Blacks traveled through to get from the South to
safety in the North. One day, when the tunnels were full of
slaves, there were two cave-ins. One was right near the entrance to this house on Poplar. The other was about a
thousand feet beyond. Well, there were all these slaves
caught between these two cave-ins. The owners of the house
tried to rescue them, of course. You know, they tried to dig
them out. But these Northerners couldn't do a whole lot be-

cause then the secret tunnels would not be a secret any more.
So all these slaves died. But they really didn't. I mean, their
spirits are supposed to be alive and roaming that house and
the land around it.

A few years ago, a bunch of us guys got this phone number
from another guy. I can't remember his name right now,
though. Well, anyway, we called it. It was the phone number
of that house. But when we called nobody really answered. I
mean, you heard someone or something pick up the receiver,
but they never said anything. Instead, you heard this breathing and then all this moaning and groaning. You could hear
chains clanking. We called the number several times. It was
always the same. I wish I still had that number, but I lost it.

83. Merom's Haunted House

There was an old house in Merom as you go toward
Graysville that looked just like a big castle or a mansion, and
us kids around Merom used to call it the old castle. It has big
silo-like pillars in the front of it, and it was really spooky
looking, and us kids would walk way around it on dark
nights. An old maid and her mother lived in the house named
Midders. My dad shucked corn for the old woman, and she
would only let him up to the back door. No one that I knew
of much had ever even been in the house. Well, one day the
old woman died and left the old maid all alone. They said the
old woman had been dead a week or more before the old
maid ever called the undertaker to come and bury her. When
the undertaker finally did come there wasn't any funeral or
anything. The undertaker just took her body and buried it at
the Merom cemetery on the old side.

From that time on the old maid stayed all alone in that big

house. She wore awful looking old clothes that were tattered and about torn off of her—usually an old shirt and a long black skirt that came down to the ground. She had one old cow that Dad said she would come out and milk in the morning if she was sure no one in the neighborhood was outdoors where they could see her. Dad would be out shucking corn in her field, and he'd see her slip out the door and look around and head for the barn early most mornings. She always wore an old floppy hat and smoked a pipe. Wasn't too long after that, I don't remember exactly how long, that we had a real bad cold spell. Someone found her froze to death outside. After that old Fred Bays bought the house, but he never would live in it. He lived in the tenant house out back and farmed the property.

It had been said in Merom that the old house was haunted. There had been a Mr. Midder who had apparently died a mysterious death in the house. There were people who said he hanged himself, and there were even some who suspicioned the old woman had done her husband in. Many folks around Merom claimed at night you could hear the old man's scream echo through the old castle walls. The house stood idle for a good many years after both women had died. It was three stories high, and finally it burned down.

84. Koleen's Haunted House

Up around Bloomfield on the other side about 15 miles out in the country, there's a small town called Koleen. It's only got a store—you know, the general type store with everything—and about five houses, but anyway there's this here house on out in the country that has weird things happen around it, especially a certain night each year. It's really weird, man. Supposedly, an old woman who was meaner than hell lived there all alone and had for several years, but she wasn't the sociable type, and being as mean as she was, no one bothered about going around the old bitch to visit her, either.

One night she was going to bed and was carrying her candle upstairs to light the way when she caught her really long black hair on fire. Well, the dumb bitch got excited and started running around shouting her head off, which naturally fed more oxygen to the fire, causing it to burn faster and harder. Well, she finally burned up, but at a certain night each year on the anniversary of her death, if you go up there and sit at the foot of the hill, around midnight you can see flames flashing in the house, and the door handle's a red-hot glow, and you can't touch it in spite of hell, for it'll burn your hand off. Then you hear all these bloodcurdling screams coming from the house, and it just plain scares the holy shit out of you. But you have to know what night to go, and you can tell around when 'cause weird things start taking place, and it all leads up to the big night when the action happens, and you can hear the screams and see the flames.

85. East Chicago's Haunted House

There is a house in East Chicago where one can hear a woman crying in pain and other scary things at night. The house has been empty for years. The story behind the house goes like this: A wealthy man had caught his wife being unfaithful to him. He waited for the opportune moment to tell her that he knew about her infidelity. When she began to deny his charges, he became so angry that he took a knife and began to stab. He butchered her to death while she screamed with pain. After he had killed his wife, the man became so insane that he felt he could go on no longer. He hung himself on one of the ceiling beams. When the police arrived, they found the man hanging from a beam with his wife full of blood beneath him. They boarded the house up and left. Now, at the stroke of midnight, if one passes the house he will hear a woman's crying and a man's moaning. The rope is still hanging on the beam. One time during the day, my friend and I went into the house and found it there.

86. Kokomo's Haunted House

I think the house has twelve rooms, and they are very large rooms. They have about twelve-foot ceilings and a fireplace in almost every room. No one has ever been able to live in this house because of the strange noises heard in and about the place. My father and mother moved into the house, as they were not superstitious.

I remember quite well, although I was quite small, an incident that would make the hair of any normal person stand on end. We were all sitting around the fireside one evening after supper, and we heard a faint noise. It kept getting louder, and it sounded as if someone was dragging a chain across the floor. It came on through the kitchen, into the dining room, and right in where we were. It scared us all stiff. This peculiar sound went on out of the front door, and we never heard it any more that night, but every night it was the same thing.

Another funny thing that happened while we were in that house was as follows: There was a large cedar tree that stood in the front lawn and is still standing the last account I had of it. We were sitting in the front room one night, and we heard

that there tree fall, and my father said, "Well, we will have to
cut that tree up in the morning." Well, we went to bed early,
and the next morning we arose with the idea of cutting the
tree into firewood, but the strange thing about this was that
the tree was standing just as straight as it is now. This was
just before we moved, and after this happened we thought it
best to move into the other house.

One day my father decided to go over and spend the night
by himself. He lit his lantern and went over to the old
haunted house. He lay down on the couch to go to sleep, and
something blew his light out. He just thought it was the
breeze that was coming through the window, so he closed the
window and lit the lantern, and just as he lit the lantern
something blew it out again. He lit it for three straight times,
and each time the same thing would happen. He left and he
said he never would try to spend another night by himself in
that house.

We moved into the other house, but we could still see
lights in the haunted house, and at times, there would be the
most beautiful music being played that one would ever want
to hear. If there is anyone that wished to visit this place, it is
still there, and you may camp there and live in the house as
long as you wish, but there has been no one that has ever
spent but one night in this horrible house. These things are
not just tales but true experiences and facts, and if you go
there and spend a night you, too, will believe that there are
ghosts and plenty of them.

87. Hill House

Now, I know that you're not going to believe this, goddamn it, but I swear on my pin that it supposedly happened.

There's this house in Rockville . . . well really, it's a little out of town . . . that's called Hill House. I guess because it sort of sits up on a small rise back off the road. Anyway, the owner or somebody of that house supposedly died, and all the relation from all around. . . . This wasn't any small house; whoever died had the cash. Well, anyway, all these people came and stayed the night before the funeral in the house. Well, when they woke up in the morning, they found every piece of their clothing gone. And get this. When they started looking around for it, guess where they finally found it? Up in these tall trees in back, so high up that no human could put it up there. I guess that it was quite a deal. I imagine that it even made some newspapers.

88. Room Changes Color in the White Castle

The White Castle at Rockville used to be where we'd go for kicks. The farmer won't let anyone in anymore. Anyway, it's a two-story house with an attic. This architect built it in the late twenties, and it's real weird. He also built a bunch of other things, some buildings in Chicago. It has an angular staircase and a big living room with a fireplace. It's made of white stucco, and so's the garage. There's a long driveway winding through the trees which overhang the drive. Joe Jackson swears that every time he's been in there the room, I guess it's the dining room, has been a different color. I can verify that, 'cause I've been there a couple of times and I noticed the paint was different. It's the room on the right when you enter the front door. I saw it dark tan once and light blue another time. Joe says he's seen it from almost black to almost white.

89. Ghost Avenges Death in the White Castle

I can't remember exactly where it was, but I feel sure it was in the Rockville area, northwest of it. Anyway, there is a large white house; it appeared to be stucco. Its shape was on the square side, and it was quite large. I was told that it was haunted by the former owner. The owner, who himself wasn't a very pleasant sort, had died a very cruel death at the hands of the townsfolk. He had willed his property to the caretaker, who was a very loyal servant. His master's last words were to avenge his cruel death. So the caretaker stole an infant of the village and raised him to take his place guarding the mansion, as the former master had requested. So the process was repeated for the age of the caretakers. Infants were stolen and trained and entertained the ghost of the old master. The present caretaker is a large man with reddish hair who walks around with a mean-looking hound and carries a gun. If he catches anyone snooping around, he catches them and takes them to the torture chamber of the house. He tortures him as supervised by the old master's ghost.

GOOD AND EVIL

90. The Devil as Escort

Many years ago a young lady became unjustly wroth towards her gentleman friend who had promised to escort her to an evening's pleasure but who, through the inclemency of the weather, did not appear. The longer she waited, the more impatient and rebellious she became towards him. Her mother tried to pacify her, telling her that the night was too cold for anyone to be out and that the young man was justified in not coming, but nothing would pacify the girl. She said she wanted to go, as she liked very much to dance and her friend knew it, and she only wished that someone else would come and take her—that she would go if the Devil asked her. The mother was very much shocked and was filled with fear at the bold, decided stand her daughter had taken.

She again tried to calm her, and while doing so, they heard the tinkling of sleighbells; they came closer and closer, and then they saw a sleigh appearing in the darkness and stopping at the gate. A very handsome young man came to the door and knocked, and when the young lady opened the door, he said that he had come to take her to the dance. The young lady said, "Why, you are not my friend." "No," said he, "but your friend sent me to take you, as he is unable to come tonight." The mother then became more uneasy than ever and begged her daughter not to go, saying, "Remember what you have just said." But the daughter was willful and again repeated the remark that she would go if the Devil asked her.

She accepted the young man as her escort, and they started through the frosty night to the scene of gaiety. They drove and drove. The night was lovely, even though cold, and her companion was gay. The young lady was enjoying herself, not thinking so much of the distance covered and the time passing, until becoming a little cold, turned to her companion and asked him if they were not about to their destination. He made an evasive answer, and she then became uneasy. He kept on driving, and finally through her urgent demand that he take her to the dance, he suddenly disappeared from her view, and she found herself dropping, dropping down into a great deep hole in the ground. Her parents, becoming uneasy when she did not come home that night, started a search; they hunted everywhere they knew, but were finally forced to give her up, for she was never seen or heard of again.

91. Devil Chased by Holy Water

Jim's aunt lived right next door to an ol' whore, who was slowly dying in bed. Everyday Jim's aunt would go over to see her and keep her company and fix her meals. Both families were Catholic, as 85 percent of Jasper's population is. One day while sitting there Jim's aunt suddenly saw a man standing over the woman and just staring at her. He was dressed in a suit and tie, and his eyes were huge, bright, and emerald-red glowing into the woman's face. Jim's aunt knew this man was indeed the devil; so being Catholic the woman had some holy water at her bedside. Jim's aunt slowly reached over and picked it up. In a split second she threw it on the man, and he vanished.

92. Jesus Saves Condemned Soul from the Devil

This's kind of on the religious side, but I had an uncle, one of Mom's brothers. He was sick better than seven years in bed. So one time he went to church. He went to church before he got sick, and he got sick shortly afterwards. And for two or three months, and maybe longer than that, he'd see a devil in his window. He'd talk about how he'd laugh at him, dance, and all. Course he's the only one that had seen him. The devil was in the bedroom window. See, he was just a-dancin' all over the place, clappin' his hands, and whatnot.

He tried to show him to the people that was a-settin' up with
him. He was tryin' to tell the people that was settin' up with
him. And this went on about a week before the man died.
And he told 'em, he said, "Christ is here starin' out the window." And he said, boy, when he did, the devil had to move.
He was there, and he could see the nail scars in his hands
and all that stuff. Happened a week or so before he died.

93. Jesus and Ghost of Grandfather Reassure the Living

A young girl who suffered from epilepsy was facing a
serious brain operation. She had a fifty-fifty chance of surviv-
ing the ordeal and naturally was very frightened. Just before
the operation—while she was waiting for the anesthetic to
take effect—she was lying in the room alone. Opening her
eyes, she saw two figures standing at the foot of her bed. One
was her grandfather, who had recently died; the other was
Christ. Her grandfather told her not to be afraid. He knew
that it was a serious operation, he said, but that they were
there to help her. If she would just have faith and believe
him, everything was going to turn out all right. Then, he took
her by the hand and told her that they would stay beside her
through the operation. Miraculously, the doctors say, she
came out of the operation and has recovered completely with
no hint of being an epileptic.

94. Answered Prayers

There is this girlfriend of mine from home that has a
really strange story that she claims is true. It seems she be-

came very ill when she was about five years old. I can't remember what she was sick from now, but all I know is that the doctor told her parents that she was going to die. Her mother became grief-stricken and began to pray to God to save her daughter. She continued to pray for a few days; meanwhile there was no change in Cathy's condition.

Cathy told me that she felt really awful and was crying because she couldn't find her mother in the room. She felt very weak. All of a sudden, she became very lightweighted, and there was a bright light in the room. Soon a stairway surrounded by clouds appeared. It looked like stairs leading to heaven. A man came down the stairs, held Cathy, and said, "Not yet, Cathy. Not yet."

He held her until she felt better, laid her back down on the bed, walked up the stairs, and disappeared. Cathy got up and ran down the corridor calling for her mother. She told her mother about the man and described him to her. Her mother cried with joy. Jesus had come from heaven to save her daughter.

95. Jesus over Fontanet

On the other side of Fontanet, before the 500 race, the weather became very rainy and stormy. Two sisters lived together in a trailer. One sister went outside to see how the storm was, and when she looked up in the sky, she saw this image [of Jesus] between two trees in the clouds. She ran back in the house and was really excited. Her sister asked her, "What are you doing? What's wrong?" So the lady told her sister to follow her as she grabbed her camera. She took a series of shots, and this picture is the only one which came out. After the image disappeared, the trees on each side were burnt on the top.

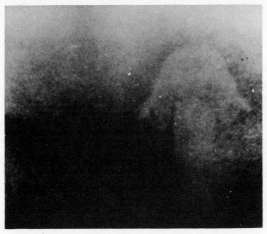

96. The Dogwood Tree

When Christ was crucified his cross was made out of the strongest tree that existed, the dogwood tree. But knowing that the wood of the tree was to be used to make the cross that Christ was nailed on, it began to shrink, wither, and twist until it was little more than a bush. Never again did it become strong enough to be used for such an evil deed. And to show its pain each year it blooms into white blossoms the shape of a cross. Each tip to the cross is stained red as if with blood, and it has a thorny center.

SPECIAL POWERS

97. The Evil Eye

Another case of the evil eye was here in Terre Haute. Sandy had a case of mononucleosis, I think it was. She was sick for a while, and they couldn't get her healed, it seemed like. It was a very slow process to get back on her feet. One day when I was there . . . this had been not too long after Nick's sister-in-law arrived to America. She's from the old school—a woman who doesn't read or write, but she knows all the house remedies for sicknesses and illnesses. It was done behind my back because I wouldn't have permitted it to be done when I was there. In any case, they went into the kitchen and took a bullet, took it apart and melted the lead from the end of the bullet. They melted it and took a bowl of water and came inside to the girl's sickbed, and they held it above Sandy and dropped the lead, hot lead, into the water. Of course, falling into the water it is going to immediately harden, and it's supposed to form, and the form that it takes in the water is the shape of the evil spirit.

98. Bloodstopping

I had a grandpa who could stop bleeding. He didn't even have to be with the person. In other words, you could take word to him. But he did have to know who it was and where the person was bleeding. Daddy had real bad nosebleeds. He just poured. And the doctors couldn't do anything. Well, when he would have one, he'd send someone down to his dad's. We all lived in Linton, but we lived several blocks apart. We didn't have a car, so whoever went had to walk. By the time the person would get to Grandpa's and tell him, the bleeding would quit. I know this happened. I was a little girl, but I remember it.

99. Blowing the Fire out of a Burned Arm

You know John, don't you? Well, his dad could blow fire. I had a burn, a great big burn on the side of my arm. I stumbled against the heating stove, and it really made a big red burned place on my arm. Anyway, they came out to our house that night. He said, "Is that really hurting you?" I said, "Yes." He said he could blow fire out. He blew in a circular motion, like little bitty circles, like you'd think of a whirlwind, you know. It quit hurting, and the red went away and everything just as soon as he blew on it. I haven't even got a scar, and it was an awful bad burn. He said he had to pass it on to a woman, from a man to a woman. That was the only way it would work. He told me he would tell me, but he never did. I didn't believe he could do it. He said that didn't matter. But, anyway, it worked.

100. Blowing the Fire out of a Burned Abdomen

I was working in a cannery running a steam cooker, and whoever tightened down the lid didn't tighten it tight enough, and it scalded my stomach, and a bunch of ladies ran up to me, and they all said, "Let's take him to the doctor!" One of the ladies said, "Henry, if you'll let me, I'll take the fire out right quick." She blowed all around on my stomach, and it took the fire out, and it never even got sore. The hide never peeled off or nothing, and I never did no more to it. I never saw anything like it before. I know some of the women working there saw it—Frances and Peg, for sure, and also John's wife.

101. Blowing the Fire out of a Burned Hand

I made me a firecracker out of powder, which I was accustomed to making out of corncobs, but I made this one out of paper. I judge I had eight drams of powder. Besides, I didn't have any fuse; I made me a fuse out of powder and paper. Alas, there was too much powder in the fuse. When I lit a match to it, the whole thing went. Then almost in one minute my entire hand was solid blisters. I got a great tin can, filled it with water, and went up the alley with my hand in a can a half a block. Grandmother said, "Oh, my, you drove the fire in with the water." She said she'd blow the fire out of my hand. She made rolling motions with her hands around mine, blowing, at the same time mumbling something. And then I had to wait a while and pierce the blisters, and they grew well. It never hurt after she blew the fire out.

102. Son Who Hasn't Seen His Father Cures Thrush

I had an old uncle, Old Uncle Otis, who lived up here, you know, where the old Steller's blacksmith shop used to be. Well, they lived there in that house. And they took children there . . . I forget what for . . . I think it was thrush. Thrush was a kind of children's rash. It was said, too, that anybody that was born without seeing his or its father, then he was gifted with a special type of curing . . . healing power. And Uncle Otis, he never did see his father, and these people were always bringing their children to him. And if my memory serves me right, he would always take the children out back by the manure pile, and Lord knows what he did to them out there. I only know that it was supposed to have cured them.

103. Rubbing Warts

One day my mother and grandmother were downtown shopping. They were in Wolford's dime store, and my grandmother saw the manager had a big wart on his neck. Well, Grandmother said, "Nellie, I could take that wart off if he wouldn't care." Mother said, "I expect he'd be tickled to death to lose it. Why don't you ask him?"

So Grandmother walked up to the manager and asked if he would care if she removed the wart. He told her he would be thrilled to death. Grandmother rubbed her hand over it and told the manager to forget about it. The manager said, "Lady, if you remove that wart, I'll buy you the finest hat in Linton." Several days later a box was delivered to my grandmother's with a beautiful new hat.

104. Burying a Knotted String to Cure Warts

I was going to a doctor for warts. Okay, I went to him for about six months, and finally I had to leave to go to school, and he still hadn't gotten rid of them. So he told me, he said, "Now, I don't know much about this, but I know this lady who is supposed to be able to get rid of warts." So he gave me her address, and I thought, "What the heck, I'd go see her; it couldn't hurt." So I called her, and she told me to come on over, so I did. She took a regular spool of thread, and she tore off a piece, and she wound it up in a little circle and tied a knot in it, and she said the main thing you have to do is believe. So she put the thread on the warts on my finger, and she told me to take the thread and bury it and not tell anyone where I buried it. And she said they'd go away as long as I believed. She told me not to think about it, but my warts aren't gone.

105. Burying a Dirty Dishcloth to Cure Warts

' Mom had this aunt . . . I think Maggie was her name . . . that came to visit with them one summer. She was real superstitious, too. My mother had noticed this wart on her arm, Mom's arm. Mom's aunt told her how she could get rid of it. Mom's aunt told my mother to take a dirty dishcloth and rub it in the dirt, dry dirt. Then rub that on her arm and then bury the dishcloth. Then, in a few days, the wart would be gone. It did; the wart went away.

106. Warts Cured by Not Looking at Them

When my mom was a girl, she had a whole gob of warts on her hands, and they went to this person that was supposed to be a witch, you know, and could witch things away and stuff like this. But at the time they didn't know that. And all the person said was that she was busy right then and to go away and not look at her hands for a week. Well, of course, she was a little kid and looked at them all the time. But when she went back, as she went in the door, she looked at her hands, and the warts were still there. And she started talking to the woman, and the woman said, "Well, let me see your hands." And my mom showed her her hands, and there wasn't anything there; all the warts were gone.

107. Seventh Son of Seventh Son Cures Warts

My sister had warts all over her body, especially her arms and legs. She had just started to school, and kids would tease her. We'd tried doctors and everything and the warts wouldn't go away. Earl's father in Roachdale is the seventh son of a seventh son. We took her to him, and he blew on her arms and legs. Within a week they went away.

108. Seventh Daughter of Seventh Daughter Has Second Sight

This friend of mine's cousin's grandmother is the seventh daughter of the seventh daughter born with a veil over her face, like a flap of skin. That means that she's supposed to be a witch. I guess she had powers of telepathy and could always guess things ahead of time. After she died this picture of her in the front room of her house changed its expression. Her daughter put it in the attic. At night she hears noises like her mother walking at night.

109. Person Born with Caul Has Second Sight

My sister was borned with a veil over her face. What I seen, as near as I can remember 'cause she was born in 1903, was that there was fuzz all over her face. She had the power to tell the future, but as far as I know she only used it once. One day her husband went over to the Wabash River to a fishing camp and when he got back he wasn't going to tell her anything about where he had been. But she said to him, "Were you out in a boat?" And he said, "No." She said, "Oh yes you were." And she proceeded to tell him that he had been on the Wabash River in a boat taking one or two women for a ride in a boat. Anyway, she told him exactly where he'd been and what he'd been doing and let him know that he couldn't get by with any hanky-panky.

110. The Fire-Letter

This fire-letter is dated about 1852. Anyone possessing such a letter will not have any fire that will burn a building completely, providing that they will read the letter aloud while the building is burning and walk back and forth before the fire. Wherever such directions are followed the fire will quit burning. As evidence of the edification of such a letter and the proper reading of it, while walking back and forth before a blaze, the following instances are cited:

Kinney's sawmill and lumberyard caught fire in the logs and lumber many years ago. The fire was blazing all through the mill and out in the piles of lumber and logs, on the south side of the railroad tracks, in Butler. Shannon W. Shultz saw the blaze and hurried to the spot with his fire-letter, which he read aloud as he walked about the yard and before the burning mill. Wherever he passed along, reading the letter, the fire died down and stopped burning.

Be welcome, fiery guest, but do not spread farther; this I count thee as a penance, in the name of God the Father, the Son, and the Holy Ghost.

I command thee, fire, by the power of God, which does all and creates all, thou wilt stand still and not go farther as certain as Jesus stood on the Jordan when He was baptized by John the Saint.

This I count thee, fire, as a penance, in the name of the Holy Trinity.

I command thee, fire, by the power of God, thou wilt allay these flames as certain as Maria retained her virginity alone of all women, as she kept herself so chaste and pure, so, therefore, fire cease thy fury.

This I count thee, fire, as a penance in the name of the Most Holy Trinity.

I command thee, fire, thou wilt smother thy heat,
in the name of the dear blood of Jesus Christ, which
He has shed for us, for our sins and crimes.

This I count thee, fire, as a penance, in the name
of God the Father, the Son, and the Holy Ghost.

Jesus Nazarenus, a King of the Jews, help us out of
these dangers of fire and save this country and limits
from all plague and pestilence.

111. Water Witch Locates Water with a Forked Stick

In the spring of 1968 my father decided we had to drill a
new well. Our old one was low on water, and it couldn't be
pumped fast enough. A friend of ours was known for witching
wells. My father had him come out one afternoon. I think he
brought his forked stick with him. He went out toward the
backyard and just stood there with his stick. Then it started
pointing. It finally went down over a pile of junk. This was
about 30 yards from our old well. My father cleared the junk off
this spot because he decided this was the spot for the new well.
The drillers didn't come until the middle of the summer. They
set up their drilling operation where my father told them to. The
new well came in at about a level of 50 feet. This is really good
because there is quite a bit of rock around and most wells go
deeper. The drillers told my father they hit a good vein. I think
they said the new pump would pump about 1,000 gallons of
water a minute. Needless to say, my father now believes in
water witching. I don't know what to think.

112. Spirit Enters Arm of Water Witch

I can tell you how to find water, and you will never run
out, no matter how dry it will get. You take a branch from a

certain tree. I can't tell you which one because only I know the right kind. When you get this here branch . . . it has to be shaped like a "Y" . . . hold both ends of the branch in front of you like this. Then walk around in the yard and wait for a feeling of a spirit move up your arm. When the spirit finds the water, the end of the branch will point to the ground. That is where the water will be. The spirit will leave your arms and enter into the ground while you dig. Then the well will never dry up. I know because that's how I found our well, and it has never gone dry.

113. Water Witch Has Electricity in His Body

I know an old well witcher in Carlisle named John who claims he's the most successful well witcher there ever was. I don't believe in it myself, but he's supposed to have had a lot of successful finds here in this area where he lives. Old John claims he has so much electricity in his body that he can't wear a watch at all. They just won't run on him at all. Why, the longest time he said he ever got one to run without quittin' was no more than two weeks.

114. Bent Wire Used to Locate Buried Pipes

If you don't really believe in water witches, I'll show you something that will. All you have to do is find a piece of wire and bend it with a 90-degree angle in it. Now place it in your palm so that part of the bend is running level with the floor. Now all you have to do with it is walk along with it pointing straight out, and every time you walk over some sort of water pipe, the thing will turn.

115. Divining Rod with Gold Piece Attached
Locates Gold

I know where there's 40,000 in gold. My device has told me. It's a $20 gold piece tied to a string which is wrapped around a piece of wood and tied. Since like things attract, if there's gold in the ground the coin starts to draw towards the gold. When the string is pointing straight down again, then we're right over the treasure. You can tell how much is down there by how fast the coin spins over the gold. You can do this with silver, diamonds, anything.

WITCHES

116. The Witch Cat

A man in southern Indiana (so we have been told for generation upon generation) owned a gristmill, and though he had sufficient help during the day, he could get no one to stay at the mill at night for more than a few nights in succession. The reason? Each night an enormous cat with fiery eyes would yowl and scream as it came closer and closer to the watcher. Though it had never actually attacked anyone, who could say that it wouldn't, for no one had ever dared stay in its path to see.

The story spread over the countryside and reached the ears of a man who said, in no uncertain phrases, "I'll stay at that mill!"—or words to that effect. He went to the mill owner, and they agreed upon wages, including board and room at the mill owner's home, the owner being doubtful but hopeful.

They ate their evening meal, it being cooked and served by the owner's wife. The watchman prepared himself with a butcher knife and went to the mill to wait. The screaming began, sounded nearer. He could now see those eyes, the approaching form, and the screams became more terrifying. He waited. Now! As the cat sprang toward him he slashed with the knife—cut off a front paw. The cat was gone.

The next morning he went in to breakfast. "Where is the Mrs.?" he asked, noticing the absence of the owner's wife. "She got her hand cut off last night," was the reply. Yes, sir! She was a witch.

117. The Butter Witch

Just east of the little town of Giro, Indiana, was once a German settlement that strongly believed in witchcraft. When anything went wrong in the daily routine of the housewife, she was certain that a neighbor was angry and getting revenge by "bewitching" the particular task.

Mrs. Brown had been laboring over her large wooden churn for hours, and yet no butter. Turning to her husband, dozing by the fireside, she quickly exclaimed, "Someone has a foot in my cream, so I'll find out who the witch is this time!" So Mrs. Brown hurriedly heated an iron and dropped it into the contents of the churn, thus burning out the foot that was in her cream. It was only a matter of seconds that she had a generous supply of nice yellow butter.

The next day, Mrs. Brown was making some calls in the neighborhood and stopped for a chat with Mrs. Jones. There sat Mrs. Jones in great pain with a badly burned foot. So Mrs. Brown turned homeward, happy and satisfied, for she had found the witch that had had her foot in the butter.

118. Witch Makes Cows Dry by Squeezing a Towel

Early in the 1800s [1900s?] a band of nomads named Griffy located in eastern Gibson County, about one and one-half miles northwest of Oakland City. They built floorless huts in a cluster around a large spring. There were thirty or forty people in the colony, all of whom were superstitious. They were looked upon as an indolent, lazy set, but had one feature about their manner of living which was commendable; they had several old people with them, whom they cared for, who were not related to them and had no claim upon them.

At one time Jonas and Casway Griffy came to see my father and wanted small change in bits and quarters for a silver dollar. One of them wanted to know if silver would melt in a ladle with lead. My father concluded that they wanted to make counterfeit coin and told them he was surprised to think they would undertake such business. They were alarmed and said they had no thought of doing wrong; they had not intended to tell, but would have to tell him to clear themselves of suspicion. They had lived for some time in Martin County before coming to this part, and they had so much trouble there that they moved away in the hope that their trouble would cease. But for several months the same trouble had come to them, and they were planning to rid themselves of evil. They wanted the small coin to melt in lead and run it into bullets for the purpose of disabling witches. They said there was an old woman who lived near them in Martin County who was a terror to all the country round. She did not fear anything, would ride with a bridle and saddle the wildest unbroken horse, and would fight any man. She had nearly killed two of their neighbors in a fight. They said that before they moved down here they had four cows but could not get any milk from two of them at any time—they were always milked dry. The old witch did not have any cows but always had plenty of milk and butter.

One morning one of our women went up to the old witch's house and saw her doing something with a towel which was hanging in a small window. While the witch's back was turned she determined to watch and find out what was being done. The witch first stuck a pin in the towel and named it for one of our cows. Then she took hold of the fringe and began to milk it as if she were milking a cow. When she had finished that cow she put another pin into the towel and named it after our other best cow and proceeded to milk her in the same way. At night she would assume the form of a black cat and go all over our homes. Old Mr. McCoy, one of our people, saw the cat go into his room. He closed the door and armed himself with an axe. Opening the door a little ways to let the cat run out, he cut off one of its ears. The next morning one of our women went over to see the old lady and found her in bed with a bandage on her head. That night she went back to Mr. McCoy's cabin, found the ear and it grew back on, except that it was cropped. After that the same black cat was seen with one ear cropped. We brought the same four cows when we moved down here. The range was good, and they gave an abundance of milk. About two months ago two of our men were in the woods hunting and saw the same crop-eared black cat. Ever since that evening our two best cows have given no milk, and we have many other troubles which we attribute to the same cause.

A few years later the section that these Griffys occupied had a terrible scourge of what was known as the black-tongue, and 15 or 20 died from the terrible disease. They attributed it all to the same one-eared cat, and as soon as they were able to get away, they moved up east on the Patoka River, and none of them were ever seen in this section again.

119. Witch Causes Cow to Give Bloody Milk

There was this old woman who lived not far from us who wanted to buy this cow from one of her neighbors, but they wouldn't sell it to her. So she put a spell on it and told them that it would give bloody milk. The next morning when they milked her, the milk was bloody like she said it was going to be. They was going to sell her then, but then she said she didn't want her. But she took the spell off, and the very next morning she gave good milk. Everyone knew she was a witch then 'cause she was just showing her powers. They said that when she was dying she said, "I'm bound for hell!"

120. Witch Hexes Well

That same old witch that lived next to us in Anderson, Indiana, when I was a little girl had a crazy daughter that stayed with her in that old house. Her daughter's name was Josie, and they say she went crazy because she saw her brother-in-law murder her sister. Mom used to send me up to that old witch's house to use their phone in emergencies because few people had phones in those days. I was always scared to death and I never tarried after I did what I was supposed to. Every kid in the neighborhood was afraid of that old woman because she was all bent over and scraggly faced and didn't ever look anyone in the eye. She told kids not to come around and bother her, and they never did. She had an apple orchard that us kids had to pass every day on the way to school. The biggest, juiciest looking apples hung out over her fence just in reach. But no kids I ever knowed of ever touched those apples because it was said they was poison. But here I'm straying from the thing I meant to tell you about

that old witch. One day an old nigger man's cow got loose
and tore up her garden when it wandered over into her yard.
She was plenty mad so she went over and put a hex on his
well. She just threw a penny in the old nigger's well and it
went bone dry. But this nigger man was from the South orig-
inally, and he knew a lot about voodoo and taking the hex off
things. He het a dime till it was red hot and threw it in the
old witch's well. From that time on the old man had water in
his well again, and the old witch's eyes became red and always inflamed, and she complained about 'em hurtin' her.
The nigger claimed that what he'd done had burnt her eyes.
She never bothered that old nigger man anymore.

121. Witch Causes Cake to Burst into Flames

Another incident that I heard about happened at an old-
fashioned quilting party. There were probably a dozen or
more women at this party, and among them was one that was
quite a lot older and was suspected by some of the others to
be practicing witchcraft. It seems everything went along real
fine until the hostess, or the lady that they were doing the
quilting for, served them some lunch. I don't know if I mentioned this before, but it seems that anyone practicing witchcraft is always giving or offering to give someone else something or doing some kind of favor for them. I don't know for
sure just why this is done, although I probably should say
was done, as it is no longer practiced around here; at least, I
hope not. I think the reason they're so generous and obliging
is that they have to gain the confidence of the person that
they want to cast the spell on.

Anyhow, this person picked out one of the other ladies and
offered her a piece of cake, and when she reached for it, it

burst into a blue flame and so did the would-be witch's
fingertips. Of course, the rest of the crowd almost panicked
and brought a pail of water, but the old lady put her hands
with the cake in it under her apron, and it was extinguished
immediately. When this was told to me it was probably several years later, and I told them that it might possibly have
been static electricity, but was told that it was utterly impossible to make a spark hot enough to burn a piece of cake. And
they said it was really scorched. And you can be sure that this
lady was never again invited to another quilting party.

122. Boiling Water Forces Witch to Reveal Herself

I will try to put together a few incidents as they were
told to me by victims and also witnesses of witchcraft as it
was practiced in this area in the late 1800s and early 1900s.
The earliest of which I have any knowledge happened in the
late 19th century, and the victim was well-known by my parents. When this person was a young girl, she was . . . seemed
to be sickly all of the time and was feeling weaker and
weaker and seemed to be near the point of death, although
the doctors could find nothing seriously wrong with her, till
one day a tramp, or hobo as they were known, who was also a
umbrella-mender, came to the home of this girl who lived on
the farm. And how he found out about her condition I don't
really know. But he probably could tell by her parents; they
were downhearted and sad. And evidently someone . . . he
told them that someone had cast a spell on them, and this
hobo told them if he was farther along in witchcraft than the
person who had cast this spell, he could produce whoever it
was that was causing the spell.

He told them that if they would do exactly what he told

them to do, he could bring the person around who was causing it, so they decided to go along with it. They were told to fill a kettle with water and build a fire under it, and when this water would come to a boil the responsible person would appear. So they got busy and filled the kettle with water and started a fire under it. It so happened when the water started to boil, that this neighbor woman came screaming across the field and really screamed, so this hobo told her that if she wouldn't take the spell off she'd have to keep on suffering, so she agreed. And the woman, this young woman, incidentally, lived to be a ripe old age, enjoyed a long married life, and raised a large family.

123. Exorcising a Witch

Jabe was bewitched; no doubt of it. Of course there was the negligible fact that he was in the mind-poisoning stages of Bright's Disease complicated with the febrile delirium of pneumonia. Nevertheless, he was certainly hag-ridden. The witch was sitting on his chest, riding with such fury that the two men sitting on either side of him holding his outstretched arms pinioned to the bed rails, were, at times, lifted from the floor.

Granny Yanders was consulted. Pursuant to her instructions a crude picture of a witch was drawn on brown paper with charcoal from Jabe's own fireplace and pinned to a "slippery ellum" tree. A dime was melted and run into a bullet mold to obtain the silver bullet with which the witch's likeness must be shot through the heart. Upon returning to the sickroom these surgeons found the operation successful. The witch was quelled. Unfortunately, however, the patient had died.

124. Killing a Witch That Causes Illness

I want to tell you a witch story, just as Grandfather gave it to me. In the neighborhood where Grandfather lived there was an old lady who lived right across the fields from his home. In those days witches were always old ladies, never men. One day a young neighbor girl was out riding, and she met this old witch, but no one knew at the time that she was a witch. The old witch stopped her and took her hand and told her how good she was. When the girl got home she took sick, for she was bewitched. They had a terrible time with the girl, for she could see the witch while the rest of them could not. She would vomit pins in strings like fishhooks. I do not know how this happened, but it must have been true, for Grandfather saw that himself.

This went on for a long time until they finally heard of a man who was a conjurer and who had power over the witches. They took the girl to him, and he said he could do anything with a witch—could either put out her eyes, take a limb, or kill her. They said, "Kill her." So he instructed them to leave the girl, go home, and tell everyone the witch was going to die in nine days, also saying he would show her illness beginning with a corn. In a few days one of the granddaughters of the witch came in and said, "Grannie isn't feeling very well; she has a bad corn, and it is bothering her very much." The corn kept on growing until in nine days the woman was dead.

The next thing was to bury the witch. Arrangements were made for her burial, so they put her in a wagon and started for the cemetery. On the way they had to pass the house where the witch formerly lived. When they got in front of the house the team, which had always been faithful, stopped. With all of the swearing and whipping they could not get them to start for some time. Two of the wheels on the oppo-

site side commenced to rise. The men finally pulled them
down, drove the witches away, and started on. They put the
witch in the grave, pulled stones on her, and, taking a drink,
departed.

125. Strange Occurrences at a Witch's Funeral

Among the early settlers around Perrysburg, Indiana,
was a family by the name of Ream. Mr. Ream was a very
religious man and always called the family together of a
morning to have a scripture reading and prayer. Mrs. Ream
was wholly out of sympathy with the habit and caused as
much disturbance and confusion as possible. Mr. Ream,
however, continued his practice and asked that the family as-
semble. He was considered a very devout man, and inasmuch
as he had met life in the destined way, his death and passing
were of the same character. But with Mrs. Ream it was quite
different. The neighbors became suspicious of her and, as it
was in a very early day, at last came to the conclusion that
she was a witch. Many untoward events were attributed to
her wiles, and when it came to her death, everyone was sure
that something would happen.

However, the usual procedure had been accomplished
without anything unusual until they reached the bridge
which crosses Eel River, when, all of a sudden, one of the
horses drawing the wagon in which the body lay, dropped,
running its leg to its full length through a hole in the bridge.
And while every male in the procession endeavored to get it
released, it was to no avail. A boy had to be sent to the
nearest home where a saw was procured and the board
around the leg severed, a part being removed. Then they
proceeded to the cemetery, but nothing more was needed to
prove that Mrs. Ream had really been a witch.

126. Silver Bullet Protects Against Witches

Shelby County at one time was very heavily wooded; in fact, trails were blazed through these forests so hunters, trappers, and people going from place to place would not become lost. Naturally, wild game of all kinds was found in these forests of this county. Before settlers could build their log cabins, trees had to be cut in order to have enough clear space to build them. At the time of this story, log cabins were few and far between. The people knew very little about their nearest neighbor, for sometimes they would be several miles apart.

There lived in one of these log cabins three sisters who were very beautiful and also very mysterious and seclusive. Eventually it was rumored by the pioneers that they were fairies or witches. They said their antics justified these reports. Some had said that when leaving their house to take a stroll through the woods, they would transfigure themselves instantaneously and change to the feature of a wild animal. Then, on returning, they would as quickly change back to human beings. The transmutation of these sisters had become known to several of the pioneers.

One pioneer who was very fond of deer hunting did not know of the existence of these three sisters. During the winter season he spent the greater part of his time deer hunting and in the past years was noted for his ability to kill deer. He took great pride in telling of his exploits in deer hunting. One year, just prior to the deer hunting season, this hunter made very elaborate preparations for a big season in the hunting of deer. He bought extra equipment of all kinds in his preparations. Shortly after he had assembled all his equipment and had put them in perfect condition for hunting, the time for hunting was at hand.

The first day he hunted, he ventured very deep in the forest, hoping to get some choice fawn. After hunting for considerable time, he discovered three fawns. Using all his knowledge of craft in hunting, he very cautiously approached the three fawns to get a choice shot. When considerable effort and time had been spent in gaining his selected position, aiming very carefully he opened fire on the three fawns. To his great surprise he failed to hit any of them. He did not as much as singe the hair of these beautiful fawns. So disappointed was this hunter that he decided to return home and examine his gun and cartridge for defects. It was very late when he returned home that evening, so he decided to postpone the inspection of his guns and cartridges until the next day.

Bright and early the next day he examined his guns and cartridges and found them to be in perfect condition. Thinking that he was a little nervous the day before, he made a target to practice shooting. After practicing for a short time, he discovered that his nerves were as steady as they ever were and that he was still the crack shot he had always been. Clinching his fists and setting his teeth, he grabbed his gun and set out again on the hunt of the three fawns. Hunting for several hours, he found them. Using all the precaution he had used the day before, he was able to get close enough to get a good shot at them. Taking very careful aim and shooting at them, he again missed. This time rage became vivid [livid?], and he returned home immediately.

The next day he decided that he would go to town and buy a different gun and a different brand of cartridges. Arriving at the store, he was greeted very warmly by his friends. At once they began to ask how many deer he had killed and all the particulars. Dropping his head, he shamefully [ashamedly?] replied that he had been unable to kill any this season so far. His friends made great merriment of this, to the discomfort of this famous hunter.

When the merriment had ceased, he then told of his experiences of his past days. Hearing his story, his friends began to offer various suggestions as to how to kill one of these fawns. An old-time hunter who had sat throughout the entire episode without making any comments now walked over to the hunter. Placing his hand on the hunter's shoulder, he offered his sympathy to him for having such bad luck. He stated that in his youth he had experienced the same thing. He told the hunter if he would take some silver coins and melt them, then mold them into bullets, he would be able to kill one of these fawns, as he thought they were the fairies or witches transmuted into fawns. Upon returning home that evening, he went to work in making some bullets from coins. He made several of these bullets and put them in his hunting belt.

Very early the next morning, he set out on another hunting expedition just as the sun was coming up. To his great surprise he immediately saw the fawns. They were running and jumping, apparently having a good time. They did not notice the hunter, and he was able to get very close to them. Taking careful aim, he shot at one of them. Just as he shot, it jumped to one side a little. This caused him to wound the fawn, apparently in the leg. The other two fawns, upon hearing the shot, immediately disappeared, but the wounded fawn could not run so fast and was left far behind. The progress of this fawn was so slow that the hunter was able to follow it and keep it in his sight. After following the fawn for a long time, a log cabin came into view. The fawn was heading straight for this cabin. When the fawn started to enter the door, it disappeared instantaneously, and the form of a beautiful young lady appeared where the fawn had stood. When the young lady entered the house, the hunter noticed that she limped some.

Deciding that he would go to the house and ask if they had

seen where the wounded fawn had disappeared, he proceeded to the door, which was left open by the young lady. Arriving at the door, he saw two very beautiful young ladies standing at the bed. They did not notice his approach, so he continued to the bed and discovered that the young woman that he had seen at the door was lying on the bed, and that she had a wounded foot. He asked the other two ladies what the trouble was, and they said that they were sisters and that the younger sister had stepped on a stone and cut her foot very badly.

The hunter studied for a few minutes and said, "You are the three sisters that the people say are the fairies. You three sisters here appeared as fawns in the forest, and I shot the one lying on the bed and trailed her here." The sisters slyly admitted that this was true. The sisters immediately disappeared after this episode. This is an old favorite legend told by old-time hunters.

MONSTERS AND SNAKES

127. The Loup Garou

It was reported many years ago that some kind of wild animal was running loose out by the old French graveyard. It was claimed that several queer animals were not animals at all but people that had been bewitched. John Vatchet claimed that one of these animals sprang at him one night as he was going through the old graveyard and that he had quite a tussle for his life.

Charles Vatchet lived down by the site where the present hospital is located. There were a number of apple trees along this street, and as this was before the time of street lights, the place was very dark. One night as Mr. Vatchet was going home, an object having the shape of a wild animal sprang at Mr. Vatchet. He cut the animal with his knife in his struggle, and the object turned into a man. He gave Mr. Vatchet his name and address (the man was from Evansville), and requested that he should not tell anyone for one year and a day or he would turn back into an animal. When the animals were injured to the extent that brought blood, the charm was broken.

128. The Princeton Monster

In Princeton, Indiana, there is a parking place out by an old oil well drilling and tanks. Many of the high school kids go there. About four years ago, a couple was parked there, and their car was attacked by what was thought to be a big man or bear. The incidents occurred several times throughout the summer. Finally, eight or nine guys decided to go out and to try to shoot the monster. They parked their cars along the road so they could turn their headlights on whenever he came. Finally they saw his shadow, and the lights were turned on. Whatever it was, it was seven or eight feet tall and very hairy. It ran on its hind legs, so it couldn't have been a bear. When it came closer, shots were fired time and time again. It soon ran off into the woods. Early the next morning, large pools of blood were found on the road and in the woods, but no trace of the monster could be found.

129. The Wampus

The first time that I heard about this I was about 14 years old. I listened to old folks at a country store tell of the scream of the wampus cat. Their tale was that this cat was the size of a panther, which was quite large for southern Indiana. According to their tale, this cat made its home along the banks of the Wabash and Erie Canal. They said that in the building of the Wabash and Erie Canal the laborers came upon the body of a young girl, 19 or 20 years old, with her throat ripped out as though done by a huge cat. They said that there were tracks around the girl's body. They said that this girl's soul went into the body of this cat. This is true . . . what I was told. On special summer nights similar to the one the girl died you could and still can hear her screaming.

When I was 16 years old I was riding my horse through the canal bottoms. I heard the scream of the woman about 12 feet from me. My horse threw me . . . this is true . . . about three miles from home. But I almost beat the horse home. This is true. I never was so scared in my life! I never rode the horse after dark since that time.

Approximately one year after this incident my brother was riding on it in the general area of the canal bottoms. He had a twelve-gauge shotgun, and as he came up over a hill he looked at the bottom of this hill and drinkin' out of the stream was the biggest cat he'd ever saw. He shot three times point-blank from ten feet. The cat was unmarked, and the cat stood there and looked at him. And to his knowledge the cat's still there because he ran and ran and ran. This was in daylight.

Even now you can go into those bottoms on hot summer nights, and you can still hear the scream. I never did believe it, but there are some strange happenings going on there.

130. The Hoop Snake

My Uncle Sterrett came over to our house when I was little and was always telling us these wild stories right before bedtime that would scare us so bad we couldn't sleep. He always had a wild look in his eye when he told us about things he'd seen. Well, he said in Arkansas there was this whip snake that used to beat people all the time around there. And he always told about seeing this hoop snake that would grab its tail in its mouth and roll itself up into a hoop. This snake had a big horn on its head or tail or somewhere, and it would get up speed rolling down a hill or something, and it would strike a tree with this horn and release this poisonous venom, and the tree would die.

131. The Milk Snake

This all happened a long time ago, but I remember my grandpa telling about it. He had this big black cow. It was the best milker he had. It throwed a big bull calf that spring, and Grandpa was sure proud of her. Well, her milk started to fall off. She didn't even give enough to suck the calf. Grandpa decided to follow her and see what was wrong. He thought that someone was milking her during the day, and he wanted to catch them.

When he turned them loose that morning, he saddled the horse and followed them out to pasture. He stayed just far enough back so as they'd not know he was there. Well, about noon that cow throwed her head up and bawled just like she was looking for her calf. Then she trotted over towards a brush pile and a old holler tree that lightning had hit. When she got there she bawled again, and out come the biggest goddamn black snake my grandpa had ever saw. That snake crawled up that cow's hind legs, and she stood real still and let him. He started to suck her. Grandpa said you could see him start to fill up. He thought he was going to bust.

When he had all he wanted, the snake just loosened his coils and dropped off the cow, and she stepped away real careful-like and trotted back to the rest of the cows. When she got out of the way, Grandpa shot that son of a bitch. He said it was bigger 'round than a good big man's arm and nearly seven feet long.

132. Child Dies When Snake is Killed

The old folks out around the hill country near Mooresville tell this story and will vouch that it actually happened. Whether it did or not, I cannot say. I shall let you judge for yourself.

A family living near Mooresville had a child of about four years old. They noticed that he would often take his bowl of bread and milk out into the yard. One day his mother followed him to see just what he did with it. He crossed the yard, went through the edge of the woods, down to a little stream nearby. Here he sat down on the edge of the water and called in his baby voice, "Nicky, Nicky, here Nicky." Something came out of the weeds nearby, and his mother could stand it no longer. But when she rushed up to the child, whatever it was had disappeared. He would not tell her what it was or where it had gone.

His mother was determined to find out about this if she had to trail the child everywhere he went. So one day she noticed that he had again taken his bowl of bread and milk and started toward the little stream. This time, she followed closely behind him and took up her post behind a nearby tree in order that she could see all that happened. The child began to call in his soft voice as before, "Nicky, Nicky, Nicky." Soon, to the mother's horror, a large snake glided silently from the edge of the stream and stopped in front of the boy. He gleefully hit it over the head with his spoon and set the bowl in front of it.

The mother, after she had gotten over her first paralyzed fright, screamed for her husband. He came on a dead run, and she snatched up the child, and her husband killed the snake. The child screamed and carried on something terrible. He said that they had killed Nicky, his pet. They tried to comfort him, but to no avail. When they reached the house he continued to cry. And day by day after that the little child grew thin and pale, always crying for Nicky. And he finally died, calling for "Nicky, Nicky, Nicky." And they say that to this day, if you go out to this certain spot and remain quiet for a time, you can hear the little child calling in his baby voice, "Nicky, Nicky, Nicky."

133. Snake Charms Girl

This little girl . . . well, when I was young, my grandmother used to tell about her. Back in them days they didn't have fancy glasses and bowls like we have, so they'd take maybe a peach or salmon can, cut out the top real smooth, and use it to eat and drink out of. They'd eat milk and cornbread a lot of times back then. This one little girl always wanted a cup of milk and bread, but she didn't want to eat it at the table. She'd take the cup and bread and go outside in the chimney corner. You know how people built their houses back then. They hadn't thought anything about it because it was warm; they thought she just wanted to get outside.

Well, she got to doing it so much, and they'd want her once in a while to sit at the table, but she didn't want to. So they followed her out there one day and watched her. When they got out there, she would take a bite of bread; then she'd take another spoonful and put it over here to the side of the log. They couldn't figure out why she was doing it, so they got a little closer. When they got up there they could see, and it was a big copperhead taking that milk and bread out of that spoon. This snake, then, too, had this little girl charmed. They got the little girl away and tore out those rocks and killed that snake. This little girl almost died, too, because the snake had had her charmed. They say to never kill a snake if you think it's got anything charmed.

134. The Beast of Busco

There is a lake in Churubusco, Indiana, called Blue Lake. One time two old guys were out there fishing and saw what they believed to be a huge sea monster. The noise that it made was kind of a sucking sound. The people in the town formed a vigilante group to investigate and to keep watch on the lake at night. They found large footprints around the lake and felt that whatever it was walked on two legs.

The men patrolled the lake at night and would hear these strange noises, but they didn't see anything. During the day they would find fresh footprints. There was always someone who reported that they had seen the monster. Some said it was a hairy thing that would come out of the water, kill small animals and return to the water. Others thought it a great sea serpent. Many who discount the monster story believe the tracks belong to a huge turtle that lives in the lake. Every few years tracks are found, and the search begins again. The last time the "Beast of Busco" stories kicked up again was in 1967. Churubusco has an annual parade called the "Beast of Busco" parade.

PART TWO

Personal Legends

FAMOUS PEOPLE

135. Prince Madoc

As the story goes, a colony of Welshmen emigrated to America in 1170 and found their way to the Falls of the Ohio, where they remained many years, being finally almost exterminated in a great battle with "Red Indians."

We are told that Owen Gwyneth, a Prince of Wales, died in 1167 and left seventeen sons. Disputes and contentions arose among them as to who should succeed his father, and Madoc, one of the sons, thinking it more prudent to try his fortunes elsewhere, set sail with a goodly company of Welshmen and traveled westward until he reached the shores of another continent. The new land offered such an alluring prospect that Madoc returned to Wales and brought back a considerable number of Welsh to join his colony in the "New World." The party of Welshmen divided; and a group ascended the Missouri branch of the Mississippi, and the other group ascended the Ohio River as far as the Falls. This occurred in the latter part of the twelfth century.

136. Johnny Appleseed

Well, now, here, let me tell you some history. Now you
know where Township Road is over by Banta. If you follow
that road south from there you'll remember that there are all
kinds of apple trees planted. See what I mean? Well, if my
memory serves me correct, though I'm not sure of the exact
date, those trees were planted by Johnny Appleseed himself.
He came right through Johnson County here, and left those
as a part of his trail. I doubt if there are many left who know
that for a fact. There are very few old-timers left around.

137. Abe Lincoln Visits Terre Haute

A tall, awkward, slouchy-looking youth drove a crude
wagon into little Terre Haute. It was filled with the possessions of a pioneer family, pots, bed covers, chairs, kettles,
rifles and all such property, for that was more than ninety
years ago. He was ungainly, his clothes were homespun, and
he stared around with eyes that were earnest and unafraid,
though the little town was new to him. He drove the wagon
to the old wagon yard at Third and Wabash Avenue, and he
slept that night in the wagon yard. Of what he did that evening little is known, but that was the first time Abraham Lincoln ever passed through Terre Haute.

Years later, in the fifties, he came in a more pretentious
manner, sprawled on the back seat of a stagecoach, which
proves without doubt that he always followed his belief that
he was one of the people. When the stagecoach stopped in
front of one of the town hotels near the Wabash River and the
door was opened for passengers, Lincoln continued to sprawl
on the seat and look at the two dolled-up men who were

ready to take their seats in the stagecoach. Suddenly, one of them said, "Will you move on another seat, my good man? Judge Hammond would like to have this seat." The tall, ungainly man climbed out of his seat, smiled, and doffed his hat. He looked around at the other passengers a minute and then climbed up onto the driver's seat and began talking to the driver of the coach. He sat beside him as the stagecoach dashed up Main Street, now Wabash Avenue, past the store of Rice, Edsall & Co., and out onto the National Road. He continued to ride on top of the coach until the halfway house was reached. It was raining then, and he jumped down. It had been raining for some little time, and the roadway was muddy. The great American, after he had jumped from the coach himself, brought a board and laid it across the muddiest place so that the Judge did not have to step in the mud.

Finally, Indianapolis was reached, and Abraham Lincoln was met by his friend, one of Terre Haute's greatest men, Col. Richard Thompson, who introduced him to the two men. They must have almost dropped dead when they realized how they had treated a man even then holding first place in the attention of his country.

138. Pearl Bryan Loses Her Head

I was only five years old then. I remember everyone talking about it. I can't make much of a story out of it. How they did it . . . she went away with two fellas. She was engaged to be married to one of these fellas, and they went on a trip to . . . I think it was Kentucky . . . and she was murdered. But I don't know the story well enough to tell it. That's been so long ago. They found her body in a river somewhere in Kentucky, but her head was gone. They never did find her head.

They identified her by the shoes she was wearing, which was from Allen Brothers store in Greencastle, and that store was right over there on the corner where Penney's are now.

They put up monuments to her grave, good-sized ones. And the first one they chipped it away, and they put up another one, and anybody that would come to Greencastle . . . that was such an unusual story . . . that any stranger that would come to Greencastle would inquire about it and find that her grave was here, and they'd go out and chip off the monument. After they chipped the second one away, they quit puttin' 'em up and haven't put anymore up since. She was distantly related to me.

139. Pearl Bryan Delivers Babies and Keeps Them

There was this woman who lived in Greencastle, and her name was Pearl Bryan. College girls who went to DePauw and who got pregnant would go to see Pearl when the baby was about to be born. Pearl would deliver the babies, and she would keep them. A few years ago under Pearl's house there were a bunch of baby skeletons found, and nobody could explain this.

140. Pearl Bryan's Ghost in Mooresville

Traditionally, there is a ghost story that has survived in Mooresville for the last forty-four years. It was in the year 1892 that Pearl Bryan of Greencastle was murdered and beheaded; her head was never found, so she was buried headless. Many communities for miles around that point reported seeing a white, headless, will-o'-the-wisp appear in marshes and lowlands or other dark and lonely places. Many of the younger folks of Mooresville and vicinity were no exception to that rule.

At a point where the road—now State Road 267—made a sharp turn immediately after crossing a little stream, every so often, especially on dark, foggy, and rainy nights, a headless woman dressed in white could be seen in the center of the road at this lonely, dark spot and could be heard to exclaim in a weird, piercing shriek, "Oh, I've lost my head." When anyone tried to approach the apparition, it would suddenly disappear.

This ghost story persisted steadily around Mooresville through the Gay Nineties. Finally the next generation of children reached maturity; the road was widened and straightened at this point; and the story became known and ridiculed as just one of Mooresville's ghost tales.

141. Pearl Bryan's Ghost in Greencastle

Pearl Bryan was a student at DePauw. She had two male medical students as two of her many friends. Somehow Pearl got pregnant, so the two medical students offered to give her an abortion. They ended up killing her and disposed of her body in Kentucky. Somehow the body got sent back to her home. One legend has it that her head was on, and another has it that it was off. In this situation, the family decided to bury her without a funeral in Forest Hill Cemetery. People started to ruin her gravestone by chipping off pieces. But even today people see her walking across the road in front of her house; some say with her head, and others say without her head.

142. John F. Kennedy is Still Alive in Dallas

Did you know that President Kennedy is still alive?
That's what I said. President John F. Kennedy is still alive
today! Oh, he's not really a human being anymore. In fact,
he's really nothing more than a vegetable. You see, I have
this friend who works with me in my office here in Bedford
who has a cousin who lives in St. Louis who has a friend that
works in the library in Dallas, Texas. Well, this girl who
works in the library is a friend of a nurse and an orderly who
work in the 'Parkland Hospital in Dallas—you know, the one
where Kennedy was taken after he was shot.

Well, anyway, this nurse and this orderly had heard that
Kennedy had not died in November 1963. What happened
was that his brain was severely damaged, but the doctors
were able to keep his body alive. In other words, the doctors
were able to keep Kennedy alive, but only as a vegetable. He
just exists. They had also heard that doctors there were working on research so that one day other brain cells might be
transplanted into the damaged parts of Kennedy's brain.

They had also heard that Kennedy was being kept on the
third floor of the hospital. Well, the orderly didn't believe a
word of it. You know what I mean—it does sound rather fantastic. And besides, everyone had seen Kennedy buried over
television. So this orderly decided to disprove this rumor by
going up on the third floor of the hospital. When he got off
the elevator, he was met by two plainclothesmen. One identified himself as a member of the Secret Service, and the
other was from the Central Intelligence Agency—the CIA,
you know. Well, they asked this orderly to see his pass. He
replied that he didn't have a pass, but that he worked at the
hospital. They then told him that no one could be on that
floor without a special pass, and that if they ever caught him
up there on the third floor again without one of these passes,

he would be in serious trouble with the Federal Government of the United States. So the orderly quickly got back into the elevator and went down and told the nurse what had happened.

After this incident, the nurse and orderly were on their toes noticing who got in the elevator and went up to the third floor. Then one day the nurse saw a lady wearing a big hat and sunglasses enter the hospital and approach the elevator. There was something very familiar about this woman, but the nurse could not put her finger on it. The nurse continued to watch the woman as she approached the elevator, and as the woman took off her sunglasses to see which floor the elevator was on, the nurse recognized her—it was Jacqueline Kennedy. After Mrs. Kennedy got in the elevator, the nurse ran over to the elevator to see where she went. And, sure enough, the elevator stopped on the third floor and then came back down, without Mrs. Kennedy.

After this, the nurse and orderly saw Mrs. Kennedy come into the hospital and go up to the third floor many times. The last time she visited the hospital was in November 1969. And this time she was with a man—a man they recognized as Aristotle Onassis from his pictures which appeared in the papers after his summer marriage to Jacqueline. They stayed up on the third floor about an hour, and then they came back down and left.

Well, anyway, this story makes me doubt whether John F. Kennedy is really dead or not. You can see that this story comes from very reliable sources. My friend who works with me here in Bedford hasn't talked to her cousin in St. Louis who has a friend that works in the library in Dallas who is a friend of the nurse and orderly who work in the Parkland Hospital in Dallas for a couple of months. But I just wish she would because I'm just dying to know if Jacqueline or Onassis have made any more trips to the third floor of the Parkland

Hospital. And some day when the doctors complete the transplants on Kennedy's brain and he's able to leave the hospital, this fantastic story will be made known to the general public. But you'll always remember that it was me who first told you that John F. Kennedy is not dead.

143. John F. Kennedy is Still Alive on Onassis's Island

JFK is not dead. At Ball State we talked about it in one class during my freshman year. It has to be the truth. First of all, no one had seen the body after it left the hospital, if the body did at all. When she [Jackie] married Onassis, no news media was allowed inside. She really didn't marry him, but had to have an excuse for being on his island all of the time. He owned an airline, and they could fly Kennedy, now a vegetable, to the island to live his life out. Also in the four years after his "death" until her "marriage" she visited Dallas over 100 times, but the "grave" only around five times. Also how could anyone have held up as good as she did during the funeral? After all she had been through, she would have shown something. He really is alive. The only reason they didn't tell the world is that it would have put the world into a shock.

ECCENTRICS

144. Martin Pirtle

There used to be an old peddler around these parts named Martin Pirtle that was a captain. The folks in Dugger and Linton used to know his antics pretty good, and the amazin' thing was that because old Mart lived like a pauper everyone thought he was poor. There wasn't nothing further from the truth. They say when he died he owned six or seven properties in Linton. Now, let me see. Where was I? I hardly know where to begin in talkin' about Mart. I've heard tell he went to buy a cow from a man once, and he took all nickels and dimes to pay him. Mart was always out for anything that was free, so he was always out lookin' along the edge of the streets to see if there was any money or anything dropped alongside the way. Mart would come to town in Dugger and snitch cookies or candy out of the barrels when no one wasn't looking, so by the time he left town to go home he'd be full and wouldn't have to eat no supper.

I've heard tell of him many a day going into the bank with a coal bucket full of pennies he'd saved to get them changed into bills. Why, if he didn't steal from the grocery store, he went in and bummed off people. He'd ask for black nannies or stale cookies or burnt ones that the store was going to throw away. When he did buy something he always made sure it was the cheapest thing there was. He had a wife and two or three kids at home to feed, so he'd go in to the butcher shops and get hogs' heads which weren't over 25 to 50 cents apiece. But when he bought somethin', he wanted all he could get out of it. They say he always told the butcher to cut that hog's head pretty well to the shoulders so he'd get more meat that way. And, oh yeah, he even told that butcher not to cut those ears off that hog's head 'cause his kids liked the ears. I never knowed of him having no steady job, only walking or riding on horseback and peddlin' his buttermilk from his cow and green beans and those kind of things. He'd come walking in with a tie and an old crusty looking white shirt that looked like it had never been washed, and he'd start his line about how thick and good his buttermilk was. Well, he had it in these big jars, and it did look pretty good, but always to demonstrate his wares old Mart would stick his old dirty finger in the buttermilk and stir it around good. There weren't too many people anxious to buy any buttermilk when he did that.

I think Martin attended every funeral and box supper there ever was in these parts. He really liked basket dinners the churches had best 'cause the food was free. More often than not, Martin would wear bib overalls, and I don't think he ever took a bath. There was a man who ran a clothing store in Linton who used to give Mart a pair of Osh-Kosh overalls free to wear and advertise his store. Well, Mart not only wore those overalls; he never washed 'em or bothered to take the store tags off. One pair soon got pretty slick, and the white tags just crumbled away with time. The funniest thing I ever heard about old Mart was the reason he attended all the funerals in town. They said he had a deal with the funeral director whose name was Akin that if he attended every funeral till he died that Akin would bury him when his time come free of charge. I think old man Akin meant this to be a joke, but Martin he took him up on it. As far as I know Akin kept that promise too.

145. Old Man Sanders' Buried Treasure

Back before the Depression there was a old man named
Sanders who owned one of the large taverns in town
[Diamond]. He had everything in that tavern a man could
want, gambling, women, and later, even during Prohibition,
he had drinks. But in the late 1920s he was getting old, about
65–70. He decided to retire, so he bought a piece of land at
the south end of Diamond and built a house. He did not trust
banks, so he kept all the money he saved somewhere buried
on his place. When the government told everybody to turn in
their gold for paper money, Old Man Sanders would have
nothing to do with that. But about two months later after the
order, he died. So before his body was cold, almost everyone
in Diamond was going through his house and digging up his
land looking for the gold coins. As far as I know no one has
found that first dollar.

146. Flo Peggy

This is about Flo Peggy. She was an old woman; she
looked like a witch. She always wore black, a big tall hat,
skirts which drug the ground, long sleeves, high collar. She
always carried a cane. She went to one grocery store —
Russell Brailey's; it was called the Clover Farm. Her house
was downtown on the square in Versailles. It was a red,
three-story house. She performed abortions in her younger
days. She died not too long ago. Her house had one big room
in the third story. It had a picture window with white, ragged, dirty curtains. You could see the rope from the window
that her husband used to hang himself. People thought she
was a witch. She had lots of money. When she died, this guy

inherited all her money. He was a shyster. He tore down her
old house and built a new one on the spot. She's buried in a
vault on top of the ground. It has her name and the dates of
her life. It says, "A friend in need is a friend indeed." The
kids used to ride their bicycles down there, and they said you
could smell her.

147. Shellshock

There's a guy around town [Terre Haute] who is always
just walking the streets. He always has about a five-day
growth of beard, and he sometimes wears his pajamas under
his pants and shirt. He's always dressed in real ragged
clothes, and he never seems to have anywhere to go, just
standing on downtown street corners. Everyone calls him
Shellshock. It seems he was a doctor's son and real rich.
Then he went to war, and he got shell shock. When he came
home he was never the same as he had been. He still has lots
of money, but he never uses any of it, just hides it in tin cans
and buries it all over town.

148. Pollie Barnett

You talk about eccentric characters, and the first person
that comes to my mind is an old lady named Poll Barnett. She
was a curious, slouchy-looking old woman that smoked a
corncob pipe and traveled all around this part of the country
on foot. She was like a wandering gypsy, and people in the
Dugger and Sullivan area often had seen her in the late 1800s
or so. She lived on whatever people would give her and al-

ways carried a cat in her arms and had one or two trailing behind her. No one seemed to know where she had come from or whether she had a home somewhere or not. Whenever I got all dirty or had my clothes all messed up, Mom used to look at me and say, "Clean yourself up; you're beginning to look like old Poll Barnett." They said Poll was leading this kind of nomadic life because she was looking for her daughter who had disappeared a long time before. Poll's supposed to be buried somewhere over in the Linton cemetery, and her tombstone has on the top of it a cat carved in stone because these animals were her constant companions. Legend has it Poll's wandering was all in vain, and she died never having found even a trace of her daughter.

149. Walking Snyder

John W. Snyder was familiarly known far and near in Blackford County as "Walking Snyder." He was thought to be unbalanced mentally, for he was under the delusion that he had three layers of skin on his feet. He believed that he had to get the two additional layers off, and it is said that in the backyard of his home, Hartford City, there were three perfect circles worn in the ground from his continuous walking. There is no telling how many pair of shoes he has worn out, for he walked for over a period of 15 years. It is also said that he walked continually when he was awake, and when anyone came along to talk with him he would break into a trot, thinking that he was losing time and getting behind. Snyder continued to walk until he died. This little incident was known for miles around, and "Walking Snyder" became more than a local curiosity. People came from as far as 100 miles to see him.

150. Crissy, the Skunk Woman

Not too many years ago, Crissy, the Skunk Woman, died. She had lived in Howe, Indiana, with her husband. They were notorious for the filth about their premises, as well as on their bodies. They lived alone and isolated from the rest of the town until their pitiful condition seemed to attract visitors out of sheer curiosity. Seeing Crissy and her shack made the visitors even more satisfied with their own things.

Then Crissy's husband became ill. He was ordered to take a bath. When he did, he died. The widow declared that his death was caused by his bathing. She vowed she would never take a bath as long as she lived. She lived alone in her shack and filth. The only company she kept were several skunks and a cat or two. This brought on her new name, "Skunk Woman."

Crissy kept her vow about bathing for many years. She continued to caress and care for her skunks and cats. The only dirt ever rubbed off her body was done so by her equally filthy clothes, as they rubbed against her body. This went on until the neighbors made it necessary for her to clean up. They built her a new home with some of the modern conveniences, including a bathtub. They tried to force her to take a bath, even to the point of bathing her themselves. Not long afterwards, Crissy died—seemingly as a result of her different way of living.

151. Martin Piniak

There is an old man who lives right now under the big bridge that divides Hammond and East Chicago. He is a hermit. He wears old patched-up baggy denim slacks, jacket, and hat with a dirty blue shirt. He has a dirty white beard; he smokes a pipe; and he is very thin. Once in awhile you can see him walking on the streets near that bridge, although they say he does not come out often—only to visit his brother who lives in East Chicago or to get something to eat. They say at one time when he was a younger man, he had a very well-paying job in the steel mills and that he had plans to get married to a very beautiful girl. Unfortunately, the girl died about a week before they were to be married. They say that the two of them were in a car accident and that he came out of it without a scratch, and she was killed. Although the accident was not his fault, he blamed himself and felt that he had nothing more to work for. So he quit his job, gave up almost all his wordly possessions to his brother, and went to live under that bridge.

They say that one Thanksgiving Day he took off all his clothes and jumped in the polluted Little Calumet River with intentions of taking a bath. Naturally the police arrested him. He stayed overnight in jail, was given a real bath, got a new set of clothes, received some shots so he wouldn't get sick from that dirty water, and was given a hot turkey dinner. That's the real reason he did it—to get a good hot meal on Thanksgiving Day. That happened a few years ago, now he doesn't have to jump in the river; the police automatically come around and arrest him at Thanksgiving, Christmas, and other holidays to feed him a good meal on those days.

152. Diana of the Dunes

A headline story of two decades ago was that of an unclad woman bathing in Lake Michigan by evening and morning twilight or the glow of the moon, scandalizing less

comely fishermen's wives and repelling advances of the
fishermen with drawn pistol. She was said to live by hunting
and fishing and gathering berries. She was called Diana of
the Dunes.

One fisherman's wife who enjoyed the grotesque said that
she lived in a wigwam before moving into a driftwood
hut—also that she wore her hair bobbed, in those days a
thing for bated breath and lifted hands, and that, lacking a
mirror, she cut it by its shadow on the beach. It was also
rumored that she made wine of berries for sale. The sensational press played her up as the spirit of the dunes, and
cinema scouts tried for pictures of supposed Dianas.

A few years later came a man. He was reported to be
anything—prizefighter, trainer, Texas snake catcher, to a
Michigan City railroad engineer. From his vacationing in the
dunes and acquaintance with Diana grew more notorious
tales, this time of free-love intimacies.

These facts do remain: In the summer of 1916 after an
all-night vigil this woman was interviewed by a newspaper
man. From that conference and subsequent discoveries it was
learned that she was Alice Gray, daughter of a Chicago
physician, precocious as a child, Phi Beta Kappa graduate of
Chicago University, European traveler for two years, and editorial secretary (of exceptional ability) to the president of the
University of Chicago. She had resigned her position because
men were paid more than women for the same work. However, her own salary was generous enough for her last
paycheck to have sufficed all winter for bread and salt and
like necessities.

The previous October she had come, slept four nights in
the open, and then appropriated a nondescript, abandoned
shack which she fitly named Driftwood, likening herself to it
as driftwood. This shanty had a fireplace, a few boxes, and a
coffeepot for furnishings.

She dressed roughly in conformity with the demands of her

surroundings. She lived quietly, secluding herself from the notoriety she resented. Nearby libraries knew her as a constant patron of philosophical works and as a writer of similar trends. She was a pleasant-voiced, gray-eyed, inconspicuous, fair-minded, incorrigible individualist, though she was appreciative of the flora and fauna and mood and color of the dunes.

Three more times she came in contact with unwanted publicity—when her hut was bought for speculation, when Paul Wilson entered her life (they were later married), and when the Wilsons were involved unjustly in a murder mystery and injured by a deputy sheriff, Mrs. Wilson having a fractured skull and her husband being shot in the foot in an altercation. During their hospitalization their dwelling was ransacked by souvenir hunters, and many of Diana's writings were destroyed.

Upon their recovery they went away on a boating tour and returned, intending eventually to settle in Texas. Her premature death in 1925 prevented their plan from maturing, and lack of cremation facilities frustrated her desire to have her ashes scattered to the dune winds.

The tragic truth of her mystery is stranger than any of the fictitious marvels. Why did she deny her social position and the personal comforts that wealth can give? Whether it was for disappointed love or for the quiet, contemplative life unhampered by the restraint of conventions has never been answered.

153. Ghost of Diana of the Dunes

This thing happened about 1905. It really happened; it's not a legend. There was this lady named Diana, and she was a female hermit. She wrote poems. She was supposed to have run around nude in the dunes and was a nature lover. The area she lived in was predominately Swedish. At the time, she was living with a big Swede out of wedlock, or common law you might say. She lived on Lake Michigan in a shanty. They say Diana was a nymph. Oh, by the way, she had a big dog, too. One night her dog ran into town howling. Everyone knew whose dog it was. So a couple of people walked out to the shanty. On the way out there, they saw one arm, and as they walked farther they saw a leg. Then they found another leg. After they got to her shack they find her torso and another arm. They never did find her head anyplace. The guy she was living with disappeared, and her dog ran away. They never could find either one. So, today, they say when you go out there you can see a veiled figure that floats down the shore. The head is visible, but the body is not. It looks like a head on a transparent body.

154. Billy Hazard

William (Billy) Hazard was one of Salem's most colorful residents in the early 1900s. Billy, it seems, had a place in Burke's Peerage Register, but he became infatuated with one of his mother's maids and eloped with her. Finally she deserted him, and he lived alone in Salem for the rest of his life. He died in the county asylum in 1913.

Billy lived as a recluse in an old brick house at the north end of Salem. Its walls were lined with cordwood, and there were no carpets on the floors. He cooked his meals in old tomato cans on a little rusty iron stove that he might have rescued from a junk dealer's pile.

Billy was very well educated, and there appears to be no doubt of his aristocratic British ancestry. Because of his eccentricities, he could truly be called a legend in his own time.

LOCAL HEROES

155. The Strongman of Salem

When I was just a little boy, they used to talk about this man who used to come to the general store in Salem, Indiana, all of the time. Now, this man wasn't real bright, but he was supposed to be very strong.

The storekeeper was a tight old man. And one day this man came in a spring wagon to the store and wanted some salt. Now salt in those days didn't come packaged like it is today. Instead, it was in a large barrel that weighed about six hundred pounds. So this storekeeper said that if he could put that barrel of salt on his wagon, he could have it. So, he just rolled that barrel over to his wagon and lifted it up onto the back and drove off with it.

They also used to say that if this man was out plowing and someone would come by and ask him directions to somewhere, this man would just pick up his plow with one hand and point out the way.

156. General Ledgerwood

There used to be a General Ledgerwood who fought in the Indian campaigns with William Henry Harrison, and he lived in Carlisle. He was supposed to be a local hero when he come back from the wars. An old elm tree used to stand in Carlisle called Treaty Elm because that was where a treaty was supposed to have been signed with the Indians at that very spot. Well, I don't remember exactly how it was, but there was a letter sent by the President or someone in his government that told old Ledgerwood that in reward for his fightin' the Indians he was supposed to go to the top of the hill where that old elm stood and that as far as his eye could see that land was supposed to be his.

157. Robert Straight

I'm from Huntington, Indiana, located 25 miles southwest of Fort Wayne. As most towns in Indiana, Huntington is basketball minded. Around twelve years ago the school system was in search of a head basketball coach. The teams had been down and lost three of the four sectionals the previous years. Robert Straight was hired, and the fortunes changed for the Vikings.

The season started off slowly, and after each loss, Mr. Straight changed the color of his shirt. He went from red (one of the school's colors), to green, and then blue. He never wore a tie or coat. Finally he put on a yellow shirt. The Vikes won the next five games, and he never changed the color. The team won the sectional, and the following year the team turned out their first of four straight regional championships. In 1964 the team made it to the final game of the state. Straight still had the same yellow shirt. At the banquet in Indianapolis the sports writers gave him a new yellow shirt because the old one was worn out. He didn't use it until the next year. He didn't win a regional after that but continued to wear yellow until he retired and had built Huntington into a northeastern Indiana power.

FOLK DOCTORS

158. Doc Cox Found Cure for Cancer

Old Doc Cox, mostly Indian he was, lived down south of Sullivan aways. He was one of these herb doctors, used all kinds of herbs, such as ginseng and plantain and a whole raft of other herbs. Old Doc Cox was never a graduate of any highfalutin' school of medicine. Still he could cure more diseases than any ten other doctors.

American Medical Association tried to shut him down for many years; that's 'cause he knew more medicine than they did. Well, anyway, old Doc found himself a cure for cancer. That's when they really did start to try to shut him down. A company over in Indianapolis sent a man over to check on him. They're one of the largest drug makers of the world. They even offered $50,000 cold cash, mind you, for his remedy for cancer killing. So they persecuted and prosecuted him for practicing medicine without a license. Sent Doc up to Michigan City prison. Old Doc died up in prison, and never did tell them drug companies the secrets so they could make a fortune off of poor folks. It's all right, though; Granny Bea knows.

159. Doc Cox Never Charged for Healing

Dr. Cox was located south of Sullivan about five miles on Highway 41. His office was there where that slaughter pen is now. He was a herb doctor, not a registered physician, but he

had quite a practice. My grandfather went to him for a can-
cerous growth that had come on his face. Dr. Cox painted it
with something and covered it. In about three or four weeks,
it dropped off. He treated hundreds of people from Indiana
and Illinois. They finally got him for practicing medicine
without a license and something about interstate law, as
people were coming from out of the state. Of course, the doctors in the area disliked his taking their patients. Dr. Cox
never charged; you gave him only what you wanted to give
him. He treated and helped a lot of people.

160. Dr. Wheat

Dr. Wheat, an herb doctor, lived in Coxville, so . . . wait a
minute . . . he had an office at the entrance of the Coxville
covered bridge, and Dad said he could remember when
people used to line their Model-T's up and down the road
waiting to get in to see him. Members of his family sold
tickets to these people to see the doctor. He was so famous
he was invited to St. Louis to lecture, and he walked there
gathering herbs on the way. When he got to St. Louis he lec-
tured using the herbs he had gathered along the way. He had
a girl which jilted him, and being a pretty eccentric man, he
took the buggy that he used to court her apart and reassem-
bled it in his living room, where it remained for the rest of
his life. He spent very little of his money and usually hid it in
places around his home. As late as 1952, I believe, people
have been finding sums of money around Coxville that he
buried.

161. Dr. Green

Dr. Green was a queer man. He never visited a patient on foot, sometimes riding his horse into the cabin itself before dismounting. He wore a long overcoat the year around and carried a hoe to gather the herbs and roots he used in his treatments. He had many superstitions, one of which was that the patient must not be moved from the original direction nor the bed moved. He carried a piece of charcoal in his pockets, and he drew a ring around the entire bed to keep off more spirits and one around each leg to prove to himself the bed was untouched.

Perhaps his greatest claim to fame was "Silver Dollar Jim." Jim, a storekeeper, had received a blow from an iron weight, which had caused a slight skull fracture. Dr. Green was called and he proclaimed the Devil to "come out of that there head, dang ye!" With no result, but more severe fits, he decided upon a rare procedure. He sent a boy to his home to get a silver dollar. "Spirit needed silver," he said. He then removed some of the bone, and thus relieving the pressure, the fits left the patient. He inserted the silver dollar, and Jim went sixty years more with the money in his skull. Many of the older residents remember the thrill of touching the "Spirit's Silver Spot" on the head of Silver Dollar Jim.

OUTLAWS

162. Jesse James' Hideout in Jay County

I don't know if I ever told you this before but Jesse
James and his brothers used to hide out in my grandpa's
hayloft down near the Ohio line in Jay County, Indiana. You
see Jesse's mother was a cousin to the Steeds, and my
grandma's name was Steed, and she lived in Osgood, Indiana. Jesse James used to come through quite often on one
of his rampages and have to lay low for a while. I've heard
tell Jesse wasn't near as bad as they said he was. It's true he
did steal from the rich and give to the poor, but he was lots of
times blamed for stealin' he didn't do.

163. Jesse James Spent the Night near Terre Haute

My father likes to tell a story that happened to his grandparents. I don't know how many years ago it was, but it was
back in the pioneer days, more or less, in this part of Indiana.
They ran a roadside inn south of Terre Haute about ten miles,
which is east of the present [Highway] 41, and at that time it
was the main road between Terre Haute and Louisville. At
that time the transportation was horses; there weren't many
buggies, if any, and travelers would stop and stay the night at
this inn, similar to the way they stay at motels today.

This one night, just a little while before dark, some man
rode in on a big white horse. The horse was all lathered up as
though he had been ridden very hard. The man wanted to

stay all night, so they put his horse in the barn and give the man his supper, and he went to bed, and so did they. The way the inn worked, the meals were included with the room and figured in the price. And the next morning they all had breakfast. They didn't have customers every night, or a lot of them, and they ate breakfast at the family breakfast table. And so they were having their breakfast as usual, and somebody in the family noticed two pearl-handled pistols sticking out of this man's coat that was hanging on the coat peg in the hallway. This was kind of unusual, particularly two pearl-handled pistols, big ones like they were, but they didn't think too terribly much about it. So the man had his breakfast and took off on his big white horse.

This was early in the morning. About noon that day the lawmen came through looking for Jesse James. They had word that Jesse James had traveled this way. They had no way of ever knowing that the man that had stayed with my father's grandparents at their inn was Jesse James, but Jesse James was supposed to have ridden a big white horse and was always wanted by the law, and it seemed probable that this was Jesse James that stayed at this inn. It just so happens that we built our house right on the very location where this inn was, where Jesse James was supposed to have stayed one night.

164. Jesse and Frank James Spent the Night near Bowman

There is a house which stands today on Indiana State Highway 56 about one mile west of Bowman, Indiana, that is supposed to be where the notorious outlaws Jesse James and his brother Frank stayed overnight one time as they passed through southern Indiana.

The story goes that the sun was just about to set as the James Brothers rode up to this old, deserted house, and therefore they decided to spend the night. They did not know that not too far behind them was a posse from the last town that they had robbed a bank in. Well, early the next morning, the posse reached this old house, which resulted in a gunfight between the posse and the James Brothers. Jesse and Frank managed to escape unharmed, but there are still bullet holes in the front of this old, deserted house which serve as souvenirs of the night that Jesse and Frank James stayed there.

165. Frank Reno

Where ol' man Everhart lives . . . now this friend of mine, this Mrs. Reeves . . . she was an Able . . . and she was born and raised out there. And said that Frank Reno was a good man. He was just like the sheep-killing dog—he didn't; he just caught wool in his teeth.

But he was a good-hearted man, and she said that when one of her brothers was born . . . why, they made you then . . . they didn't get you up to walk around the next day. They made you lay in bed eleven days and wouldn't comb your hair, and they wouldn't let you sweep under the bed, nor would they allow anybody to sweep under and change your bed . . . had to lay right there in the gook! Bad luck to move you! For nine days you're like that!

Anyways, and she said her mother was in bed with one of her brothers . . . I forgot now which one she said it was . . . and their house got afire and burnt. And they carried her out on a bed and carried her into the barn loft. And she said that they didn't have . . . my land, they didn't have no insurance or anything 'tall about it. She said that when Frank Reno . . . he was gone, and he happened to come back . . . he heard

about it by hook or crook—you know no telephones, no nothing. And he come back, and she said he come down there in
the barn and just turned his pockets . . . they was neighbors
there . . . he turned his wrong-side out and give her dad, ol'
man Able, every dime he had, and she said, "Marguerite, it
was rolls and scadoodles and scadoodles of money." And
said, "Now take this and build you a house." And she said
with what they could salvage, planks and stuff out of the
river, and what Frank Reno give 'em . . . that house right
where Bud's dad lives is the house. Built with Reno money.

166. Al Capone's Country Home near Chesterton

As you drive up Indian Boundary Road near Chesterton,
Indiana, you cross a bridge and go up through a grove of
trees, and on the right is an estate called Palomara Farms,
and it's a large plantation . . . kind of like a big manor and a
group of caretaker's buildings set on a lake. The grounds are
cornfields and woods, and nobody lives there except for a
caretaker. At one time this was Al Capone's country home, a
place where he and the syndicate could hide out and carry
out their dirty dealings. And they said several of Al's boys
were picked up here and arrested during a big raid on the
place at the end of Al's reign. They say that the syndicate still
owns the place 'cause people come and go, but nobody
knows where they're from, and the farm is not being used to
grow crops.

167. Al Capone in Jasper

I guess back in Prohibition Jasper was really a swinging
little town. Al Capone used to come down from Chicago. You
know how the Dutch and their booze are. Well, Prohibition

sure didn't stop any of 'em. They used to make the stuff and
then ship it off on turkey trucks. They put the moonshine on
the trucks and would cover it with crates of turkeys. Ol' Al
Capone would come down to the K. of C. in Jasper and gamble like hell and line up his booze. Hell, it was his old
hangout—really put out damn good booze. I remember when
I had to go to court in Martinsville and the judge found out I
was from Jasper; he started telling he how he used to go
down there during Prohibition times. Says it's the best goddamn booze in the country.

168. Al Capone in Terre Haute

I guess that a private club near Terre Haute is pretty famous for its gangsters. Oh, not anymore. But I guess back
during Prohibition Al Capone and his gang used to hang out
there and drink and gamble. I've never been there, but I
guess all the rooms have a door. That way you can get in
without anyone seeing you and get out if there's a raid or
something. I guess that's why it's so popular with kids. A lot
of people sneak out there without their wives. That's probably why they built it that way—to beat Prohibition.

169. Al Capone's Hideout near Edwardsport

Al Capone had a hideaway in the river bottoms in the
southern part of the state west of a little town on Highway 67
called Edwardsport. This hideaway was built as a double
corncrib out in the commons where it wasn't likely anyone
would happen to be around. The corn would be in the cribs

on each side, but in the middle of the crib or the driveway was two rooms. One was for his automobile, and the other was for Al's comfort while dodging the police. It has been said that Al's places of hiding were very plush and elaborate and had all the facilities that there could be this far out in the country. People nearby knew what the corncrib was really for, and out of their own good judgment for their safety would not relay the information to the police. This is supposed to be one of Capone's hideaways that was never bothered.

170. John Dillinger: Hoosier Robin Hood

Collector: You mean Dillinger was sort of a Robin Hood? Do you mean by that that Dillinger gave to the poor?

Informant: That's right! He gave me money more than once, ten dollars at a time. And that was when ten dollars was something hard to latch onto. Hell, yes, he used to give me ten dollars or so, and he'd say, "Here, kid, go have yourself a good time." He was a hell of a nice guy, John Dillinger, and so was Harry Pierpont and Baby Face Nelson. Why, they used to give away whiskey . . . to us kids, you know that? My old man would've shit, you know that? They was the nicest fellas. They used to work in people's gardens, and once I saw Pierpont and Baby Face Nelson clearing land for one of my neighbors.

Collector: What do you think about the fact that Dillinger stole money and perhaps killed people?

Informant: Johnny got a real raw deal when he was real young; you know how the law operates. Well, times were rough and money was tight, real tight, and Dillinger wanted money—fast. But he was real nice, not selfish like most. He'd give you the shirt off your [sic] back, but he'd steal your money.

171. Dillinger Robs the Rockville Bank

About the only thing I can tell you is I was here that day that it happened, but I didn't pay any attention to it 'cause there wasn't much to it, see. He didn't get it done, see. He said this was one place he failed, see. And he walked in there, see; and they didn't have any alarm down there or nothin', see. Had a hole in the wall back there and a feller with a shotgun laying back there, laying right there aside of it. 'Course I knew the shotgun was there because I worked as a plumber, there, see. And when he came in down there they found out that fellow was down there, see. And this fellow picked up this scatter gun, see, a barrel about that long [about two feet] and pointed it at them and told 'em either get out or there'll be hell to pay. Then they pulled their guns and backed out, and that was the end of it. That's all there was to it. He always said that was the only one he ever failed at, see. I can't remember when it was; it just slips my mind.

172. Dillinger Robs the Greencastle Bank

Well, mister, I can tell you some stories about John Dillinger. When I was a kid, I went to School Number 5 down there on the old state road, and one day me and another boy was down there by the bridge when this big black car came whizzing by. Right after, here came the police. They stopped and asked if we had seen a car and did we see which way it went. We told them, and they said it was John Dillinger, and he had just robbed the Greencastle bank.

173. Dillinger Wouldn't Rob the Carbon Bank

Once Dillinger walked into the bank in Carbon and walked right up to the window. Old Jed Marshall, the head of the bank, he nearly peed his pants, but Dillinger just wanted change for a couple fifties he had stole somewheres else. Damn it, if that wasn't the funniest thing I ever heard of. Jed just shit, but John Dillinger would never rob the Carbon bank in his life. You know that?

174. Dillinger's Hideout at Highrock

Back in the twenties and thirties the countryside of Indiana and surrounding states lived in fear of such notorious men as Baby Face Nelson, Bonnie and Clyde, and John Dillinger. Highrock was supposed to be a haven for one of these notorious men, John Dillinger. For years Dillinger robbed area banks and hid out at Highrock.

Highrock is located about ten miles south of my hometown in Glendale, Indiana. The only thing Highrock is made up of is a large wall of rock with the White River running by the front of it. High upon this rock, apparently after a long and hard rain, Dillinger carved his name and right under it a small handgun. He must have really got into carving guns. Some of the money Dillinger had stolen from banks he hid in the wooded area surrounding Highrock, or so the legend goes.

The last time I visited Highrock was about five or six years ago. Last weekend I was working at a man's house that lives about two miles from there, so I decided to go over and check it out again and see if the name and gun still remained. The only thing I found was a cable across the road which used to lead back to a field that you had to walk across to get to High-rock. The man I was working for said that the cable was put up by the farmer that owned the field that you had to cross to get to Highrock.

175. Dillinger's Hideout in Indianapolis

Well, we were delivering papers down the alley one day, heading back home down the alley by the wall, up there by Raymond Street. It was three houses east of Delaware, where it comes out there, you know. Well, they had this car pulled out with bullet holes all through it and blood all over the backseat. All over the backseat! And we had never gotten into the backyard because there was this monkey they had tied up out back, and sometimes we would just throw a newspaper into the yard, and that son of a bitch would tear it up like nobody's business. And there never seemed to be anybody present around the house, but it was as though you knew that they were there. They always had measles signs or some-thing posted so that we never went up, but from everything that I and your Uncle Ray could gather, it was a hideout of Harry Pierpont, one of Dillinger's gang, and Dillinger always used to come there to hide or visit.

176. Dillinger's Hideout in New Discovery

John Dillinger had a hideout up in the New Discovery area. It was made out of oak logs and had great big oak frames built on runners so they could slide over the windows. It looks like a little fort when those oak panels are closed. It's not too far off the road, and, in fact, quite a few people knew it was there, but everyone was afraid to say anything. The last I knew of him being in these parts was when I was plowing that sand farm I used to own on the county line road. I was coming out at the end when I saw a car coming. When it passed, I saw four men sitting with machine guns inside. They just looked up and waved, and I'll be damned if I didn't just wave back and stare. I couldn't be certain, but since it was so close to Terre Haute, and he was definitely there during that time, I'd say it was him. Later I found out they'd robbed the bank.

177. Dillinger's Hideout at Rocky Forks

Dillinger and those fellas used to come in here and hide in the hills a lot. There was that house back the lane down there where they stayed. This guy named Pickett moved in here one time all of a sudden, right into the back two rooms of the Taylor place down there. He was married to Harry Pierpont's sister. Once, a long time after that, the cops raided the valley and shot up Pickett's house. But they all lived back there along the old lane, and they used to come in from the other road, from the east, but nobody knew that. And then there was old Al House, the train robber; he lived back there, and Dillinger knew him. There was this big still back there. It produced over ten thousand gallons a day—the biggest ever found in Indiana. But the cops broke it up. That Al House was a mean son of a bitch. Yeah, all those guys lived back there at one time or another: Dillinger, Pierpont, Baby Face, Al House—all those guys, you know what I mean?

178. Dillinger's Sidekick Buys a Car in Brazil

Sure, I know about John Dillinger. But I know more
about his sidekick, old Harry Pierpont. He was a killer. Why,
that son of a bitch would as soon kill you as look at you. He
was a killer. Hell, he used to work out at the gravel pit there.
Everyone said he was a hell of a nice guy. But he'd kill you.
Back in the early thirties, old Roy sold him a car, a big new
car. So, old Roy asked him how he'd like to pay for it, and
Pierpont said he'd just pay cash. Now this was back in the
days when money was hard to come by. Well, Roy told Pierpont to bring that car back in either 30 days or, let's see,
10,000 miles, I believe. Well, they say when Pierpont
brought that car back, there was 40 or 50 thousand miles on
it. You see, he used to hang around with Dillinger, used to be
his driver. Old Roy looked at that speedometer, and he damn
near shit.

179. Ghosts of Dillinger's Victims

Informant: You ought to come back this evening when
Foxy's here if you want to hear some Dillinger stories. He says
he knew that Pierpont that run around with him personal.

Collector: But you live up around Rocky Forks, Cliff, and I
want to hear some stories about Dillinger hiding out up
there.

Informant: OK, Jesus Christ! They say old Dillinger used
to hide out up there in the valley. He used to just go around
and kill the shit out of people and rob the hell out of the
banks and then go up to Rocky Forks and lay low. Well, I
guess one time there was 16 deputies from Parke County
come down there and went after him, but he killed every last

one of them. He buried them right behind the cabin while some of them were still alive, and I guess that sometimes their ghosts get up and raise hell up and down that valley.

180. Dillinger's Fat Lady

There's a big white house on a desolate road in a farm area around Crown Point, Indiana, where a big fat lady used to live. The road that goes by the house is nicknamed "The Big Mary Road" because her name was Mary. They say that Mary loved John Dillinger, and he came to her house when he escaped from the Lake County Jail. They caught him out there on a full moon, and they claim that any time a cop car drives by there on the night of a full moon they'll always see that old fat lady out there glaring at them as they go by.

181. Why the Lady in Red Betrayed Dillinger

Collector: Now, Cliff, I know you must have heard more stories than that. Come on!

Informant: Damn it, I told you you should come back and talk to Foxy. All right, here's a story you can use. Do you know anything about when Dillinger was killed?

Collector: Yeah, in Chicago, in 1934. He was pointed out by a woman in a red dress as he came out of a theatre. Right?

Informant: Right. Well, at least part right. But you don't know why she turned him in, I bet. Well, I guess old Dillinger had him 16 inches, and he used to just rip that bitch a new asshole every night, so she couldn't take it and turned him in. How's that?

182. Dillinger's Long Penis in the Smithsonian

At work we started talking about some of the greatest lovers of all time, and Phil happened to mention the fact that John Dillinger was not a lover even though he had a 23-inch penis, soft. He said they called him Wailing Willy. So I asked him why he wasn't a great lover with a penis that big. He said he didn't have enough blood to support an erection. He said everytime it got hard he passed out from lack of blood to the brain. I asked him if this was true, and he said that it was and that John Dillinger's penis is in a glass case located in the Smithsonian Institution. I asked him if he had seen it, and he said no, but his wife and Mike, a friend of theirs, saw it when they were in high school. I asked him how he found out about it, and one person offered it as part of the information when they were playing Jeopardy, and another supported it as being true.

183. Dillinger's Long Penis in the Smithsonian Must Be a Horse's

I heard a story about John Dillinger the other day from this Marilyn at work. But I don't believe it, I don't think. Well, Marilyn asked me if I believed the story about Dillinger's you-know-what being on display in the Smithsonian Institute. I said I didn't know anything about it, and she said that they had it pickled and in a jar there and that it was 22 inches long. She said it was true, she saw it, but she didn't really believe it was Dillinger's. She said it must have come from a horse or something. That is really gross. I don't really believe, do you, that they would put something like that on display?

184. John Dillinger is Still Alive

Well, I followed John Dillinger's career pretty close when he was robbing all those banks back in the thirties. I think just about everybody did then, and when they said he got shot up in Chicago, I just couldn't believe it.

After he was killed they took his body to Mooresville and put it in a funeral home, and this friend and I decided that we'd go up and see him. So we got there and had to stand in line for a long time before we got inside. We got up to the casket and looked down, but the man we saw lying there sure didn't look like John Dillinger. I know 'cause I'd seen him in person before.

Well, like I said, we just didn't believe what we saw. The man lying there was real small, narrow shoulders and all, and he had a real small forehead. You know, his hair came down low on his forehead, but Dillinger was a big man, and he had a lot of muscle on him, and he had a real high hairline. They say Dillinger had this plastic surgery, but I don't see how they can take a big man and make him as small as that guy lying in that coffin was.

Just to show you how much we didn't believe it was John Dillinger, when the guards told us to move on out, we went around to the front and stood in line to go past and see him again. So we got back inside and looked, and now the both of us know that it wasn't John Dillinger, and we even talked to Dillinger's father, who was standing there, and told him it wasn't John. But his father said it was. We had an idea that John got some guy to take his place, and his dad knew it but didn't want to say anything because if he did the police would be going after him. That's one reason why I don't think John Dillinger got shot in Chicago.

185. Dillinger Seen at State Fair after His Alleged Death

I'd say it was about three years after Dillinger got shot in Chicago that some friends and I went to the [Indiana] State Fair, and we were all walking around the midway. The others wanted to ride one of the rides, but I didn't, and so they went ahead, and I stood there and watched. In back of this ride there was this tent, and the man barking outside said you could see a new type of canning machine. So while the others were riding, I decided to go inside the tent.

I got inside, and I'll tell you the truth, I didn't believe what I saw. There, as plain as the nose on my face, was John Dillinger showing the people how to run the machine. I'll bet my jaw dropped down to the ground, and when I looked around, my jaw sure as heck wasn't the only one touching the ground. I'll tell you that.

Like I said, there was no doubt in my mind that the man I saw was John Dillinger. I just stood there and stared at that face and build. So after awhile I began looking around at the people inside the tent again, and up towards the front and to my right, I saw John Dillinger's father standing there. Like I told you before, I knew exactly what he looked like from that time I went up to the funeral home there in Mooresville. Standing next to Dillinger's father, I saw his [John's] sister, Audrey, and standing next to her was some other girl I didn't know. But they were all together watching the show.

Pretty soon the show ended, and I was real curious to see if the three would go up to where John was standing. So I kinda waited around, and, sure enough, the three of them walked up to John and started talking to him. And they were laughing, too, you know, like they knew each other real well. I didn't want them to think that I recognized them, so I left the tent and went back outside. That's the end of the story. I never saw any of those people again, and I really didn't need to because at least I knew John Dillinger was still alive.

186. Belle Gunness

There is a farm in LaPorte on McClung Road where a woman named Belle Gunness lived. It was about 50 years ago because I can remember my folks telling about her. She was a very large woman—big and strong and not nice looking at all. She would advertise in out-of-state newspapers for male companions. She said she was lonely. Since she owned this 80-acre farm, one of the stipulations in the ad was that the man have some money. They would come; she would take their money and kill them. When she was found out and they started digging on the farm they found seventeen bodies. They were all cut up and put in gunnysacks. Belle had a daughter that graduated from high school in LaPorte and was supposedly sent off to college. But no one ever saw her after that. They think that one of the bodies that they dug up was her daughter.

The way she was found out was a brother of one of the victims was suspicious because he never heard from his brother after he left for Indiana. So he came to LaPorte to find him. The house on the farm burned down, and the body of a woman was found in the ashes. But a local dentist said it wasn't Belle. The bridgework of the body they found was not that of Belle Gunness. It is thought that she killed someone and planted the body in the house and set fire to it. It was believed but never proven that a local attorney and possibly even the sheriff helped her escape for money.

The neighbors said that she was a very good-hearted person and did a lot for other people. It was the neighbor lady who felt later that she had done something to the daughter. I don't think she ever married any of the men.

PART THREE

Place Legends

BOTTOMLESS LAKES

187. River Pirate's Treasure in the Prairieton Blue Hole

The Blue Hole is a body of water, lying near the river bottoms, south of Prairieton, Indiana. Until recently it was believed that it was a bottomless hole, filled with water. It was also believed that there was a mysterious current which could suck a body down into an underground river, never to be seen again. Because of this belief, many legends and stories have evolved. One of the strangest involved a car and its occupants being swept off the road by a giant tidal wave and drug into the Blue Hole, never to be found. It was also reputed that a river pirate's treasure was buried somewhere at the bottom of the lake and that the strange occurrences were due to a series of traps which the pirate had set to protect his treasure. There are also stories that the Blue Hole is inhabited by a prehistoric water monster who lives in the depths of the back waters. The strange happenings are also attributed to it.

188. Wagon and Bus Lost in the Prairieton Blue Hole

The Blue Hole is supposed to be bottomless, and I know divers that have been 65, 75, and 85 feet down and couldn't find bottom. Well, back at the turn of the century, a double team of horses, a wagon, and a load of straw went over the cliff, and all they ever found was one blade of straw, and none of the wagon, horse, or men. A few years ago a bus drove off into it full of children—a long time ago, 20 or 30 years—and they never found a trace of them.

189. Large Catfish in the Prairieton Blue Hole

The Blue Hole is a circular lake that is approximately 50 yards in diameter and said to be bottomless. Many scuba divers have tried to reach the bottom but could not stand the pressure and had to return. Some have tied weights on the end of ropes in an effort to measure its depth, but the ropes were not long enough. There have been many large objects, such as cars, thrown in the Blue Hole that have sunk and never been recovered. There is also supposed to be a huge catfish with a head the size of a rain barrel living in the Blue Hole. The Blue Hole is located southwest of Terre Haute off Highway 63.

190. Bootleggers Throw Victims in the Prairieton Blue Hole

During the bootlegging days the syndicate or bootleggers would tie a rock around the person's neck they wanted to get rid of and would throw him into the lake [Blue Hole]. It is

supposed to be bottomless, but I heard that it leads underground to the Wabash River. I think that it is only about 100
feet deep, though.

191. Ghosts of the Prairieton Blue Hole

There is a strip pit located outside of Terre Haute, Indiana, which is called the Blue Hole. It has always been a
favorite swimming pit. Some years ago, a large group of boys
went swimming there. They were gone for a long time, and
their parents became concerned. They went to the hole looking for them, but all they found was their equipment and
clothing. The boys never returned, and their bodies were
never found. Everyone believes they all drowned in the Blue
Hole. No one goes swimming there any more because they
say if you do, the ghosts of the boys will come up out of the
water and chase you away.

192. Train Lost in the Seymour Blue Hole

My father and I loved to go fishing. There was a very
clear pool of water called the Blue Hole just a few miles from
our home. Well, a long time ago, during a storm, a train left
the rail trestle over the Blue Hole, and three cars and an
engine went to the bottom. Divers dove to try and retrieve
the cars by chains and a large crane, but when they got to the
bottom of the pool there was nothing there.

After continued efforts to find the cars and engine, railroad
engineers and scientists pronounced the pit bottomless. One
of them said there was quicksand down on the bottom and

that it swallowed up the cars, engine, and crew. Nobody really knows about what happened to them, but my dad said that there was fish in there as big as I am.

Once a fella was driving across the bridge when he saw a buffalo [carp] swimming on the top of the water. My dad was there, and he said that guy got out of the car and dove in after the big carp and wrestled him and brought him in.

193. Bottom of the Seymour Blue Hole Appears and Disappears

Well, that, a . . . Listen, honey, that is a hole, and nobody knows . . . and nobody knows anything about it, only just that hole. And do you know that there's a whole train in there? Yes, ma'am, engine and five cars! Yes, that's a-there, engine and five cars. Must be quicksand. And, oh, one day you'll found a bottom, and next day you won't. It must be the . . . You suppose it could be attached to an underground stream like a lost river down by Harrisburg?

194. Half-Moon Springs

Jonathan Lindley settled around 283 people near this place. They came from North Carolina, and they were Quakers. These people used this spring to wash their clothes in, to swim in, to water their horses in, and carry water to their homes. This Half-Moon is one of the deepest springs around these parts. For a long time people thought it was a bottomless lake. Just recently they have found out that it is close to 55 feet in depth. A lot of soldiers have drowned in this spring, but their bodies were never found. One man even lost his wagon and team of mules in the springs. They took big cranes with hooks on the ends of them to try and fish out the wagon. Nothing was found. This spring has been investigated by scuba divers and spelunkers, but no evidence has been found as to the disappearance of these people and their property. They do think, however, that there is a possible underground stream that could have washed this stuff into another branch.

HOOSIER: ORIGIN
OF THE STATE NICKNAME

195. A Hoosier is a Husher

Early in 1819 many squatters, principally from Kentucky, had built cabins and had made some improvements on a part of the public domain. Some of these squatters hastened back to Kentucky to tell their friends that the country was now opened for settlement and to insist on coming to the "New Purchase." They gave such glowing accounts of the soil, fine timber, abundance of wild game, and the level country that they were deemed to some who heard them as extremely visionary.

Many of their listeners were the Pennsylvania Dutch who had always lived in a mountainous region. They were especially incredulous. After listening to what they regarded as exaggerations, they would turn away and say to others, "Well, he is a hoosher" (meaning a husher, a silencer).

This epithet became proverbial until all who returned from Indiana were facetiously called "hooshers." This, my Kentucky parents told me, was the origin of the name "Hoosier," as it was pronounced later.

196. Another Kind of Husher

This is another tale that I have known for many years. I don't remember where I first heard it. This legend also answers the question "Where did the Hoosiers get their nickname?"

Back when flatboat travel was one of the few ways to get to St. Louis and New Orleans, many Indiana men hired out as boat hands. The men were quite muscular from the farm work that they had done as children and again from the hard work that they did on the flatboats. These men were big enough to hush any man who said anything that did not agree with their opinion; consequently, they acquired the name "Husher," which later developed into our present-day Hoosier.

197. Who's Your Daddy?

Do you know how Indiana got the nickname Hoosier? When it was first settled everyone ran around saying, "Who's your daddy? Who's your daddy?"

198. Those Damn Hoosiers

It's funny how we got our name, Hoosier. When this state was first here there was this guy from Kentucky came up, and he was sort of drunk, and he knocked on this guy's door. Well, the guy inside the house was kind of drunk, too, so he says, "Who's der?" The Kentuckian walked off and said, "Those damn Hoosiers."

199. Who's There?

I can't remember where I first heard this story, but the story answers a question often asked about how we Hoosiers got our nickname. Long ago when Indiana was first being settled it was not uncommon for the new settlers to stop by the cabins as they went on their journey. As the new settlers stopped before the cabins, they would shout to the occupants, and in typical, friendly Indiana fashion, the people would shout out, "Who's there?" Of course, heard through the heavy, wooden doors, the question was somewhat distorted and came out sounding more like "Hoosier?"

200. Hows Come and Who's There?

Shortly after Indiana was admitted to the Union as a state in 1816 the language of the people living there was considered to be somewhat different from the rest of the country. Many natives of Indiana commonly said "hows come" you do this or that, and this was considered to be rather strange language by some people from other areas of the country. Along with this saying and others the people of Indiana had another very distinct saying. When someone came to visit a person's home, after knocking on the door, they were greeted with a "Who's 'ere?" Evolving from this the saying gradually became "Hoosier," and the people of Indiana became known as the "Hoosiers."

201. Whose Ear in the Jar?

When my dad was running for office this man was telling me how the name Hoosier came about. He said that when the state capital was in Corydon there was a tavern that most of the people went to and there was a jar on the bar that had an ear in it, and when strangers came in they would ask, "Whose Ear?" In time this phrase became popular and was eventually shortened to Hoosier for a nickname for people that came from around there.

202. Whose Ear on the Floor?

Taverns at that time had sawdust on the floors, and it wasn't uncommon for two men to get to fighting. They'd kick and scratch and bite and maybe bite somebody's ear off. The next day some guy would come in, kicking through the sawdust, and kick up an ear. He'd say, "Whose ear?" And that's where the word Hoosier comes from.

203. A Hoosier is a Hayseed (or a Diseased Calf)

"Hoosier" was at one time a slang word in the South referring to a "jay" or "hayseed." The term originated from

England where "hoose" was a common name for a disease of calves. This disease causes the calves' hair to turn back, and it gives them a wild, staring look. The coonskin caps which the pioneer men and boys wore made their hair lay funny, and the homemade whiskey produced the wild-eyed look. Thus, the word "hoosier" was used to describe these early pioneers, and then it was later applied to all Indiana folk.

PLACE-NAME LEGENDS

204. Alum Cave

The post office named it Alum Cave, and the reason is because there is a small canyon of pure white limestone, which doesn't occur in Clay County except in spots. The stream is alum water, and there are balls of alum all along the stream edge. It is a very unusual canyon, and many slaves hid in it and outlaws. Alum Cave had one side in Sullivan and one side in Brazil, and it had ten saloons and one general store. There was always a knifing there every Saturday night, and it was so wild that even the sheriff wouldn't go in. The only man from outside Alum Cave itself that would go into that town over a weekend was a doctor. After the town was moved, the decent people hated the town of Alum Cave so much that they tore down all of the buildings.

205. Bloody Corners

In 1853 the Pennsylvania Railroad was laid through this area, connecting Fort Wayne with Chicago. Working on the track were Irish immigrants. One group was quartered in Etna Green and another in Bourbon. On payday a good share of the wages fell into the hands of the local saloonkeepers. When the workmen were properly fortified with whiskey, they fell to bragging about who were the best workmen. After considerable argument they met midway between the towns and engaged in a fight, which turned out to be a bloody affair. Tradition says that some were killed and the bodies were placed in the roadbed then being prepared for the tracks. Be that as it may, the battle site was ever after known as Bloody Corners.

206. Boggs Creek

Just a little piece from where Mount Pleasant used to be there was the first settlement in and around here. The ferry boatman settled there, and pretty soon a couple more families come in, including Boggs who built at the mouth of the Boggs Creek. That's how Boggs Creek got its name, but, anyhow, this was new territory and the Indians was dangerous, so they had guards posted there ever' couple nights or so. The last night they didn't have a guard, and the Indians attacked. When the guards come in the next day they found Boggs' cabin burnt down and his wife and children's heads split. They never did find Boggs, but everybody said he spent the rest of his life huntin' down them murderers.

207. Dead Man's Bridge

There's an old bridge southwest of Advance off [Highway] 74 called Dead Man's Bridge. The legend that goes with it has been told for quite a long time. There was supposed to be an old man, a criminal maybe—there are a lot of different versions now—who was found under the bridge, or parts of his body were found there. However it happened, it's supposed to be true. He was supposed to have been missing for a long time, and when they found the pieces of body it was just assumed it was this missing man. Our parents remember the legend from when they were young, and for years and years the boys have taken the girls out there to try and scare them.

208. Dead Man's Hollow

In December of the year 1874, a man by the name of Barber and some friends of his were coming back from Eugene, Indiana, where they had just spent a considerable portion of the evening drinking and playing cards. As the wagon was ascending the farther side of the deep hollow, Barber fell out of the back of the wagon. Unknowingly, the others continued their journey to Browntown, a small community of seven or eight houses.

When they arrived and discovered Barber's absence, they were not concerned for him and allowed that he would be home by the following day. The next day came and passed, and still Barber did not return. As more days and finally weeks passed, people began to get suspicious. They accused a couple of his friends of his murder. There was even a trial held for one of these men, but since there was no proof of what happened to Barber, he went free.

About a year later, a man and his dog were hunting in the hollow. The dog began to bark and tug at something under a bridge at the bottom of the hollow. When the hunter went to investigate, he found the dog pulling on a boot which had a man's leg in it. It was assumed that this leg belonged to Barber. From then on the hollow was known as "Dead Man's Hollow."

209. Devil's Tea Table

I've always heard from the very old people that the rock is called Devil's Tea Table because when settlers first came down the White River there were Indians in this part of the country, and they had a lookout on that rock because you can see a large stretch of the river from there. I understand they also used this rock for ceremonies or such, and of course they must have built fires there. So the white settlers called it Devil's Tea Table because it was shaped like a big table and the Indians used it. I've never seen any written record; that's just what I've been told. Perhaps there is a record somewhere; I can check the state and county records and find out.

210. Dutchman's Bridge

Seven and a half miles south of town [Terre Haute] there's an old covered bridge called the Dutchman's Bridge. It's called the Dutchman's Bridge because when it was built there was a Dutch family in a covered wagon on a rainy night; they spent the night in the bridge, and the woman delivered a baby that night. It's haunted because in the early

1930s when the KKK was very active in Indiana they hung a
nigger down there, and a man and a woman who lived down
there started through the bridge on the opposite end of the
hanging. When they came to the dead man the horse reared,
and they took off some other way.

211. Elkhart and Mishawaka

There's this story about the naming of two cities in the
northern Indiana area. A long, long time ago when savage
Indians lived in this part of Indiana, there was a famous Indian chief who was a hero-like image to his people. He always wanted to be remembered even after he died. The same
Indian chief had a beautiful daughter, and he wanted his
princess daughter to be remembered too. Well, anyway, the
Indian chief's name was eventually given to his main camp
on the river here. His daughter, the beautiful princess, had
her name used in naming a smaller camp a couple a miles
away on the same river. The Indian chief's name was Chief
Elkhart, for whom Elkhart was named. Today, there is a city
near there often called the "Princess City," after Chief Elkhart's daughter; her name was Princess Mishawaka. This is
the name for the city called Mishawaka, Indiana.

212. Gate to Hell

Years ago, something happened in a field around this
area. It has been told that there is a hole as big as an acre
sunk into the ground. No one knows for sure what was the
true cause of it. Many people believe that there was an

earthquake in that part, and it has caused the ground to gradually sink into a very deep hole. Still there are others who just say that it is a large sinkhole and it is due to the contour of the formation of the earth around southern Indiana.

It is said that when you look into the hole that it is so deep that you can see trees growing in the bottom of it. Also, that when you look you are looking at the top of the trees which are way down in the bottom. No one has been able to give a logical explanation of what caused it, but it is thought around here that people have ventured into the sinkhole and never returned. Some people even call it the Gate to Hell.

213. Gordon's Leap

This is true. There was a Dr. Gordon in Versailles. There had been a strange death. Gordon thought an old man's wife had poisoned him and wanted an autopsy. The family wouldn't let him. One night real late, he dug up the body. When he got the casket open, the cops and the family came out. Gordon took off running. There's a 200–250 foot drop cliff at the edge of the cemetery. At the foot of the cliff is Versailles Lake. Gordon fell off and broke a leg. He swam away, and no one ever saw him after that. Now this is called Gordon's Leap.

214. Hangman's Crossing

There's a place in Seymour where the railroad track crosses west Second Street that is called Hangman's Crossing. According to my grandfather, it was named in this manner. About a hundred years ago a train was held up at this spot by the Reno brothers . . . supposedly the first train robbery in the United States. Well, the Reno brothers were later captured and were being transported to jail, and some men stopped the train they were riding on and took them and hung them from a tree at the site of the original robbery.

215. Hell

During the boom days of the stone industry, Laurel, Franklin County, Indiana, became noted as a tough town. This reputation was further developed by a conductor on the old Whitewater Railroad. When a drunk man without a ticket boarded his train, the conductor lost all patience and remonstrated with him. Said he, "Where do you think you're goin'?" With a resigned grin on his face, the weak one replied, "I'm goin' to Hell." The conductor kicked the man off the train at the next stop, which happened to be the little town of Laurel. When the story got about, as stories do, Laurel acquired the nickname of "Hell." And although it is a quiet little town not deserving of this name, it is still known throughout this section of the state by that title.

A traveling man visited this territory and inquired of a rustic native the distance to several different places, being answered each time with the same remark, "Seven miles." Exasperated, and feeling that he was being made the butt of a crude joke, he thought to put an end to the horseplay by asking, "Well, how far is it to Hell?" This time he received a new reply; "You're there now!" said the country lad.

216. Hobart

One of the stories of how Hobart, Indiana, got its name is common knowledge in Hobart, and it goes something like this. There was a wagon train of settlers coming west back in the early days. The first wagon was driven by an old man, and his team of horses was headed by a horse named Bart. When they got into this area, the old man decided he liked it here and that they should settle here. So he yelled, "Whoa, Bart!" to stop his horse, and they just decided to call their settlement Hobart because that's what it sounded like when the old man yelled to stop his horse.

217. Hymera ("High Mary")

I'm not exactly sure just what class it was . . . I think. . . . Oh, yes, it was . . . Mr. Morris, my high school literature teacher, told us one time how Hymera got its name. He said that the postmaster in the town had a very tall daughter, and when the people saw her taking his lunch to him they would say, "There goes High Mary." You know like high, meaning tall. They kept this up, and pretty soon the town itself got the name of Hymera.

218. (Hymera ("Hi, Mary")

Hymera, Indiana, did not always have that name. It used to be called Philadelphia, Indiana. When it was a town of about 200 people, it had a makeshift post office. The woman that worked in the post office was named Mary, and everyone

that passed by would wave and call, "Hi, Mary." It soon became so widely known that the town officially changed its
name to Hymera.

219. Indian Rock

Where my Uncle Albert Cooper lived right south of the
Cooper Chapel right across the field, down in toward the
river, a big rock is there, and that was known as the Indian
Rock. The Indians was there; there was Indian beads all
around there. Oh, Ronnie, it's bigger'en this room, an' they
was never known to ever moved it, but it's supposed to guard
some kind of treasure. There's carvings, Indian carvings, all
over the rock. And it's just about a half a mile from the Dar-
win Road right there before you get to the chapel.

220. Jack's Defeat Creek

There was this Indian that lived around Monroe County
one day. And some white men came along and gave him
some firewater, and he drank a lot of this firewater. There
was this little creek close to their camping area. And he said,
"I think I can jump over that creek." And these two white
men bet him that he couldn't do that. And I believe that they
bet him. They put up a horse and some furs or something. So
Jack takes a big running leap and went half way over the
creek and ends up in the middle and has to swim over to the
other side. And so he lost his bet, and they decided to name
the creek Jack's Defeat Creek.

221. Jasper

Yeah, the people around Jasper have always been religious people. Back in the beginnin' when they was going to name the city they had a hard time decidin' what to call it. They had a bunch a commissioners, and they voted on it an' decided to name it after one of the founders' wives. Her first name was Eleanor, and that's what they was going to call the town. 'Cept this woman, bein' very religious, wanted to name it after something in the Bible. She found this here passage in the Book of Revelations which said that the city was built on precious stones and that jasper was the foundation stone. I guess she wanted this here town to stay for a long time.

222. Kokomo

Chief Kokomoko was known to be a seven-foot Indian, one of the last of the Miami Indians. The Miami Indians were spread throughout Howard County. David Foster, one of the early settlers, named the city of Kokomo after Chief Kokomoko. There are old trading post records stating that on June 27, 1838, Chief Kokomoko bought a barrel of flour for $12 for his squaw. The chief died and is thought to be buried in Kokomo near Kears Sawmill between Superior Street and the Wildcat Creek in the middle of what is now Buckeye Street. He and two other Indians were moved to Pioneer Cemetery. There is a monument near Kautz Field in his honor. It has been said that he was an Indian chief, but was actually just an ordinary Indian.

223. Lick Skillet

Lick Skillet was the former name for North Vernon. The train used to go through there and stop, and every time it stopped, the conductor could see the dogs and cats licking the skillet. The housewives would set out the pans and skillets for the animals to clean. So it was named Lick Skillet. Later it was named North Vernon because it was three miles up the pike from Vernon.

224. Loogootee

Ever since I was old enough to go to school I've been hearin' how Loogootee got its name. It was at the time they were building the B. & O. Railroad through the Midwest to St. Louis. At the time they had already built it to Shoals, but didn't know whether to go on to Mount Pleasant or make a straighter route through what's now called Loogootee. This guy named Gootee who owned this land offered his land to the railroad for a very good price. The engineer, who knew that Gootee's son was in love with his daughter and knew how she felt about his son, said, as a joke, that he'd let his daughter marry Gootee's son if he would name the town after him. Of course, Gootee agreed, and the Lowe girl married the Gootee boy. It didn't take long for the name Lowe-gootee to catch on then.

225. Mecca

Mecca is a town, and it was first settled about the early 1840s. In 1898 they built a tile plant, and so they needed workers, and they needed cheap workers, so they sent over to the Near East and got these Moslems, in that general area. They lived there outside town, and when they got paid, they'd come to town and say it was almost like coming to Mecca, and so they called the town Mecca.

226. Monsterville

It all started when two reputable businessmen were fishing in the pumphouse pond. They supposedly noticed what they described as a seven to ten foot tall, white and shaggy-like creature. They went closer somewhat to investigate it and was sure it wasn't a man. They shot at it pointblank with a shotgun. The creature was unharmed, and they ran. They went back to Clinton police station and reported the incident. Because of the businessmen's reputation the incident was printed in the paper. After the printing of the article, several people became interested and went out there to see it. They found nothing. The monster was referred from then on as the Sheik by the people. Several people claimed to see this. One woman in Centenary saw it in her backyard. One teacher and her class claimed to have seen it running along a fence row. A farmer reported a dead cow which was mysteriously killed. Other than that, the reports are scattered. The place received the name of Monsterville because of this.

227. Montezuma

Well, the supposition is that Montezuma was named after the Aztec Indian chief Montezuma. I found an old map once that had all this area recorded as the Montezuma Plains. It's thought that the Aztecs and Incas were in this area before the Plains Indians ever came. There's been a piece of Spanish chain mail found over in Illinois, and other things have been found that indicate the Aztecs might have been here. Then, of course, there used to be an Indian settlement here. Supposedly it was called Montezuma, too. This used to be a Wea Indian reservation, the Sugar Creek Reservation. There must have been white people here, too, because some of the burials in the old cemetery go back to 1811, and this area wasn't opened up for sale until 1823.

228. Nigger Hill

I know the story of Nigger Hill. It's way back, and, oh, I don't remember when, but a way back, I guess in the days of the Civil War maybe when the Negroes were kind of down. And we had a Negro schoolteacher, and nobody liked him, but he was really a good teacher, and, I don't know, he did something to a white child, and they took him on the hill and hung him. And now supposedly in the dark of the moon, you can hear this Negro scream up there. I've never heard it, but that's what it's supposed to be. I don't really believe it. I don't know anybody that's ever heard it. We got two other things called Devil's Elbow—it's a road—and Hangman's Crossing, but I don't know why they're called that.

229. Noblesville

John Conner and James Polk founded the town of Noblesville, Indiana, in 1823. At that time Polk was engaged to marry a woman from Indianapolis by the name of Kathleen

Noble. Polk built a new home for his bride in the center of
his newly discovered town. He planted a garden of vegeta-
bles in an outline which spelled out her name. He thought
that this would symbolize his great love for Miss Noble.
However, Miss Noble was not pleased; instead, she was
greatly enraged and insulted by the vegetable garden. Thus
she broke her engagement to Polk.

Sometime later a couple passing through the territory came
to the Polk cottage, which was deserted, and saw the garden
which he had planted. The man turned to the woman and
asked, "What is the name of this town?" His wife replied that
this must be Noblesville because the garden said so.

230. Orland

The village was first known simply as "The Vermont
Settlement." When a post office was established in 1837 the
idea of a real name was concentrated upon; and, inspired
probably by their beautiful millrace and grove of trees about
it, "Millgrove" was proposed, only to find that was already
the name of a post office in Indiana. Music was the center
around which their social life moved, and it was not strange
that a quorum could be considered present at a choir re-
hearsal. At one of these meetings they agreed that Col. Cha-
pin, their leader and also postmaster, should name the town.
Taking up his hymn book he said, "Our dear old hymn book
shall have its part in the honor. The first tune to which it
turns open shall be the name of our town." It fell open to the
old hymn "Orland."

231. Pie Town

They've called upper Alton "Pie Town" for years and years. Some old-timers don't call it by any other name. There was a federal penitentiary in town during the Civil War. Soldiers used to bring prisoners in and march them right through the town. Then sometimes just the soldiers would come through on their way to and from the wars. You know, my mamma was living during the Civil War; my father fought in it. Poppa didn't see much action, but he was in it just the same. I wasn't born yet. Those soldiers would march through town, to and from the war, and the women would know that they were coming. They'd all bake a lot of pies, as many as they could afford, and when the soldiers marched through, they'd run out along the streets and give the pies to the soldiers. You know, they didn't get much to eat, sometimes nothing at all. The soldiers spread the word around and upper Alton began to be called "Pie Town." For years and years the paper was called the "Pie Town Journal."

232. Pinhook

My roomate's grandparents live in Pinhook, Indiana. Her grandparents told me this story. During the 1800s in Lawrence County near Bedford, Indiana, there was an owner of a general store who did not have a liquor license. So what he would do is pour the customer a glass of liquor and take a woman's long old-fashioned hat pin, bend it, and hook it over the shot glass. The customer was not buying the drink but the pin that was hooked over the glass. So he could not be arrested for selling liquor because he was selling the pin and giving the drink away. So whenever anyone said "Let's go to

Pinhook," one knew they were going to get some booze. Eventually the area round the general store came to be known as Pinhook, and it is on the map today.

233. Pumpkin Center

So you want me to tell you how some of these parts got their names, huh? Well, why don't you go to the damn library? When I went to college nobody ever told me anything; I had to find out things for myself. You kids have it too easy, and you can tell those people in Terre Haute that's what I think. I'll tell you one story because I don't think you will find it in any library. It seems that back when things were just getting started around here, there was this farmer who had the biggest goddamn pumpkin patch in the state just up north of here. Well, now, this old son of a gun was real proud of his pumpkins. One year he grew a pumpkin that weighed 107 pounds. I know 'cause my uncle told me about it when I was little. Well, anyway, this old guy was so proud of his pumpkins that one day he put this sign up that said "Duncan's Pumpkin Center of the World." Well, folks thought this was real funny, and they started just calling his place "Pumpkin Center," and that's what people call it to this day, and that's all I'm saying.

234. Santa Claus

Several families settled in the area and decided that they should have a name for their community. They decided on Santa Fe. They applied for a post office to make it official. On Christmas of 1855, everyone was greatly excited at the thought of going to their own brand new post office for their Christmas cards and gifts instead of having to ride to Dale. Unfortunately, a large white envelope with important seals arrived the day before Christmas to find out that a town in Indiana already was named Santa Fe. Determined to get their post office just as quickly as possible, the citizens of Santa Fe decided to discuss the matter that very night, Christmas Eve. While they were singing the whole world outdoors became filled with an intense blinding light, and a little boy came rushing in. "The star! The star! The Christmas star is falling!" Everyone rushed out just in time to see a flaming mass shooting down from the heavens and crash into a low, distant hill. They considered it an omen of good fortune. Returning to the meeting, it seemed a most natural thing for all the folk to agree that the name Santa Fe should be changed to Santa Claus.

235. Shake Rag School

The Shake Rag School outside Freelandville, Indiana, got its name back in the days when there were no telephones in town. To show that school was in session, the teacher would put a rag in the tree outside the schoolhouse. When the wind blew, it would look like the tree was "shaking the rag"—hence, Shake Rag School. Later on the name was changed to Robbins School because three-fourths of the students were named Robbins.

236. Spook Hollow

Down in Ballhinch near Sugar Creek is a place they call Spook Hollow. It's real foggy and dark down there, and that's why a lot of the kids like to park down there. But they say that there is a nutty old guy who hangs out around there and bugs the parkers. This one girl was in the hospital for three months once in shock just because she saw this old guy. You know her, Nancy James, no relation. I guess these kids were laying down in the front seat of the car . . . I don't know what they were doing . . . and she looked up and saw this spooky guy looking in the window. She said he had sort of glowing blue eyes like they did in "The Village of the Damned" and that he had a white beard and sort of bluish all over like he'd been drowned or dead a long time. Her date said she screamed and screamed, and after that she was in shock for three months because she was so scared of this guy.

237. Tampico

I heard this about sixty years ago. In the early days Tampico was called "Pico." It was the trading point for the German settlement ten miles east of Brownstown. Well, one of these old Germans that got his English pronunciation fouled up when he got excited or mad went to Pico to get some large spikes to use in building his barn. After driving all the way to Pico, he was told that they had no spikes that large. He became very angry and cried, "Well tam (damn) Pico anyhow; I will trade in Brownstown." After that they started calling Pico "Tampico."

238. Tecumseh

I asked Gary if he knew any stories, and he asked me if I knew how Tecumseh got its name. I said, "It was named after an Indian." He said, "Yeah, but you know how the Indian got his name?" I said, "No, I've never thought of that." So he told me this story. There was this band of Indians that had a powwow where the town is now. The chief's name was Tee. A couple of warriors went through the woods and found this huge river. They ran back shouting, "Tee, come see!" Tee come see!" So that's how Tecumseh got its name.

239. Toad Hop

About forty years ago a man by the name of May built two houses down along the road beside of what is now U.S. 40. Well, this here fella was quite a drinker. It seemed like every night he would come home and be just terrible drunk. Well, this went on for a couple years, and finally some of his relatives begin buildin' some homes down in there where he was at. Well, after a while some more people started buildin' down there till there was a pretty good bunch of houses down in there. Well, one night there in the summer he come trudgin' home all drunk and fell down right in the middle of one of the dirt roads that ran through there. Just as he fell down a toad hopped by right in front of him. He got up and says to himself, "Toad Hop, yep, that's where I live, Toad Hop."

240. Thorntown

Thorntown was an Indian town. There was this Indian princess, and she was in love with a warrior. They both lived there. She was unable to marry him, though, because he was either killed in battle or her father had promised her to someone else. Anyway, she was heartbroken about the whole thing. So she went running through a woods full of thorns and briars and thick bushes that hadn't been cleared away. Somehow she got tangled up in the briars and fell, and a thorn went through her heart and killed her. Since she was so pretty and everything the people around there were broke up about it and named the place Thorntown. The name stuck and that's what it's called today.

241. Wilson Creek

Wilson Creek was named from this man, this four foot nigger named Wilson. And how he ever got here, there was never no history on him unless he come in here with the Indians. He trapped with rocks and triggers, dead falls. He didn't have no gun, but he done his killin' with a knife. He'd get a bear, he'd get a bear to stand on its hind feet, a-wrestlin' with him and cut him under the left foreleg here right in his heart. Kill him! That's the way he killed bears. That's the way history gives it. And he's buried there on one of them creeks somewheres now.

PART FOUR

Modern Legends

LEGENDS NOURISHED BY THE AUTOMOBILE

242. The Vanishing Hitchhiker

One rainy night two men were driving along a country road when they saw a girl dressed in a white party dress walking along the side. They stopped and asked her if she wanted a ride. She got in the backseat and told them that she had been away for a couple of weeks and that she was going home. She gave them directions, and the men took her to a small farmhouse. The girl thanked them and got out of the car. She walked into the yard, but instead of going up to the front porch, she walked around the side of the house. All at once she just disappeared.

The men got worried so they went up to the house and knocked on the door. Finally, a woman opened the door and asked them what they wanted. The men explained about the girl and wanted to know if she had gotten into the house safely. The woman's face went as white as a sheet. She ran into the living room and brought back a picture. She asked the men if that was the girl they had given the ride to. The men said that it was and asked why she was so frightened. The woman said, "This is my daughter. She was killed in an automobile accident two weeks ago. We buried her in her white graduation dress." The men thought that maybe they had dreamed it so they went back to their car. There in the backseat was a puddle of water where the girl had sat.

243. Death Car Sells for $25

I heard' several years ago about this real rich guy who was driving down a real deserted road in his Corvette and had a heart attack and died. They say he laid there for months before anyone found him. His body had decomposed, and the smell was terrific, I guess. A car dealer fixed up the car and put in new upholstery and everything, but the smell of death was still in the car, and it just would not go away no matter what they tried. I think it was for sale on some car lot in Chicago or Indianapolis. But no one would buy it because of the awful odor, so the car dealer put it up for sale for $25, and still it didn't sell.

244. Couple Killed in Death Car

This car that everyone calls the death car really did exist. My brother was going to buy it and clean it all up, but someone got it before he did. Evidently, a girl and guy were killed in this car in a wreck, and the bodies weren't found until three months later. You can imagine how bad the car smelled, but my brother figured if he could get the car cheap

enough—by the way, the car was a Stingray—that he could
figure out some way to clean it up and get rid of the smell. I
don't know who has the car now.

245. Lawyer Killed in Death Car

In Indianapolis not long ago this man in his middle
fifties who was a lawyer was driving down an old country
road. He was driving his sports car, which was a Jaguar. For
some unknown reason he died, and his body set in the car for
two weeks before he was found. Because he sat there so long
in the car, his body began to decompose, and the smell
seemed to penetrate into the car. This very expensive sports
car was sold by an auto dealer in Indianapolis for $50. The
reason it sold so cheap was that the smell of death was still in
the car, and there was no deodorant that would take it away.

246. Boy Commits Suicide in Death Car

I can remember when the boy was found down by
Jericho back in about 1960, and he'd been dead for about a
week in his car. They say he drove back into the stripper hills
where his car couldn't be seen and ran a hose from his
exhaust back into his car and took his own life. This was
mid-July and extremely hot, and he had closed all the windows up tight. The undertakers had gone after him in a panel
truck that they never could get the death smell out of and had
to finally get rid of. They had to take a shovel and scoop that
boy out of the car and put what was left of him in a plastic
bag. His car was like brand-new, so they tried fumigating it

and everything to get the stink out. But nothing worked. I'm not sure whether they burned his car or had a dealer take it away from here and sell it cheap, but I do know for a truth you can never get rid of the death smell.

247. Assailant in the Backseat Foiled by Truck Driver

It's a true story. This woman in Indianapolis was shopping late one night at a shopping center. She was by herself, and she had to drive quite a ways to get home. She was driving down the highway, and she noticed this semi followin' her with his brights on. It really made her mad. He wouldn't dim his lights, and then he started blinking them. Finally she came to a turn-off and thought she'd get rid of him. But the truck turned, too. Then she started to get scared. She was on a county road that no trucks hardly ever used. She speeded up and tried to lose the truck, but he kept right with her. Finally she got to her lane and turned in. The truck turned in, too. She was so scared she jumped out of the car and ran in the house. The trucker didn't try to follow her. He ran over to her car and jerked the back door open. There was a man all crouched down in the backseat where the woman couldn't see him, but the trucker was up so high he could. So remember, always look in the backseat before you get in the car. If that woman had a-been smart she'd a-kept her doors locked when she parked the car.

248. Assailant in the Backseat Foiled
by Station Attendant

One night a woman pulled into a gas station. The gas
station attendant came out, and she told him to fill the tank.
He did this and came back to the window to get the money.
She gave him a five dollar bill, and he said he didn't have
change, that he would have to go get some. Not too long after
that he came out again and told her that money was counterfeit and that she would have to come into the station and wait
until the police came. The woman was really surprised; she
was just a housewife. She argued that it could not be true for
a few minutes, but he insisted that she had to come into the
gas station to wait for the police. So she got out and went in.
When they got inside, he told her that there was a man in the
backseat and that he just wanted to get her out of the car.

249. Convertible Filled with Concrete in LaPorte

There was a fellow in LaPorte who was in the cement
business. He suspected that his wife had been seeing another
man. He came home early one night in his cement truck and
found a strange brand-new convertible in his driveway. So he
took the spout of the cement truck and filled the convertible
with cement. This same story was said to happen in Des
Moines, Iowa, and also in Indianapolis.

250. Convertible Filled with Concrete in Plainfield

While my dad and I were sitting in the Blue & White
truck stop on I-65 near Plainfield, Indiana, I overheard these
men talking, and one of them told a story about another

trucker whose wife was running around on him. And so one
day he went home to find the neighbor man's car out front.
Well, it so happened that this trucker drove a cement truck,
so he just backed the funnel up to the man's car, and filled it
plumb full of cement, then left and went on his way.

251. Mooresville's Gravity Hill

There's a real spooky hill on Keller Road just outside
Mooresville, Indiana. When you park your car on the hill and
put it in neutral, there's a force of gravity that will pull the
car up the hill backwards. It's a real funny sensation. There's
supposed to have been an Indian witch doctor buried in the
hill that the road is built on. Recently, when the road was
resurfaced with asphalt, the workmen questioned whether
the hill would still be the same. To their amazement, the hill
still has its uncanny force of gravity.

252. South Bend's Gravity Hill

There is this hill that is in South Bend. You drive to the
bottom of the hill; it's not real steep, but it is a hill. You can
see it. You park your car at the bottom, and you put the car in
neutral. The car coasts up the hill for about 100 yards. They
say that it has been checked by scientists from Notre Dame
and that they cannot figure it out. There is only one other
place in the world like it. It's someplace in Florida. It sure is
weird.

PARKING LEGENDS

253. Hook Man

This young couple is out parked on a country road. The girl is real nervous and uneasy. It seems that there had been a report out about an escaped criminal in the area. He was supposed to be dangerous, a mad killer. They called him the Hook because one of his hands was missing, and he wore a hook in place of it. He was supposed to have used it on all of his victims. Anyway, the girl was real uneasy for some reason. Supposedly, they were not aware of the escaped killer. She kept saying she had an uneasy feeling, but she did not know why. The guy finally got mad at her. He thought she was just making up excuses because she didn't want to park. Finally he lost his temper and stepped on the gas. He really tore out of there fast. He didn't say a word on the way home. When they get to the girl's house, he just got out and went around to open her door. When he got to the door, there was a hook hanging on the handle.

254. The Boyfriend's Death in Gary

There's this story back in Gary about a fella and his girl who used to always park around the mental asylum. Now the girl didn't go for it too much, but the boy was a bold, big fella who was never afraid, said, "Now it's gonna be okay. We'll go over there, and we'll park." So they went over there, and they parked the car and were talking awhile . . . they had a con-

vertible. Well, they parked for awhile and got their smooch-
ing and stuff done, and the boy decided that it was about
time to take the girl home. Well, the girl agreed, and he tried
to start his motor; but, unfortunately, he found he was out of
gas. Well, he didn't quite know what to do, and it was awful
dark outside . . . no moon . . . and he didn't think it would be
too good of an idea to take the girl with him to go get some
gas. So he left the girl in the car and said, "I'll be back. I'm
gonna go get some gas, and whatever you do, don't let anybody come in, and lock your doors. Don't let anybody get in
the car. She said . . . the top was up . . . she said, "Fine,
okay."

Well, he got out of the car, and she locked the car. He
started walking on down the road . . . so she thought. Well, he
never returned, and he never returned, and he never returned. Well, she was getting panicky, but she still remembered the point that he said, "Now don't ever leave the car."
Well, soon she fell asleep in the car, and about 5:30 or 6:00
when the sun was coming up she heard a knock on the window, and she woke up and was startled to find it was an
officer.

Well, the officer told her to roll the window down. She
rolled the window down, and the officer said, "Now, ma'am,
we're gonna take you back home," he said, "but just promise
me one thing—that whatever you do you won't look back at
the car." She said, "But why? Does it have something to do
with my boyfriend?" "No," he said. "Just come with us, and
just don't look back." Well, she said, "Okay." So they left the
car, and they were walking to the squad car, and she wanted
to look back so bad . . . Oh, I blew it! . . . She wanted to look
back so bad, and as they were walking back she told the
policeman that during the night she had heard some unusual
scratches on the top of the car, but she didn't know what they
were. She had wondered if somebody had tried to get in or

anything. The cop said, "No, it's okay. Whatever scratches you heard weren't anything. Just forget about them." So she said, "Okay." So walking back to the car she had to turn around and look. Her curiosity was up, so as the policeman walked ahead of her she turned around, and she found out what the scratching was on top of the car. Someone strung her boyfriend up by the legs and stripped him of all his skin, and the only thing that was scratching on the top of the roof of the car was his fingernails.

255. The Boyfriend's Death in Munster

This is true also, and it happened on Werewolf Road in Munster, Indiana. This boy and girl were parked on this Werewolf Road. When he tried to start his car, it wouldn't turn over. So he told his girlfriend that he was going for help. He told her to wrap up in a blanket and keep the doors locked and not to let anyone in. He left, and she waited, but he didn't come back. After awhile she heard this knocking on the back window of the car. But she was so scared that she was afraid to look. Finally a flashlight was shined into the window. She heard someone say, "Open up, open up; this is the police." After some identification she opened the door. The policeman said whatever you do don't look back, but just get in our car. When she was getting into the police car, she turned her head and saw her boyfriend hanging from a tree upside down with his head knocking on the window.

256. The Purple Lady

My brother's a nut about all these legends. He even goes out to the places to see what they're like. He tells this story about the Purple Lady and says it's true. I don't know if I believe it or not. It doesn't sound very likely. Well, south of Terre Haute down by the covered bridge there is an abandoned road. They say that when couples used to park there this lady in purple velvet came out with a dead baby. She would ask the couple to take it, and if they didn't she put it under the wheels of the car so that they would run over it. I guess this happened to several couples. Really weird.

LEGENDS INSPIRED BY THE TELEPHONE

257. Man Believing in Afterlife Has Phone in Mausoleum

A few years ago, this real influential man from West Terre Haute died, and the family had him buried in an expensive cemetery mausoleum. In his will, he stated that he wanted a telephone installed inside the mausoleum with him because he believed that some day he would come back to life, and he had told his wife that he would call her when he did. Several years later his wife suddenly died of a heart attack, and when the police found her, she was still holding the phone in her hands. They checked the mausoleum where the husband was buried, and they found his receiver off the hook. The mausoleum phone was removed a few days later. Quite a few people believe this really happened.

258. Man Fearing Live Burial Has Phone
in Mausoleum

Collector: What have you heard about the Martin Sheets mausoleum?

Informant: Well, I used to work at the telephone office across the street where he lived there on Ohio. He used to come out every morning in his underwear—trap-door in the back—to get his paper. Well, anyway, after he died he was buried out to the Highland Lawn Cemetery. They said over at the other office—the old Citizen's—that he had a telephone put in there 'cause he was afraid that he'd be buried alive, and he'd come to life, and no one would know he was in there. That was the only way he could get to anyone. He had the phone put in, and the number came in on the board. And the girls didn't like to sit on that board. They was scared to death—what if that light would come in?—wouldn't know what to do. They'd probably fall over.

259. The Baby-Sitter and the Phone Call

There's this girl, and she was baby-sitting for a couple in this house, and it was about 12 o'clock, and she had just put the children to bed. There was one little boy and two girls. So she was expecting a phone call from her boyfriend about 12 o'clock. So the phone rang, and she answered it, and all she could hear was some man breathing very heavily into the phone and growling. So she hung up the phone and thought it was just a prank call, but the same thing was repeated a few minutes later, so she got scared and called the police and wanted to have the call traced. The police told her next time to stall as long as possible so they could trace the call.

About five minutes after she called the police she received a phone call from the man, and all she could hear was growling and heavy panting. So she held the phone for about five minutes so the police could check the call. She hung up, and the police called her back and said they'd be right out because the phone call was coming from an upstairs extension in the house. At that time the girl heard the extension phone slam in the background and heard someone going down the backstairs and crash through a window.

The girl, I guess, went insane and just froze in a state of severe shock. When the police got there they found the girl standing in the same position holding the phone. They found the children upstairs all sliced to pieces in big chunks as if someone had ripped them apart with their teeth. They never found the man, and the girl is still in a mental institution.

VACATIONS

260. Vacationist Falls Out of Travel Trailer

A couple of years ago, this dentist in Brazil thought it was about time he and his wife took a vacation. They had both worked pretty hard, and he decided that they really needed a vacation. He thought if they were going to make a trip out west he might as well do it right. He went out and bought a brand-new camping trailer and a new car to pull it. The trailer wasn't just one of these foldout deals. It was a big furnished trailer.

Well, they went to Colorado and stayed two full weeks and really had a wonderful time. The only thing hampering their good time was that the husband had done all of the driving, and was really pretty tired. He didn't think his wife was a good enough driver to drive on strange land, especially with all the new equipment he had bought. He had tried to be very careful, and nothing had gone wrong. Things were going very smooth.

Well, they got all the way to Marshall, Illinois, when they stopped to get something to eat. The man was just exhausted from doing all the driving. They were trying to drive straight through without stopping overnight. They spent so much time on the way out there, they wanted to make up for it coming back. As I said before, though, the man was very cautious not to get a speeding ticket. Anyway, after they stopped in Marshall to eat, the man decided to let his wife drive the rest of the way home. He was so exhausted he could hardly keep his eyes open. It was only about 35 miles to their house, and she was familiar with the highway, so he felt pretty confident about letting her drive the rest of the way. He even decided to crawl back in the trailer and lay down. So he undressed down to his boxer shorts and must have just went right to sleep.

When the woman had driven all the way to Fruitridge and Wabash, she had to come to a stop for the red light. Well, her husband felt the car stop, and opened the back of the trailer to see where they were at. Just as he opened the door, the light changed, and the woman pulled off. The trailer gave a little jerk, and the man fell out. There he was in the intersection with just his shorts on. Well, he ran into the Clark gas station there on the corner. Incidentally, his wife didn't know he had fallen out and kept on driving. Meantime, the man gets this gas station attendant to drive him home in a truck. They passed his wife on the highway, but she didn't even see them. The man tells the driver how to take a shortcut, so they beat his wife home. She still doesn't know he's not in the back, and she gets caught in a traffic jam in Brazil.

Meantime, the truck driver drops the guy off at home. He didn't have a key to get in, so he gets a lawn chair out of the garage and lays down on it. They live in the country, and he wasn't too worried about anyone seeing him in his undies, so he just sat the chair in the driveway. Well, he dozed off, and just about that time his wife pulled in the driveway safe and sound. Halfway up the driveway, she sees her husband sitting in the chair. Well, it scared her so bad that she stepped on the gas instead of the brake and ran the whole damn thing right through the garage.

261. The Runaway Grandmother

Well, one time there was this family that was going on a trip up in Canada. I heard this was true, and the girl was from Bloomington. Anyway, they took their grandmother along because she lived with them; she was pretty old. They were way up in some Canadian woods; you know how they just go on and on for miles. The grandmother died, and they didn't know what to do; they couldn't bury her up there, so they wrapped her up in a blanket and rather than keep her in the car they put her on the baggage rack on top. So they headed for the nearest town and had to stop and eat. And when they came out, the car had been stolen and supposedly they haven't heard from Granny since.

TEENAGERS ALONE

262. The Licked Hand

There's a story about a dog, too, and an escaped convict. It goes like this: In a little town south of here—ever hear of Farmersburg?—there was supposed to be some escaped convict loose. He was supposed to be a murderer, a psycho. Well, anyway, there were these two girls, real good friends. The parents of the one were gone for the night, so the other girl was to stay with her at her house. Just the two girls and the dog of the girl who lived there. For some reason, there were two beds in the room, and the girls slept in separate beds. Well, they'd heard about the man breaking out, and they were scared, so the girl who lived there sent her dog over to sleep with her friend so that she'd feel better.

Sometime in the middle of the night, the girl who lived there got scared and reached down to the side of her bed to pet her dog. When she did, the dog licked her, and she felt better about it all and went on back to sleep.

In the morning, she got up and saw that sometime during the night her friend had been killed. Her throat was slit and so was the dog's. She thought about it, trying to figure out when it could have happened, since she remembered petting the dog. Well, her folks came home, and there was a great big mess and all that stuff, and then it was all about forgotten. Then about twenty years later, when this chick had grown up and all, she got a note from this guy, the murderer. They'd never caught him somehow. The note said, "I'm coming to see you. I had my chance once before, but I didn't take it. Not only dogs can lick."

263. The Surpriser Surprised

This guy was going with this girl, and they'd been dating
for a long time. Well, she was up in bed, and her parents
were down in the basement, but he didn't know that they
were in the house, so he went on up. Well, since he thought
that they were out and so did she, he went to bed with her.
But that didn't work out too well. The furnace shut off. Well,
he started downstairs to check on the furnace, and she went
with him. They got close to the door downstairs to the basement, and it opened for them, and the lights went on. There
they were in their birthday suits, right in the middle of a surprise party that her folks were giving for her graduation. All
of her friends and her parents and everything. It happened to
one of my fraternity brothers, or at least he says it did, and it
doesn't seem likely that he'd create it about himself.

FOREIGN MATTER IN FOOD

264. Kentucky Fried Rat in Shelbyville

Did you hear about Colonel Sanders' chicken? There
was this woman who went into Colonel Sanders and ordered
white meat. Well, instead of giving her white meat, she got
dark. She asked them why she got dark meat, and they said
that it was a fried rat. I think it was in Shelbyville.

265. Kentucky Fried Rat in Elwood

You should have heard what I heard about the Colonel Sanders in Elwood. Steve told me that a guy bought some chicken there and ate the chicken, but he thought it tasted funny. Upon further investigation, he found out he had eaten a rat.

266. Kentucky Fried Rat in West Lafayette

I heard something about the Colonel Sanders in West Lafayette last weekend. There was this guy who ordered a thing of chicken, and he noticed a piece that looked funny and had part of a tail stickin' out of it. It turned out to be a rat.

267. Kentucky Fried Rat in Terre Haute

A friend of mine told me about the Colonel Sanders at 8th Avenue and Lafayette [in Terre Haute]. A guy told her on a date one night. There was this couple on a date who stopped at the Colonel's and got a bucket of chicken. They were goin' on a picnic, I think. Well, while they were eatin' the chicken, the girl bit into a piece that tasted funny. She and her date looked at that piece of chicken and found out it was a fried rat.

268. Tacos

There was a taco stand in Gary that was very popular. Everyone went there. It seems that a lot of people in town were missing their pet cats, and some other people reported hearing cats yowling over at the taco stand. The police investigated and found that there were hundreds of catskins out back of the taco stand, and they closed the stand down. I heard that they had the best tacos in town.

269. Booze from Formaldehyde

During Prohibition days it was said that people would drink anything. Well, this is a true story. There was a setup joint in Terre Haute that bought bootleg from some students at I.U. in Bloomington. They said they made it in the labs in their spare time. No one doubted their word. One day the police caught the boys running the stuff and arrested them. When they questioned them, they finally told them where and how they made the booze. It was made from the preserving solution that covered the cadavers at the I.U. Medical School. The story was never released for fear the customers would harm the boys.

270. The Stolen Whiskey Bottle

A lady was going to the doctor for an examination. The doctor had asked that she bring a sample of urine. She looked around the house for a bottle to put it in. Finally, she found an empty whiskey bottle, so she put the urine into it. When she got in the car she laid the bottle in the front seat. On the way to the doctor's, seeing that she had time, she stopped at the K-Mart to get some things. It was summertime; the car windows were down. After she got back to the car from her shopping, she became almost hysterical from laughter, for her bottle of so-called whiskey was gone.

DEPARTMENT STORES AND SHOPPING CENTERS

271. Department Store Snakes

I heard this one from Mom, and the lady that told her swore to God it was true. It's the same old story about the snakes in the discount store. She went—where was it?—to K-Mart and tried on a blouse or a dress or a coat or something, and when she got home there was a welt on her arm, and she didn't know what it was. And it got to hurting her, and she went to the doctor, and he said, "There's nothing that can be but a snakebite." No, he didn't tell her what it was, but he kept asking her where she had gone and where she had been.

Well, she went back to the store and looked for the dress, and it was still there. They got the dress and took it to the manager's office and told him that she thought that they should tear open the dress because there was something suspicious about it. So they tore it open, and they found these little baby snakes in it. The fabric had come from Singapore or somewhere. The eggs had been in it, and the heat in the store hatched them out. The store gave her so much money to shut up about it. It was $200 they gave her, I think.

272. Assailant Mutilates Boy in Shopping Center Rest Room

One day the mother of my friend came home from Terre Haute shopping and was not only upset but very sick. She told us about while shopping at Meadows Center there was a clerk or someone who told her about how somebody had hidden in the rest room, and when a little boy went in this person had taken a knife and cut him up. This little kid about four had gone in by himself while his mother was shopping. Anyway, when the mother went to find him she found blood all over the floor and parts of him all over. This person told my friend's mother she had seen the blood. This was about four years ago. Also I heard a bunch of colored boys or white boys chopped up a little colored boy there, too. I know I was afraid to go in the rest rooms in the basement of Meadows for a long time.

273. Assailant Emasculates Boy in Shopping Center Rest Room

About ten years ago my mother told me this story, and I can't tell you how strongly that I believed it was true. She said that she heard that there was a man from Louisiana who would wait in rest rooms and attack children when they came in. She said that this happened to a six-year-old boy at Meadows Shopping Center. He walked into the rest room, and the man pulled out a knife and cut his peter off. I wouldn't go into a rest room by myself for nearly a year. An article also came out in the Terre Haute paper denying this incident, but that didn't mean anything to me.

274. Woman Who Buys Returned Dress is Embalmed Alive

I was down at Bea's, and she started to tell a story about this that happened in Chicago at Marshall Field's. I finished the story for her, only it happened here at Root's. A local woman shaved her armpits and went shopping. She bought a dress, and when she wore it the first time got terribly sick and died. When the family checked into it and an autopsy was performed they found a colored family bought the dress and used it on a dead relative. Embalming fluid had seeped out onto the dress. After they had her laid out for showing, they returned the dress to the store and got their money back. When this woman who had recently shaved wore the dress the embalming fluid in the dress penetrated her skin and killed her.

275. Teenager Who Buys Returned Dress is Embalmed Alive

This lady died, and she wasn't very old. A couple of her sisters went out to buy a dress to bury her in, and they couldn't decide between this yellow one or the purple one, so they took both of them with them to get approval from the rest of the family. They left both the dresses at the funeral home and later decided on the purple one, so they called the undertaker. I don't know if the undertaker didn't understand, but he had the yellow dress on her the next morning when the family came in. They told him about the mistake, and he exchanged the dresses, and they returned the yellow one to the store. A few days later a girl bought the yellow dress and wore it to a dance. During the dance she began sweating because the place was really full. After a few minutes she dropped dead. The stuff the undertaker had used had been so thick on the dress that it had killed her.

COLLEGE LEGENDS

276. The Cadaver Arm in Nursing School

There was a sorority initiation of a girl who would never get scared of anything. She was a nurse who was in training at one of the hospitals where they always had a lot of accidents. The girls initiating her decided to try and scare her by placing an amputated arm in her closet and hang it from the light switch. They left the house and decided not to return till late since they knew she got off work late. They stayed away until about midnight, and since they didn't hear anything, they crept back into the house to see what had happened. They came in and looked for the girl. To their shock they found her eating the arm, and her hair had turned white and was on end. She had just gone crazy.

277. The Cadaver Arm at Indiana University

There was this girl at I.U., see, who was a student at the med school. Anyway, nobody liked her. In fact, they all hated her because she was always trying to act like she was better than everyone else. One night some guys cut the hand off a cadaver and tied the hand onto the light cord in her room. When she came in later that night, she yanked hold of this bloody stump of a hand and screamed. The girls found her sitting on the shelf in her closet, eating the hand, and her hair had all turned white.

278. The Roommate's Death

There were once two girls who were supposed to be staying in a dormitory over Christmas vacation, and everyone else had already left, and the dorm director had left, and they were the only two girls who would be staying there. Well, the dorm director before she left told them, told the two girls, to make sure that they keep all the doors locked and don't answer the door for anyone during the evening because there was supposed to be a cat . . . well, what was known as a hatchet man . . . he was supposed to be out. So the girls promised, of course, you know, because they didn't want to get hurt either.

So it was late one night, and one girl was upstairs . . . it wasn't a very big dorm . . . they had kind of a library-study downstairs, and one girl was upstairs in her room, and the other one wanted to go down to study, and the one girl said, "Well, I really don't think you should, but, well, if you want to go down there, well, go ahead, but be very, very careful, and be sure the door is locked." So the girl went downstairs, and it got rather late. It was about 12:00 or 12:30, and the girl upstairs heard this very funny, heavy noise like someone walking, kind of dragging themselves up the steps. And, of course, she was a little bit shook. She didn't know what was going on, so she grabbed her desk and some other things and shoved them against the door, and this draggin', heavy draggin' feet just started walking, and she could hear it coming down the hall toward her room. Of course she was panic-stricken; she didn't know what to do, so she just kept pushing things against the door and standing by it and had it locked and everything so that nobody could get in.

Well, the dragging steps just came closer and closer and stopped by the door, and whoever it was started scratching at the door . . . started gnawing at it and kept scratching and wouldn't stop. Well, she was absolutely horror-stricken, and she went in the corner and just sat there and just kinda cringed up in the corner. The scratching continued for a long time, and then suddenly it just stopped. And, well, she didn't want to open the door or anything, so she just left it that way, and she stayed that way the whole night. She was kinda cuddled up in the corner by her bed . . . in the corner of the room.

Then the next morning when she woke up she didn't hear anything, so she figured it's daylight, and she couldn't figure out what happened to her roommate. She didn't know what had happened to her, and she figured, well, something must have happened because, you know, he had to get through the downstairs. So she thought she better go down and find out, so she took all the things away from the door.

When she opened the door, she saw her roommate with a hatchet in her head. She was the one that was scratching at the door, trying to get in so she could be saved. And if she would have made it in time, she probably could have saved her or done something.

279. Roommate Decapitated at Ball State

A girl in a dorm at Ball State came in from a date late one night and heard her roommate humming. She didn't want to turn the light on because her roommate had been in bed for a while. She figured her roommate was happy about the date she had, and that was why she was humming. She asked her if she had had a good time, but she didn't receive an answer. The humming grew louder.

This sort of made the girl mad because her roommate wouldn't answer her, so she asked her again if she had a good time. No answer again, but the humming grew louder. Finally the girl wondered what her roommate was humming about, so she decided to turn on the light. Sitting on her roommate's bed was the date her roommate had had that night swinging her roommate's head back and forth as he hummed a song.

280. Jeane Dixon Predicts Ax Murder at Indiana State

Well, by now just about everybody's heard the story of Hatchetman but I'll go ahead and tell my version. It went around about every university in the country, I think. It was during my sophomore year, 1968, and supposedly Jeane Dixon had made a prediction about it, and this was why it was believed so strongly. This man was supposed to come to a women's dorm that started with the letter C. And he was supposed to break into the dorm and kill all the girls with a hatchet. It was supposed to happen on a certain day, but I can't remember the date now. But it was in the newspapers and everything. And lots of girls went home that weekend because they were afraid to stay in the dorm. And supposedly one of the fire hatchets in our dorm was stolen. My dorm was Burford, but Mrs. Burford's first name was Charlotte, so there was the letter C. The Colfax girls were really scared too.

281. Ghost of Burford Hall Barfs

About two weeks before Christmas vacation a girl on second floor of Burford Hall [Indiana State University] went down to the bathroom early in the morning. As she was heading down she heard sounds as though someone were barfing. But when she got into the bathroom, although the sounds were still there, no one was in the room. From that night on, for two weeks straight, sounds began to be heard on each floor. They were in the halls and sometimes in the rooms. The girls could hear sounds like someone barfing, laughing, or moaning, but no one ever saw anyone.

The hall director checked out the elevator shafts and the vents for a tape recorder, but none was found. Then one night a girl was walking down the hall. Her name was Brenda, and no one had ever called her anything but that. As she walked down the hall a voice called, "Bren, Bren," but again no one was around. She had a gift from her hall Santa on the shelf by the door, and the next morning the "da" of her name had been scratched out, leaving only "Bren." When the kids left school for vacation, the noises still hadn't been explained.

282. Ghost of Burford Hall Moans

Just before Christmas vacation this year the girls in Burford Hall kept hearing funny noises like a ghost. They came real late at night or early in the morning. It made about three different sounds. One was a moaning sound, and another was of a woman laughing hysterically, and another was of a woman or child crying. The girls all got up and went out in the halls to look around. At first they thought it was somebody with a tape recorder or record playing a trick, but they looked everywhere. They searched the stairwells from top to bottom and didn't see a thing. The noise moved from floor to floor, so whoever was doing it had to move around, but nobody was ever seen on the stairs. Finally, it just went away as quick as it had come, and nothing else was heard about it.

283. Ghost of Burford Hall Screams

This is the story of the Burford Hall ghost at I.S.U. It took place my sophomore year, 1968. A lot of strange things started happening in Burford Hall—things like girls would go to bed at night and lock their doors and set their alarm clocks for the next morning, and they'd wake up the next morning and their doors were open and their alarms had been pushed in. Their alarms never went off. This was one of the first things that happened. Then the girls on fourth floor started hearing this scream every night and heavy breathing, so they got pretty scared.

This kept continuing with the doors and alarms, and it got so none of the girls would go to bed. Well, the rumor had gotten around down to my floor that the master key to the dorm had been stolen, so we were afraid that someone was breaking in every night and doing all of this. We really didn't know what was going on, but every night the whole dorm was up walking around searching for this ghost. Besides that, someone dumped a bucket of water down the stairwell and scared everyone. Strange noises started happening. The toilet would flush, and someone would scream. And this continued for about a week until finally things got back to normal. Nobody really to this day knows what was going on.

284. Why Indiana State Has No Sorority Houses

The sorority girls on this campus [Indiana State University] will never be allowed to live in sorority houses like they do at other schools. A long time ago some old guy had a granddaughter who couldn't get into a sorority. When the grandfather died, he left the school some land they needed,

with the provision that the school could have it as long as
they wanted if they didn't allow any sorority girls to have
sorority houses. So as soon as the first sorority house is built,
the land goes back to the family and the school's out of luck.
This can't ever be changed because the guy that made the
provision is dead and no one else can change it.

285. Why Purdue Had No Sororities

At Purdue University a man donated land. He had one
stipulation to this donation. He said that the university could
not have sororities or the land would have to be given back.
Everyone says this is because he was jilted at one time by a
sorority girl. Purdue now has sororities. The word sorority is
a more recent term than fraternity, and when the girls formed
their organizations at Purdue they called them fraternities.
That is why they don't have sororities.

286. Bird Man of I.U. Gives Signal for Panty Raid

When I was a freshman, there was this guy who lived in
a dorm who made a loud sound like a bird. At night, you
could hear this sound all over campus, and this call became
the signal for a panty raid. He usually would make the sound
through a loudspeaker or something like that because it was
really loud. Then all the guys would meet together, and the
girls would get prepared.

287. Bird Man of I.U. Recorded Call for Panty Raid

Do I remember the bird man? I used to go with him! He lived in Briscoe Quad, and about once a week he would give the call for a panty raid. I don't know exactly how he got the call to carry so far. I think he recorded it on tape, then used a microphone or something like that. He was finally caught and expelled from school, but I think he is back now.

288. Bird Man of I.U. Yells from Dorm Roof

I don't know if the story is true about the Bird Man at I.U., but I have heard several other students talking about it. He supposedly stood on the roof of his dorm and yelled out some stupid bird call as a signal for a panty raid. I heard he was expelled from school for doing this, but I don't know where he is supposed to be now. He's probably in Washington!

HAIRDOS, COSMETICS, PILLS, AND DRUGS

289. Spiders in the Beehive Hairdo

When I was in high school, thé big thing was for girls to tease their hair. Now this looked nice on a lot of kids, but some girls carried it to extremes. They had these huge, bouffant hairdos, and they sprayed really stiff with as much hair spray as they could get on. We used to wonder if some of these girls ever bothered to wash their hair so they could get all that sticky stuff out. One day we heard about this girl who went to a high school in Evansville who had just died because of teased hair. I think some of the teachers were trying to scare us into not teasing our hair anymore. Anyway, this Evansville girl had had one of these bushy teased hairstyles, and she'd kept lots of spray on it. They said she hadn't washed her hair for three months. One day while she was sitting in class, she just keeled over, and when the teacher went to check on her, she saw blood trickling down her face. When they got her to the hospital, they found that a nest of black widow spiders had made a home in her hair and had finally eaten into her scalp.

290. Cockroaches in the Beehive Hairdo

I first heard this when I was about a freshman in high school and a lot of girls were teasing their hair and wearing these beehive hairdos. Well, we heard about this one girl who went to a high school out in the country who had teased and sprayed her hair a whole bunch. She apparently hadn't washed her hair for a long time because her health teacher and school nurse were always after her about washing it. Anyway, one day she was walking down the hall, between classes or something, and she passed out, right there on the floor. When they got her to the hospital, the doctor checked her head and found it was starting to bleed and was starting to run down the sides of her face. When he poked into her hair he found cockroaches had made a nest in her hair and had started to eat down into her head. They say some of the brain was exposed. I thought it was a pretty ridiculous story myself, but a lot of the kids believed it and stopped teasing their hair.

291. Ants in the Beehive Hairdo

When I was a freshman in high school, I heard the story about a girl and her beehive hairdo. She never washed her hair but just sprayed it with hair spray every morning. One day she dropped dead right in the classroom. The reason was a colony of ants had been living in her beehive hairdo and had eaten through her skull.

292. Maggots in the Beehive Hairdo

A girl had her hair done in a beehive style and didn't lift it up for months. Later, there were maggots and bugs in it.

293. Face Cream

When I was in high school I worked as a carhop at a drive-in restaurant one summer. This woman used to bring her parents in all the time in a little Volkswagen. The older lady's face was eaten away, like she had leprosy or some disease. When I finally asked my boss about this, she said that the lady had bought some face cream many years ago from a traveling salesman. Gradually it had eaten away her skin and left it marked for life.

294. Diet Pills

A few years ago there was a company who put out sure-fire diet pills, guaranteed to lose weight in no time. People began to take these pills, and in no time the people were losing weight. After a few weeks these people began to lose too much weight. So the government investigated. They opened the pills and found the head of a tapeworm. Tapeworms are hard to get rid of. They had the person starve himself for days. Then they set a bowl of hot milk in front of the person. He had to keep his mouth open. After a while the tapeworm began to come up his throat 'cause he smelled the milk. They kept moving the bowl further away until the tapeworm was completely out.

295. The Headless Head

In Brazil, around 1947, it was said that there was a man down in his basement. He was one of the first persons to try LSD, and he had the weird notion that he had to make a coal fire in a gas furnace. So he started to make the coal fire. He couldn't see very well in the basement, anyway, because it was so dark. The flame all of a sudden burst out at his face, and the door of the furnace swung shut and held his head in there. His head was cut off, of course, and people say that he holds a lantern in the house at night and makes weird noises while looking for his head.

OCCUPATIONS

296. The Truck Driver and the Motorcycles

Say, I heard a good one this morning in at Setty's. I was talking to a fella, and he was telling me about a friend of his that was sitting in the Blue Bonnet up at Brazil the other day, and a truck driver came in and sat down at the counter. He ordered a cup of coffee and a piece of pie and was just sitting there and drinking his coffee and eating his pie and mindin' his own business when a couple of fellas in leather jackets came in. These two fellas walked over and stood behind this truck driver and kind of looked at him and then looked at each other; then they both set down, one on either side of him. Well, one of these guys picked up a saltshaker and was foolin' around with it a little bit; then he just unscrewed the top off it and dumped the whole bottle of salt in that truck driver's coffee. The truck driver just stood up and backed up from the counter and kind of eyed these guys for a minute; then he went up to the cashier and paid his bill and walked out.

These two guys in the leather jackets just laughted and got themselves a cup of coffee. They set there a while and drank their coffee, and then they got up and walked out, too. Well, it wasn't no time till they came runnin' back in. They was yellin', "Who was that truck driver? What kind of truck was he driving?" Of course, nobody knew who he was. This fella said he went outside to see what had happened to get these two guys all riled up, and when he got outside, there lay two brand-new Harley Davis [Harley-Davidson] motorcycles smashed into the asphalt drive. That truck driver had run right over them and smashed them flat.

297. The Avon Lady

Mabel was telling me just the other day about something that happened to a friend of her niece. She was all alone in her house because her husband was at work. Ordinarily, she wouldn't have even answered the door because she is the timid type who's afraid of everything, but her Avon lady called her up the day before and said she would be over the next day if it would be all right. And so, since she was expecting her, when the Avon lady rang the doorbell, she went right to the door and let her in. And so, they were just sitting there talking, and she was trying to decide what she wanted, when the Avon lady asked if she could use the bathroom. Well, the lady sat there and sat there, and the Avon lady never did come out. Her husband had always told her not to try to do anything by herself, so she went over to the neighbors after she had waited for about an hour for her to come out. The neighbors come over to the house with her to see if anything had happened to her. They knocked on the door, and when there wasn't an answer, they opened the door and there was a man standing there naked with a knife in his hand.

298. Steelworker Falls into Furnace

In one of the Gary steel mills a man fell into one of the red-hot furances. Later the impression of his body was discovered in sheets of metal.

UFO'S

299. Flying Saucer Causes Machinery to Stop

Danny was working on the road over by Brazil one evening when this flying saucer went over. All the lights on the machinery went out, and all the equipment stopped. And after the saucer flew over they tried to turn the machinery back on, but it wouldn't start. But the mechanics couldn't find anything wrong with it.

300. Flying Saucer Spits Fire and Burns Person

It was about ten years ago, and it happened late at night. I was walking down Highway 63 near Graysville. The weather was very cold, and I was all bundled up. All of a sudden, I heard a roar and an enormous ball of fire swooped by me. I was found by the roadside early the next morning, and they took me to the Sullivan hospital where I was treated for serious burns over my entire body. The doctors said the burns would have been fatal if I hadn't been wrapped up in so many clothes. I can't tell you how scared I was. I was attacked by a flying saucer that spit fire!

301. UFO Appears as Bright Light

Me and Dad seen it, and Dad don't scare easy. It was at Sugar Creek at Camp Atterbury. Sugar Creek's wide . . . can't throw a rock across it. Well, we made camp, and it rained half

the night. About 3:00 A.M., we decided to check fishing lines
... no lights and no fire because of the game warden. So we
rowed right down the middle of the creek. All of a sudden, it
came like daylight. Light stayed great big ... enormous ...
no noise. This thing hovered and went back and forth. It
made no noise. Dad's been in Okinawa and war and things,
and he turned white. This happened about 1964–65 when
those UFO's were being reported.

302. UFO Appears as Spinning Light

My two cousins were driving home one night, and they
were coming from a ball game in the country, and all of a
sudden there was a bright spinning light showed up behind
them. So they went on for two or three miles and finally got
scared and turned around. When they did, the bright light
went up, and as they went down the road the light came up
behind them and followed them some more. And after a
while the light went up in the air.

303. UFO Appears as Silver Sphere

This story happened near Frankfort, Indiana. One of my
good friends was driving her children to school for a summer
reading program. When they left home, the children noticed
a silver sphere, which seemed to be high in the sky, but it
was following the car. The lady had seen it, but she didn't
say anything for fear of scaring the children until she found
out if it was really following the car. The children did say
something about it. So then they kept their eyes on it. It fol-

lowed them to school. The people at the school saw it, too.
She let the children out and started home after making sure
the children were safe. The people at the school watched it
follow her home. The people in her town saw this and
noticed that the sphere seemed to stay over her house.

She went back after the children, and it followed her again.
But it was not close enough so that they could tell what it
was. It seemed to be really high in the sky. She watched it
follow her, and again the people in the school saw it follow
her. She drove back home, and again they kept their eyes on
it. This sphere made no attempt to approach her or harm
them in any way. It stayed hovering over her house for a few
hours. Then the townspeople watched it float away, and they
have never found out what the sphere was or have never
seen it again.

304. UFO Appears as Blue Saucer

When we lived out on the corner in Cass I saw a real
flying saucer just as plain as anything, but at that time I didn't
say much 'cause people were kind of upset about them. It
was late at night, and I had to get up and take your older
brother to the bathroom. He was only about three at the time.
As I was taking him back to bed I happened to look out the
window up at the sky just to see what kind of night it was. I
saw this big flying saucer making its way at about treetop
level across the stripper hills of Number 10 Mine, and then it
dropped out of sight. It went behind the trees and over the
stripper cuts which blocked my view. I suppose it was in
sight just about a minute or so, but I got a good look at it. It
was shaped like a saucer with a dome in the center and a
kind of halo around it. The most memorable thing about it

was that it was the most brilliant blue I ever saw. It had blue florescent lights, and sparks were just shooting out from it. It would go along at a certain level and then drop suddenly and raise again. I wasn't the only one that seen this saucer. Ralph Edwards said later he had six or seven calls that come in from Linton that night reporting a mysterious object in the sky.

305. UFO Burns Spots on Field

Several years ago, when I was in high school, I heard this story about UFO's. There was a farmer near Loogootee who had just cut his hay during the day and left it in the field to dry. The next morning when he went back to the field, there were three large circles burned into the field. There were also impressions where some kind of legs had set down. There were four of these for each circle. No one could figure out how these perfect circles got there. The owner of the field says three UFO's from outer space set down there and burned the spots.

SOURCES AND NOTES

The following short-title listings and abbreviations are used throughout the notes:

Baughman: Ernest W. Baughman, *Type and Motif-Index of the Folktales of England and North America*, Indiana University Folklore Series, No. 20 (The Hague, 1966).

Brown: *The Frank C. Brown Collection of North Carolina Folklore*, VI–VII, ed. Wayland D. Hand (Durham, 1961–1964).

Hyatt: Harry Middleton Hyatt. *Folklore from Adams County, Illinois* (Hannibal, Mo., 1965).

ISUFA: Indiana State University Folklore Archives, Department of English, Indiana State University, Terre Haute, Indiana.

IUFA. Indiana University Folklore Archives, Folklore Institute, Indiana University, Bloomington, Indiana.

Motif: Stith Thompson, *Motif-Index of Folk-Literature*, 6 vols. (Bloomington, Indiana, 1966).

Randolph: Vance Randolph, *Ozark Superstitions* (New York, 1964).

Type: Antti Aarne and Stith Thompson, *The Types of the Folktale* (Helsinki, 1964).

WPA: Works Progress Administration. Indiana Files of the Federal Writers' Project, Cunningham Memorial Library, Indiana State University, Terre Haute, Indiana.

1. ISUFA. Collected in Covington, November 1972, from a 19-year-old female student. Brown 97: "Prenatal fears cause birthmarks in children."

2. WPA. This memorate (personal belief tale) is from Huntington County. A ball of fire as a portent of death is common in American folklore. Randolph writes, "Some old folks claim to have seen a ball of fire travel across a field and down the chimney of a house where someone lay sick; this is a sure death sign . . ." (pp. 303–306). Cf. Baughman E350.1.6(c), "Lights seen on or near property of person about to die"; Motif D1812.5.0.3, "Behavior of fire as omen."

233

3. ISUFA. Collected in Mooresville, December 1968, from a 55-year-old housewife. See note 2.

4. WPA. This text from Randolph County involves a bird as a death sign. One of Hyatt's informants offered a similar account: "When my grandmother died, a big white bird flew through the house one night, and she died the next morning" (9723). Generally any kind of bird in the house is a sign of death (Brown 5280). Motif D1812.5.0.2, "Omens from flight of birds."

5. ISUFA. Collected in Worthington, May 1971, from a 34-year-old housewife. Brown 5019: "To dream of seeing a coffin is a sign of death."

6. ISUFA. Collected in May 1972 from a 20-year-old female student from St. Anthony. Brown 5604: "A falling portrait foretells that the original [i.e., the subject of the portrait] is near death."

7. ISUFA. Collected in Whiting, January 1969, from a 48-year-old housewife. Cf. Brown 5082: "The breaking of a dish in one's hand is a sign of death."

8. ISUFA. Collected in Shelburn, May 1968, from a 20-year-old female student. This tale incorporates the familiar motif that rapping is a death warning (Baughman D1827.1.3.1*). As Randolph points out, "If you hear raps, knocks, ticks, or bells, with no apparent cause for these noises, it is a sign that death is coming to someone near you" (p. 302). Also see Hyatt 9959–9972 for other accounts of rapping on doors and windows as death signs.

9. ISUFA. Collected in Mooresville, December 1968, from a 55-year-old housewife. See note 8.

10. ISUFA. Collected in Indianapolis, May 1967, from a 70-year-old housewife. Seeing a wraith of a person is a sign that he or she will die. Brown 5139: "If you see anybody coming toward you in a room, very distinctly, and the person is not there, he will surely die soon." Motif E723.2, "Seeing one's wraith is a sign that person is to die shortly."

11. ISUFA. Collected in Terre Haute, August 1968, from a 29-year-old female office clerk. Motif V233, "Angel of death."

12. ISUFA. Collected in Terre Haute, May 1971, from a 40-year-old department store saleswoman. Brown 5404: "The clock stops when a person dies." Brown 5052: "It is a sign of death for a clock to stop." Brown 5408: "Sheets and white spreads are put over . . . the clock . . . in the presence of a dead body." Brown 4915: "If you hear singing or music in the night, it is a token of someone's death."

13. ISUFA. Collected in December 1970 from a 20-year-old male student from Jasper. Motif E766.1, "Clock stops at moment of owner's death."

14. ISUFA. Collected in Mooresville, December 1968, from a 52-year-old male sheet metal worker. For variations of beliefs about feather crowns, also called heavenly crowns and angel wreaths, see Randolph, pp. 320 ff.

15. ISUFA. Collected in Jasper, March 1968, from a 67-year-old salesman. See note 14.

16. WPA. This tale was collected from a pioneer resident of Starke County in Knox in 1936. The major motif, Baughman D1810.8.2.3, "Murder made known in a dream," has been reported from Ontario, Illinois, Kentucky, and the Ozarks. Another motif in the tale is K2116, "Innocent person accused of murder."

17. ISUFA. Collected in Indianapolis, October 1968, from a 50-year-old female teacher. This legend involves the widespread theme of the live burial (Motif S123). Frequently in such tales the person accidentally buried alive is awakened when a robber opens the coffin to steal a ring or jewels (See text 18). In other developments of the story, when the body is exhumed for some reason at a later date, it is found turned over with its hair torn out or rubbed off. Before embalming, of course, it was quite possible that occasionally someone might have been buried alive. This possibility, at least, gave rise to a number of legends about people in cataleptic trances who were victims of live burials.

18. ISUFA. Collected in December 1968 from an 18-year-old female student from Newburgh. Type 990, "The Seemingly Dead Revives." Motif K426, "Apparently dead woman revives when thief tries to steal from her."

19. ISUFA. Collected in Linton, May 1971, from a 53-year-old male owner of a body shop. Brown 807: "An amputated limb, if buried crooked (in a cramped position), will cause the patient pain until it is taken up and straightened."

20. ISUFA. Collected in Terre Haute, August 1968, from a male informant in his fifties. Motif J1769.2, "Dead man is thought to be alive." Though not actually supernatural, this tale presupposes belief in ghosts. For versions of this popular story, see Richard M. Dorson, *American Negro Folktales* (New York, 1967), pp. 329–330, and William Lynwood Montell, *Ghosts along the Cumberland* (Knoxville, 1979), pp. 202–204.

21. ISUFA. Collected in Bedford, August 1968, from a 40-year-old housewife. See note 20.

22. ISUFA. Collected in Linton, December 1969, from a 16-year-old male student. Cf. Motifs E700, "Soul," and E751.1, "Soul weighed at Judgment Day."

23. ISUFA. Collected in Shelburn, May 1968, from a 21-year-old

female secretary. Motif N384, "Death from fright," and
F1041.7, "Hair turns gray from terror."

24. ISUFA. Collected in Bedford, July 1969, from a 20-year-old
female student. Motif E422.1.11.5.1, "Ineradicable bloodstain
after bloody tragedy."

25. ISUFA. Collected in May 1968 from a 20-year-old male student from Kokomo. See note 24.

26. ISUFA. Collected in Hammond, December 1969, from a 20-
year-old housewife. Motif F974.1, "Grass will not grow where
blood of murdered person has been shed."

27. ISUFA. Collected in Terre Haute, May 1969, from a 21-year-
old male student. See Ronald L. Baker, "Legends about Spook
Light Hill," *Indiana Folklore*, III: 2 (1970), 163–189, for an
analysis of the Spook Light Hill legend complex. The main
motif is E530.1, "Ghost-like lights." Cf. Motif E421.3, "Luminous ghosts."

28. ISUFA. Collected in Terre Haute, December 1972, from a 20-
year-old male student. See note 27.

29. ISUFA. Collected in Terre Haute, March 1972, from a 23-
year-old female secretary. See note 27.

30. ISUFA. Collected in Terre Haute, January 1972, from a 21-
year-old female student. See note 27.

31. ISUFA. Collected in Perth, November 1970, from a 33-year-old
male factory worker. See note 27.

32. ISUFA. Collected in Terre Haute, April 1968, from a 21-year-
old female student. Motif 491, "Will-o'-the-Wisp (Jack-o'-
Lantern)."

33. ISUFA. Collected in Lewis, October 1971, from a 61-year-old
male farmer. Motif F491.1, "Will-o'-the-Wisp leads people
astray." See note 32.

34. ISUFA. Collected in Clinton, February 1973, from a 20-year-
old male student. See Gary Hall, "The Big Tunnel: Legends
and Legend-Telling," *Indiana Folklore*, VI: 2 (1973), 139–173:
Motifs E421.3., "Luminous ghosts," and E422.1.1, "Headless
revenant."

35. ISUFA. Collected in Shelbyville, April 1971, from a 22-year-
old female clerk and student. See Larry Danielson, "The Revenant Plays the Organ," *Indiana Folklore*, I: 1 (1968), 52–54.
Motif E554.1, "Ghost plays organ."

36. WPA. Familiar motifs are found in this ghost story from Henry
County. Baughman E425.1.1, "Revenant as lady in white";
E402.1.1.6, "Ghost sobs"; Baughman E332.2(h), "Ghost seen
in road at night"; and Baughman E421.1.1.2(b), "Horse sees
ghost and is unable to proceed on way." This legend also illus-

trates that frequently informal place names are derived from local legends, as the scene of the haunting was once called "Ghost Hollow."

37. ISUFA. Collected in Dugger, January 1972, from a 59-year-old housewife. Motif E402.1.4, "Invisible ghost jingles chain."
38. ISUFA. Collected in Princeton, March 1969, from a 22-year-old female practical nurse. Motifs E419.7, "Person with missing bodily member cannot rest in grave," and E402.1.1.2, "Ghost moans." Cf. Motif E422.1.2., "Armless revenant."
39. ISUFA. Collected in East Chicago, November 1969, from an 18-year-old female student. See Philip Brandt George, "The Ghost of Cline Avenue: 'La Llorna' in the Calumet Region," *Indiana Folklore*, V: 1 (1972), 56–91. This legend complex is a localization of a familiar legend type, "The Vanishing Hitchhiker," Motif E332.3.3.1. See note 242.
40. ISUFA. Collected in Hammond, May 1969, from a 21-year-old male student. See note 39.
41. ISUFA. Collected in East Chicago. January 1969, from a 21-year-old male student. See note 39.
42. ISUFA. Collected in Hammond, December 1968, from a 20-year-old salesman. See note 39. This text is interesting, for it is a blend of texts 39, 40, and 41.
43. ISUFA. Collected in Terre Haute, December 1970, from a 22-year-old female student. See Ronald L. Baker, "The Face in the Wall," *Indiana Folklore*, II: 2 (1969), 29–46. The main motifs in this legend complex are: E422.1.11.2, "Revenant as face or head"; E411.10, "Persons who die violent or accidental deaths cannot rest in grave"; E334.2.2, "Ghost of person killed in accident seen at death or burial spot."
44. ISUFA. Collected in Terre Haute, March 1972, from a 22-year-old female clerk. See note 43.
45. ISUFA. Collected in Terre Haute, March 1970, from a 21-year-old female teacher. See note 43.
46. ISUFA. Collected in Terre Haute, August 1969, from a 21-year-old male student. See note 43.
47. ISUFA. Collected in Indianapolis, September 1970, from a 20-year-old female student. See Linda Dégh, "The Haunted Bridges Near Avon and Danville and Their Role in Legend Formation," *Indiana Folklore*, II: 1 (1969), 54–89. There are a number of ghost motifs in this legend complex. The main ones are Motifs E332.1(a), "Ghost appears at bridge," and E334.2.2, "Ghost of person killed in accident seen at death or burial spot," E402.1.1.3, "Ghost cries and screams." Text 53 is a variant of this legend. See note 53.

48. ISUFA. Collected in November 1970 from a 21-year-old male student from Indianapolis. See note 47.

49. ISUFA. Collected in Indianapolis, July 1969, from a 20-year-old male student. See note 47.

50. ISUFA. Collected in May 1972 from a 21-year-old male student from Indianapolis. See note 47.

51. ISUFA. Collected in Indianapolis, April 1968, from a 19-year-old female student. See note 47.

52. ISUFA. Collected in May 1971 from a 20-year-old female student from Indianapolis, See note 47.

53. ISUFA. Collected in November 1969 from a 19-year-old female student from Washington. See Linda Dégh, "The Negro in Concrete," *Indiana Folklore*, I: 1 (1968), 61–67. Dégh discusses the social injustice theme in this tale and relates it to the ancient ritual of foundation sacrifices. See Motif S261, "Foundation sacrifice." In this motif, a human is buried alive in the foundation of a bridge or building. Text 47 is a variant of this tale. See note 47.

54. ISUFA. Collected in June 1971 from a 19-year-old female student from Columbus. While several ghost motifs appear in versions of this tale, the most persistent is Motif E402.1.1.6, "Ghost sobs."

55. ISUFA. Collected in North Vernon, August 1969, from a 20-year-old male part-time factory worker and student. See note 54.

56. ISUFA. Collected in Sullivan, December 1968, from a 27-year-old male student. The main motifs are E272, "Road-ghosts," and E422.1.1, "Headless revenant."

57. ISUFA. Collected in Sullivan, May 1968, from a 21-year-old male student. Motif E402.1.1.1, "Ghost calls." See note 56.

58. ISUFA. Collected in Sullivan, April 1972, from a 20-year-old female student. Motif E599.7, "Ghost carries lantern."

59. ISUFA. Collected in Sullivan, May 1970, from a 33-year-old male bank cashier. Motif E422.1.11.2, "Revenant as face or head." See note 56.

60. ISUFA. Collected in Lyons, December 1970, from a 17-year-old female student. Motif E422.1.11.1, "Revenant as an eye."

61. ISUFA. Collected in December 1968 from a 21-year-old female student from Martinsville. See William Clements and William E. Lightfoot, "The Legend of Stepp Cemetery," *Indiana Folklore*, V: 1 (1972), 92–141. As Clements and Lightfoot note, there is considerable variation in this legend. The black lady appears in most versions of the tale, although she may be a ghost, witch, disfigured human being, or simply a woman in black. Baughman E574(bc), "Woman in black."

62. ISUFA. Collected in December 1970 from a 19-year-old female student from Martinsville. See note 61.

63. ISUFA. Collected in Leavenworth, March 1970, from a 20-year-old female student. See F.A. de Caro and Richard Lunt, "The Face on the Tombstone," *Indiana Folklore*, I: 1 (1968), 34–41, and William Clements, "The Chain," *Indiana Folklore*, II: 1 (1969), 90–96. Motif N270, "Crime inevitably comes to light." Cf. Motif D1316.1, "Stone reveals truth."

64. ISUFA. Collected in Paoli, June 1971, from a 40-year-old housewife. See note 63.

65. ISUFA. Collected in Terre Haute, March 1972, from a 16-year-old male student. See Ronald L. Baker, "Stiffy Green," *Indiana Folklore*, III: 1 (1970), 113–127. Motifs E421.3.6, "Ghosts as dogs with glowing tongues and eyes"; E521.2, "Ghost of dog"; D1380.16.1, "Magic statute of dog protects." Cf. Motifs A673, "Hound of hell," and B15.7.1, "Cerberus." In some versions of the tale Motif B301.1.3, "Faithful animal doesn't allow anybody to come near master's corpse," is suggested.

66. ISUFA. Collected in West Terre Haute, July 1971, from a 23-year-old female secretary. See note 65.

67. WPA. Orville L. Funk, in *A Sketchbook of Indiana History* (Rochester, Indiana: Christian Book Press, 1969), p. 85, says, "It is said, even now, that on a windy, stormy night, if you are traveling on the river and you reach the vicinity of Locust Point, you can hear old McHarry shouting across curses at all who pass on the river below." Motif E334.2, "Ghost haunts burial spot." Cf. Motif E545.0.1, "Words uttered from the tomb."

68. ISUFA. Collected in Terre Haute, December 1969, from an 18-year-old female student. Motif E402, "Mysterious ghostlike noises heard."

69. ISUFA. Collected in January 1969 from a 20-year-old male student from Indianapolis. See note 68.

70. ISUFA. Collected in May 1971 from a 21-year-old female student from Princeton. Type 1676B, "Clothing Caught in Graveyard." Motif N384.2, "Death in the graveyard; person's clothing is caught."

71. ISUFA. Collected in East Chicago, April 1969, from a 48-year-old housewife. See note 70.

72. WPA. Road ghosts, often encountered in American legends, sometimes are ghosts of animals. This text from Hamilton County illustrates a common tendency to rationalize supernatural elements in American folk narratives. The main motifs in the tale are E272, "Road-ghosts," Baughman E402.2.3,

"Hoofbeats of ghost horse," and E521.1, "Ghost of horse." For motifs of sounds mistaken for ghosts, see Baughman J1782.3 ff. A version of this tale in the ISU Folklore Archives was collected in Noblesville in December 1967 from a 66-year-old female retired teacher.

73. ISUFA. Collected in Lebanon, December 1968, from a 23-year-old vending salesman. Several ghost motifs appear in versions of this legend, including E272, "Road-ghosts," E421.3, "Luminous ghosts," and E422.1.1, "Headless revenant."

74. WPA. Motifs in this text from Harrison County are E413, "Murdered person cannot rest in grave," and E422.1.1, "Headless revenant."

75. ISUFA. Collected in Lewis, November 1971, from a 61-year-old male farmer. Motif E415, "Dead cannot rest until certain work is finished." Cf. Motif E336, "Non-malevolent mine ghosts."

76. ISUFA. Collected at St. Mary-of-the-Woods, December 1968, from a 19-year-old female student. See Michael L. Crawford, "Legends from St. Mary-of-the-Woods College," *Indiana Folklore*, VII: 1/2 (1974), 53–75. Motifs E415, "Dead cannot rest until certain work is finished," Baughman E422.4.4(ea), "Female revenant in garb of nun," and Baughman E338.7*, "Ghosts haunt educational institution."

77. ISUFA. Collected in Worthington, May 1971, from a 53-year-old male owner of a body shop. Motif E443.8, "Ghost laid by Bible."

78. ISUFA. Collected in April 1969 from a 20-year-old male student from Greenfield. See Magnus Einarsson-Mullarky, "The House of Blue Lights," *Indiana Folklore*, I: 1 (1968), 82–91, and Linda Dégh, "The House of Blue Lights Revisited," *Indiana Folklore*, II: 2 (1969), 11–28. Dégh discusses the factual background of the legend. Persistent motifs in the versions of this tale are the dead wife in a glass coffin and the blue lights surrounding the casket or the house. Motifs F852.1, "Glass coffin," T211.4.1, "Wife's corpse kept after death," and E530.1, "Ghost-like lights."

79. ISUFA. Collected in Hobart, April 1970, from a 20-year-old female student. Motifs T211.4.1, "Wife's corpse kept after death," and F852.1, "Glass coffin."

80. WPA. This text from Jackson County contains several ghost motifs: E402.1.1.2, "Ghost moans," E235.2, "Ghost returns to demand proper burial," and E422.4.3, "Ghost in white." Cf. Motif T211.4, "Spouse's corpse kept after death."

81. ISUFA. Collected in Terre Haute, January 1969, from a 21-year-old female student. This tale is discussed in the introduction. Although a ghost does not appear in all versions, often the house is said to be haunted, and the ghost moans. Motifs E281, "Ghosts haunt house," and E402.1.1.2, "Ghost moans."

82. ISUFA. Collected in Terre Haute, March 1972, from a 16-year-old male student. See note 81.

83. ISUFA. Collected in Sullivan, January 1971, from a 64-year-old housewife. Motifs E281, "Ghosts haunt house," and E402.1.1.3, "Ghost cries and screams."

84. ISUFA. Collected in Lyons, November 1970, from a 19-year-old male student. Motifs E281, "Ghosts haunt house," E402.1.1.3, "Ghost cries and screams," and E337.1.2, "Sounds of accident re-enact tragedy." Cf. Baughman E337.1.2(b), "Cries of children burning in house after parents left them alone."

85. ISUFA. Collected in East Chicago, November 1967, from a 22-year-old male student. Motifs E281, "Ghosts haunt house," E402.1.1.2, "Ghost moans," and E402.1.1.3, "Ghost cries and screams."

86. WPA. This story from Howard County incorporates several common motifs of haunted houses: Baughman E402.1.4, "Invisible ghost jingles chains"; H1411, "Fear test: staying in haunted house"; Baughman E530.1.0.1(c), "Building seen to light up strangely at night when unoccupied." Cf. Motifs E1887.2, "Deceptive nocturnal noise. Wood-spirits imitate falling of trees"; Baughman E402.4, "Sound of ethereal music"; and Baughman E402.1.3, "Invisible ghost plays musical instrument." The first part of this tale is a memorate, as it is a first person narrative of an encounter with the supernatural.

87. ISUFA. Collected in Rockville, November 1968, from a 21-year-old male student. Baughman E281.0.3*, "Ghost haunts house, damaging property or annoying inhabitants."

88. ISUFA. Collected in Clinton, July 1969, from a 23-year-old male teacher. Motif D492, "Color of object [magically] changed."

89. ISUFA. Collected in Terre Haute, November 1968, from a 21-year-old male construction worker. Motifs E281, "Ghosts haunt house"; P361, "Faithful servant"; E234.3, "Return from dead to avenge death (murder)." Cf. Motif R10.3, "Children abducted."

90. WPA. Sometimes in Western folklore Satan appears as a handsome young abductor (Motifs D303.3.1, "The devil in human form," and G303.9.5, "The devil as an abductor"). This tale

from Miami County includes those motifs, but the main motifs are Baughman G303.10.4.4, "Devil appears to girl who wants an escort for a dance," and Baughman C12.5.3(a), "Girl says she will go to dance even if she has to go with devil. The devil escorts her." Baughman, however, reports these motifs only from Quebec. Another motif in the legend is F92, "Pit entrance to lower world," a common legendary access to hell.

91. ISUFA. Collected in Jasper, May 1970, from a 26-year-old male student. Motif G303.16.7, "Devil is chased by holy water."

92. ISUFA. Collected in Lawrenceburg, December 1968, from a 59-year-old male laborer. Motif G303.16, "How the Devil's power may be escaped or avoided."

93. ISUFA. Collected in Shelburn, May 1968, from a 21-year-old female student. Motifs E320, "Dead relative's friendly return," and E363.4, "Dead reassures the living."

94. ISUFA. Collected in January 1972 from a 19-year-old female student from LaPorte. Motifs D1766.1, "Magic results produced by prayer"; V52, "Miraculous power of prayer"; D2161, "Magic healing power"; and F950, "Marvelous cures." Cf. Motif E63, "Resuscitation by prayer."

95. ISUFA. Collected in Terre Haute, April 1973, from a 21-year-old female student. For a version of this text, see Kenneth A. Thigpen, Jr., "Adolescent Legends in Brown County: A Survey," *Indiana Folklore*, IV: 2 (1971), 187.

96. ISUFA. Collected in August 1969 from a 20-year-old student from Gas City. Motif A2721.2, "Tree cursed for serving as cross."

97. ISUFA. Collected in Terre Haute, April 1970, from an Eastern Orthodox priest, age withheld. Motifs D2071, "Evil Eye," D2064.4, "Magic sickness because of Evil Eye." Cf. Motif D2176.3, "Evil spirit exorcised."

98. ISUFA. Collected in Worthington, May 1971, from a 34-year-old housewife. See Richard M. Dorson, *Bloodstoppers and Bearwalkers* (Cambridge, Mass., 1952), pp. 150–165. Cf. Brown 879–883.

99. ISUFA. Collected in Worthington, May 1971, from a 34-year-old housewife. Brown 993: "To cure a burn many old people look at the burn, repeat some mysterious words to themselves, and blow the burn."

100. ISUFA. Collected in Cayuga, May 1972, from a 65-year-old male retired laborer. See note 99.

101. ISUFA. Collected in Clay City, December 1972, from a 76-year-old retired businessman. See note 99.

102. ISUFA. Collected in Bargersville, October 1968, from an 83-year-old female retired teacher. Brown 413: "A person who has never seen his father can cure a child of thrash by blowing his breath in its mouth."

103. ISUFA. Collected in Linton, May 1971, from a 53-year-old male owner of a body shop. Cf. Brown 2695 and 2696, both of which involve rubbing warts to remove them.

104. ISUFA. Collected in May 1972 from a 20-year-old female student from Evansville. Cf. Brown 2439: "Steal string, tie as many knots in it as there are warts to remove, then bury the string."

105. ISUFA. Collected in Feburary 1970 from a 23-year-old hospital technician from Linton. Brown 2594: "If you steal a dishrag and bury it, it will cure your warts." Cf. Brown 2602, 2609.

106. ISUFA. Collected in December 1971 from a 19-year-old housewife from Anderson. Brown 2687: "Never think of warts or look at yours, and they will disappear."

107. ISUFA. Collected in January 1972 from a 20-year-old female student from Bainbridge. The same belief that the seventh son of a seventh son can blow off warts is reported in Wheaton Phillips Webb, "The Wart," *New York Folklore Quarterly*, II (1946), 98–106. Cf. Brown 2421, Hyatt 4021, and Motif D2161.5.7.

108. ISUFA. Collected in Terre Haute, July 1969, from a 20-year-old student and postal worker. Motif D1825.1, "Second Sight"; Brown 5588: "A seventh daughter, born on Christmas Day, possesses mysterious (witch-like) powers." For more information on the magical powers of the seventh or tenth daughter, see Erich Seemann, "'Die zehnte Tochter': Eine Studie zu einer Gottscheer Ballade," *Humaniora: Essays in Literature, Folklore, Bibliography*, ed. Wayland D. Hand and Gustave O. Arlt (Locust Valley, N. Y., 1960), pp. 102–114.

109. ISUFA. Collected in Cayuga, May 1972, from a 75-year-old male retired carpenter. Motif D1825.1, "Second Sight"; Brown 245: "A child born with a veil over its face will see in later life many supernatural things, such as ghosts, spirits, and apparitions hidden from the eyes of ordinary man."

110. WPA. This account with accompanying fire-letter is from Dekalb County. The letter belonged to Shannon W. Schultz of Butler and was printed by A.C. Gruhlke of Waterloo. The main motif is D2158.2, "Magic extinguishing of fires." Related motifs are D1266.1, "Magic writings": D1766.1, "Magic results produced by prayer"; D1382.7.1, "Magic hymn protects from fire"; and D1566.2.4, "Runes quench fire." Frequently in fire

charms the name of the trinity is invoked, and one folk belief is that walking around a fire will stop it (see Brown 994 and 5844).

111. ISUFA. Collected in Roachdale, August 1969, from a 20-year-old female student. See Hilda E. Webb, "Water Witching as Part of Folklife in Southern Indiana," *Journal of the Folklore Institute*, III (June 1966), 10–29. Brown 5869–5882.

112. ISUFA. Collected in Terre Haute, May 1969, from a 73-year-old retired railroadman. See note 111.

113. ISUFA. Collected in Dugger, December 1971, from a 75-year-old male retiree. See note 111.

114. ISUFA. Collected in Bargersville, October 1968, from a 28-year-old male plumber. See note 111.

115. ISUFA. Collected in Terre Haute, March 1970, from an 87-year-old retiree. Randolph, p. 88, says, "Many hillfolk are interested in the search for lost mines and buried treasure, and some of these people have tried to use the witch stick in their quests. If a man is looking for buried gold, he fastens a gold ring to the end of his stick, if it is silver that he expects to find, he splits the end of the wand and inserts a silver coin. . . . Witch sticks thus equipped for treasure hunting are sometimes called 'doodlebugs'. . . ."

116. WPA. This tale from Posey County is a variant of a well-known migratory legend, with versions reported from Asia as well as from Europe. The motif is D702.1.1, "Cat's paw cut off: woman's hand missing." As in this Hoosier version, frequently a man spending a night in a mill cuts off a cat's paw and the next morning discovers the miller's wife has lost a hand. See F.A. de Caro, "The Witch Cat," *Indiana Folklore*, I: 1 (1968), 21–24.

117. WPA. This Knox County legend shows a witch in a familiar role as meddler in the dairy. The main motifs are D2084.2, "Butter magically kept from coming"; Baughman G271.4.1(k), "Breaking spell on cream that refuses to become butter by putting hot iron in the cream, thus burning the witch"; Baughman D2084.2(dd), "Hot iron put into churn"; and H56, "Recognition by wound."

118. WPA. This legend from Gibson County includes a number of familiar witch motifs, including D1385.4, "Silver bullet protects against giants, ghosts, and witches"; G221.3, "Witch has extraordinary bodily strength"; G241.3, "Witch rides on horse"; D2083.1, "Cows magically made dry"; Baughman D2083.3.1(h), "Witch transfers milk by squeezing or drawing on towel"; G211.1.7, "Witch in form of cat"; Baughman G275.12(bc), "Cat injured; witch shows same injury"; and

G263.4, "Witch causes sickness." A version of this tale in the ISU Folklore Archives was collected in Cannelburg, July 1969, from a 68-year-old male retiree.

119. ISUFA. Collected in Greensburg, April 1969, from a 47-year-old female owner of a nursing home. Motif D2083.2.1, "Witches make cows give bloody milk."

120. ISUFA. Collected in Dugger, November 1971, from a 59-year-old housewife. Motifs D2080, "Magic used against property," and G271.4, "Exorcism by use of sympathetic magic." Cf. Motif G257.1, "Burning object forces witch to reveal herself: sympathetic magic."

121. ISUFA. Collected in Jasper, March 1968, from a 67-year-old male laborer. Cf. Motif G265.8.1, "Witch bewitches household articles," and Baughman G257.1(e), "Burning cake stuck with pins forces witch to reveal herself."

122. ISUFA. Collected in Jasper, March 1968, from a 67-year-old male laborer. Motif G257.1, "Burning object forces witch to reveal herself: sympathetic magic." Cf. Motif G257.1(d), "Boiling needles and pins forces witch to reveal herself."

123. WPA. The style of this legend from Sullivan County is more literary than oral, but the text preserves familiar folklore motifs, especially Baughman G271.4.2(ba), "Shooting witch picture or symbol with silver bullet breaks spell," and G241.2, "Witch rides on person." Other motifs are G263.4, "Witch causes sickness" and G271.6, "Exorcism of the witch by countercharm."

124. WPA. This legend comes from Red Key in Jay County. A central motif in the story is G263.4, "Witch causes sickness," a common theme in British and American folklore. Other motifs include Baughman G265.11*, "Person or animal admired by witch becomes ill"; Baughman G263.4(a), "Witch causes victim to vomit foreign objects"; G271.6, "Exorcism of witch by countercharm"; Baughman G265.6.3(a), "Witch causes horse to balk"; G265.8.3.2, "Witch bewitches wagon"; E431.10.1, "Corpse buried under stones." Stones are placed on graves to prevent the return of the dead. Cf. Randolph, p. 228, and Motif G278.1, "Marvelous manifestations at death of witch."

125. WPA. The major motifs in this Miami County legend are G285, "Witches avoid religious ceremonies," and G278.1, "Marvelous manifestations at death of witch." The Bible sometimes is used in exorcism (Motif G271.2.5) or recognition (Motif G257.2) of witches. Other motifs suggested by the legend are G273.4, "Witch powerless to cross stream," and Baughman G265.5(b), "Witch maims horse."

126. WPA. This well-wrought text is from Shelby County. Seven

other supernatural legends from Shelby County are in the WPA
files, suggesting a rich belief tradition was once in this county.
Although this text is literary, the legend type is familiar in
American oral tradition, but it usually involves witches, not
fairies (see Christine Goldberg, "Traditional American Witch
Legends: A Catalog," *Indiana Folklore*, VII: 1/2 [1974], 91–
92). Motifs in the legend include F234.1.4.1, "Fairy in form of
doe" (Cf. G211.2.4 "Witch in form of deer"); D1385.4, "Silver
bullet protects against giants, ghosts, and witches"; D2086.2,
"Guns rendered ineffective by witch"; and H56, "Recognition
by wound."

127. WPA. This werewolf story (Motif D113.1.1) was collected from
an elderly French woman in Vincennes. Legends of the *loup
garou*, common among French-Americans and French-
Canadians, were brought to the New World from France. See
Paul Sebillot, *Le Folk-Lore de France* (Paris, 1904–1907), I,
284–285; II, 205, 206, 373, 437; III, 54–56; IV, 210, 240, 304;
Richard M. Dorson, *Bloodstoppers and Bearwalkers* (Cambridge, Mass., 1952), pp. 69 ff.; Paul A.W. Wallace, *Baptiste
Laroque, Legends of French Canada* (Toronto, 1923), pp.
42–46. Typically a *loup garou* is freed from his animal form by
cutting him. See Harold Thompson, *Body, Boots, and Britches*
(Philadelphia, 1940), pp. 115–116. Motifs D712.6, "Disenchantment by wounding," and D712.4, "Disenchantment by
drawing blood."

128. ISUFA. Collected in Princeton, May 1970, from a 41-year-old
male industrial engineer. Parking legends of this sort are not
uncommon in Indiana (cf. note 226). Often the monster is huge
with shaggy hair (Motif F531.1.1.6.3, "Giants with shaggy hair
on their bodies"), but sometimes it is rationalized and becomes
an animal, such as a panther. For other references to hairy
monsters resembling the Himalayan Yeti or Bigfoot, see James
P. Leary, "The Boondocks Monster of Camp Wapehani," *Indiana Folklore*, VI: 2 (1973), 188.

129. ISUFA. Collected in Evansville, April 1971, from a 40-year-old
male oil company representative. Motifs F401.3, "Spirit in
animal form," and F401.3.3.1, "Waumpaus: monster with huge
dog tracks."

130. ISUFA. Collected in Sullivan, January 1971, from a 75-year-old
male retired miner. Motifs B765.1, "Snake takes tail in mouth
and rolls like wheel"; B765.10, "Snake cracks self like coach
whip and chases man." Cf. Motif X1321.3.1, "Lie: hoop snake."

131. ISUFA. Collected in Terre Haute, March 1970, from a 74-
year-old male retired streetcar man and bus driver. Motif
B765.4, "Snake milks cows at night."

132. WPA. This story from New Albany is a variant of an international tale, Type 285, "The Child and the Snake." The central motif is B765.6, "Snake eats milk and bread with child." Motif F1041.1.1, "Death from broken heart," is found in some texts, and Motif E402.1.1.1, "Ghost calls," appears in this text. The story is No. 105 in the Grimm collection and has been given literary treatment by Charles Lamb. See Butler Huggins Waugh, Jr., "'The Child and the Snake,' Aarne-Thompson 285, 782C, and Related Forms in Europe and America: A Comparative Folklore Study," Diss. Indiana University 1959.

133. ISUFA. Collected in Vallonia, January 1972, from a 59-year-old housewife. See note 132.

134. ISUFA. Collected in Terre Haute, May 1970, from a 19-year-old male student. Motifs B875.3, "Giant turtle," and H1331, "Quest for remarkable animal." See John A. Gutowski, "The Protofestival: Local Guide to American Folk Behavior," *Journal of the Folklore Institute*, XV (May-August 1978), 113–132, for a discussion of this legend and related tall tales and how a popular festival was inspired by the Beast of Busco legend. For a fuller account, see John A. Gutowski, "American Folklore and the Modern American Community Festival: A Case Study of Turtle Days in Churubusco, Indiana," Diss. Indiana University 1977.

135. WPA. This Clark County legend seems to be a composite text based in part on written sources, but legends of Madoc can still be collected in Clark County. In April 1975 an 80-year-old female informant claimed she saw Welsh drawings of stick men with swords in a cave near the Ohio River when she was a young woman. Other informants in Charlestown said they had seen Welsh writing in caves near the Ohio, but they could not find the caves to show me the writings. John Filson, author of the first history of Kentucky in 1784, believed the legend and discussed it with several people while collecting materials for his book. See *Filson's Kentucke*, ed. Willard Rouse Jillson. The Filson Club Publications No. 35 (Louisville, 1930), pp. 94–98; Reuben T. Durrett, *Traditions of the Earliest Visits of Foreigners to North America*. The Filson Club Publications No. 23 (Louisville, 1908), pp. iii–xv, 17–69, 117–119, 124–134, 137–150; Richard Deacon, *Madoc and the Discovery of America* (New York, 1966).

136. ISUFA. Collected in Bargersville, January 1969, from an 81-year-old businessman. Other accounts (six from Allen County and one from Jay County) are in the WPA files. Also in the WPA files from Allen County are several affidavits attesting that Johnny Appleseed's grave is located on the W. S. Roebuck

farm, while others say the grave is in Archer Cemetery. A Johnny Appleseed Commission, appointed by the city of Fort Wayne, on the basis of an article published in the *Fort Wayne Sentinel* (October 21–23, 1871), decided on December 27, 1934, that "Johnny Appleseed was buried in the burying grounds of David Archer." See Richard M. Dorson, *American Folklore* (Chicago, 1959), pp. 232–236; Robert Price, *Johnny Appleseed, Man and Myth* (Bloomington, Ind., 1954); Robert Price, *John Chapman: A Bibliography of "Johnny Appleseed" in American History, Literature and Folklore* (Paterson, N.J., 1944).

137. WPA. This tale from Vigo County suggests Motif J910, "Humility of the great." As B.A. Botkin notes in *A Treasury of American Folklore* (New York, 1944), " . . . Lincoln was great because he was not afraid to be common" (p. 250).

138. ISUFA. Collected in Greencastle, August 1969, from an 81-year-old housewife. Pearl Bryan, a pregnant Greencastle girl, was murdered by her boyfriend, Scott Jackson, and his accomplice, Alonzo Walling. Her headless body was discovered on February 1, 1896, near Ft. Thomas, Kentucky, and she was buried in Greencastle. She is the subject of a popular American folk ballad. See G. Malcolm Laws, Jr., *Native American Balladry* (Philadelphia, 1964), pp. 192–193; Ann Scott Wilson, "Pearl Bryan," *Southern Folklore Quarterly*, 3 (1939), 15–19; and Anne B. Cohen, *Poor Pearl, Poor Girl!* (Austin, 1973).

139. ISUFA. Collected in Greencastle, November 1978, from a male informant, age and occupation withheld. See note 138.

140. WPA. This story of a headless revenant (Motif E422.1.1) comes from Morgan County. Other motifs in the legend are F422.4.3, "Ghost in white"; F91, "Will-o'-the-wisp"; Baughman E419.7.1*, "Ghost returned to search for head"; and E402.1.1.1, "Ghost calls." This legend is especially interesting because unlike the ballads of Pearl Bryan it deals with the headless ghost, a common legend theme. Since the tale involves Pearl Bryan, it is included in this section with the other tales of Pearl Bryan instead of with the other ghost legends, where it could have been included. See note 138.

141. ISUFA. Collected in Greencastle, December 1973, from a 20-year-old male student. See notes 138 and 140.

142. ISUFA. Collected in Bedford, February 1969, from a 20-year-old female office worker. See F.A. de Caro and Elliott Oring, "JFK is Alive: A Modern Legend," *Folklore Forum*, II (March 1969), 54–55, and "New Kennedy Lore," *Folklore Forum*, III (March 1970), 65, 71. The cover story of *The National Tatler*, July 11, 1971, exploited this legend.

143. ISUFA. Collected in Huntington, March 1972, from a 22-year-old male dairy worker. See note 142.

144. ISUFA. Collected in Dugger, January 1972, from a 68-year-old male retiree. Motifs W153, "Miserliness"; W115, "Slovenliness."

145. ISUFA. Collected in Diamond, November 1970, from an anonymous middle-aged male informant. Motifs W153, "Miserliness"; N511, "Treasure in ground."

146. ISUFA. Collected in August 1969 from an 18-year-old female student from Versailles. Motifs W153, "Miserliness"; W115, "Slovenliness." Two supernatural motifs are suggested: E538.2, "Ghostly rope of suicide appears," and G259.2, "Witch recognized by odor."

147. ISUFA. Collected in Terre Haute, March 1969, from a 25-year-old male student. Motifs W115, "Slovenliness"; N511, "Treasure in ground." Cf. Motif N511.1.8, "Treasure buried in chest, cask, kettle, or cannon barrel."

148. ISUFA. Collected in Sullivan, January 1972, from a 64-year-old housewife. The story of Pollie Barnett is well known in Sullivan and Greene counties. The main motif is H1385.2, "Quest for vanished daughter."

149. WPA. A motif in this tale from Blackford County is H1110, "Tedious tasks." Motifs suggested are F551, "Remarkable feet," and F1015, "Extraordinary occurrences connected with shoes."

150. WPA. The main motif in this legend from LaGrange County is W115, "Slovenliness."

151. ISUFA. Collected in Hammond, January 1972, from a 20-year-old female student. Although informants disagree about what urged Martin Piniak to become a hermit and live under a bridge, recurring motifs in his story are T211.5, "Man becomes a hermit after his wife's death," and T93.2, "Disappointed lover turns hermit." See Elena Bradunas, "An Urban Hermit," *Indiana Folklore*, X: 2 (1979), 159–163.

152. WPA. The WPA files include not only this text of "Diana of the Dunes" from Lake County but also similar accounts from Porter and LaPorte counties. The story of Diana is still popular in the area. Baughman F567.1, "Wild woman. Woman lives alone in woods like a beast."

153. ISUFA. Collected in Gary, December 1968, from a 20-year-old male student. Motif E422.1.11.2, "Revenant as face or head." See note 152.

154. WPA. This tale from Washington County includes Motif T93.2, "Disappointed lover turns hermit." See Warda Stevens Stout, "William Hazzard [sic]: The Story of an Irish Nobleman Who

Became Salem's Town Outcast," *The Salem Leader and the Salem Democrat*, February 26, 1969.

155. ISUFA. Collected in Mitchell, December 1967, from a 46-year-old optometrist. Motifs F610, "Remarkably strong man," and F624.4, "Strong man lifts plow." A Washington County informant said the reason the man was so strong was that he had "a double set of ribs."

156. ISUFA. Collected in Dugger, December 1971, from a 75-year-old male retired miner. Motif Q111.8, "Large quantity of land as reward." Cf. H1584.1, "Land measured according to amount within person's view."

157. ISUFA. Collected in Huntington, April 1972, from a 21-year-old male student. In Indiana, basketball is a tradition. Although the game is not folk, it takes on aspects of ritual for Hoosiers who play and observe the game, and players and coaches become folk heroes. In modern folklore, coaches frequently have items of clothing they feel are lucky and wear them every game. Cf. Motifs N135.3. "The luck-bringing shirt," and Z148, "Yellow a lucky color."

158. ISUFA. Collected in Terre Haute, July 1971, from a 76-year-old male retiree. Doc Cox was an herb doctor who allegedly discovered a cure for cancer. He is still remembered in Sullivan and Vigo counties. For more discussion of herb doctors, see Randolph, pp. 92–120. Cf. Motifs D1502.10, "Magic cure for cancer," and F950, "Marvelous cures."

159. ISUFA. Collected in Terre Haute, May 1971, from a 45-year-old male supervisor in a chemical plant. See note 158.

160. ISUFA. Collected in Terre Haute, December 1967, from a 20-year-old male student. Dr. Wheat shares qualities with other herb doctors (see note 158), but he also takes on characteristics of other local eccentrics since he was a disappointed lover who buried his money. See Motifs T93, "Fate of disappointed lover," and N511, "Treasure in ground."

161. WPA. In this tale from Pike County, the healer is a power doctor (see Randolph, pp. 121–161) as well as an herb doctor (see note 158). He is a power doctor because he uses charms (magico-religious healing) to combat illness caused by the Devil, but he also uses herbs and roots for curing (natural folk medicine). Some motifs in this legend are D1385.5, "Metal as defense against spirits"; D1385.7, "Magic circle averts sorcery"; and G303.16.19.15, "Devil cannot enter magic circle made to keep him out."

162. ISUFA. Collected in Dugger, December 1971, from a 59-year-old housewife. Jesse James is the most famous of Ameri-

ca's romantic outlaw heroes. This tale shows him in the typical
role of the good outlaw, a friend of the poor. While legends of
Jesse James are common, Jesse, like Sam Bass, a Hoosier train
robber who moved to Texas, is a ballad hero, too. See G. Malcolm Laws, Jr., *Native American Balladry* (Philadelphia,
1964), pp. 176–177; Richard M. Dorson, *American Folklore*
(Chicago, 1959), pp. 238–243; Homer Croy, *Jesse James Was
My Neighbor* (New York, 1949).

163. ISUFA. Collected in Terre Haute, April 1971, from a 47-year-
old male florist. See note 162.

164. ISUFA. Collected in Princeton, March 1969, from a 44-year-
old male garage owner. See note 162.

165. ISUFA. Collected in Seymour, April 1971, from an 80-year-old
housewife. Frank Reno was one of four outlaw Reno brothers
from Seymour. The Reno brothers, it's said, had the first organ-
ized gang in the United States and were the first train robbers.
On October 6, 1866, in Seymour, they took around $10,000
from the Ohio and Mississippi train. On December 11, 1868,
vigilantes broke into a New Albany jail, where Frank, William,
and Simeon Reno were being held, and hanged the three
brothers and another outlaw named Anderson. See Jeffrey
Schrink and Frances Schrink, "Hangman's Crossing," *Indiana
Folklore*, XI: 1 (1978), 87–97. In this text Frank Reno is the
noble bandit who helps the poor and unfortunate. See note
214.

166. ISUFA. Collected in Chesterton, August 1969, from a 20-
year-old female student. Unlike Frank Reno and John Dillinger, Al Capone is not a noble robber in Hoosier folklore, for
this informant calls Capone's activities "dirty dealings."

167. ISUFA. Collected in Ireland, August 1969, from a 21-year-old
male student. This text and the following one show Al Capone
in a familiar role—gambling and providing illegal booze during Prohibition.

168. ISUFA. Collected in Terre Haute, July 1969, from a 23-year-
old male student. See note 167.

169. ISUFA. Collected in Lyons, December 1970, from a 52-year-
old male store manager. Again, Capone is not the noble robber
protected by the people because they love him. In this tale
Capone's hideout is not revealed to the police out of Hoosiers'
"own good judgment for their safety."

170. ISUFA. Collected near Carbon, June 1971, from a 52-year-old
male farmer. John Dillinger, truly a noble robber in Hoosier
folklore, is discussed in the introduction. For more on Dillinger, see Robert Cromie and Joseph Pinkston, *Dillinger: A*

Short and Violent Life (New York, 1962), and Jay Robert Nash, *Bloodletters and Badmen: A Narrative Encyclopedia of American Criminals from the Pilgrims to the Present* (New York, 1973), pp. 159–178. For a discussion of the noble robber in international folklore, see Eric Hobsbawm, *Bandits* (n.p., 1969), Chapter 3. For an account of the "Robinhooding" of American outlaws, see Kent L. Steckmesser, "Robin Hood and the American Outlaw," *Journal of American Folklore*, 79 (April-June, 1966), 348–355.

171. ISUFA. Collected in Rockville, October 1970, from an anonymous male informant. See note 170.

172. ISUFA. Collected in Brazil, June 1971, from a 55-year-old male factory worker. See note 170.

173. ISUFA. Collected near Carbon, June 1971, from a 52-year-old male farmer. See note 170.

174. ISUFA. Collected in December 1978 from a 21-year-old male student from Montgomery. See note 170.

175. ISUFA. Collected in Indianapolis, January 1969, from a 43-year-old male welder. See note 170.

176. ISUFA. Collected in Rosedale, May 1969, from a 65-year-old male retiree. See note 170.

177. ISUFA. Collected near Carbon, June 1971, from a 52-year-old male farmer. See note 170.

178. ISUFA. Collected in Brazil, June 1971, from a 71-year-old male bartender. See note 170.

179. ISUFA. Collected in Brazil, June 1971, from a 28-year-old male bartender. Motifs S123, "Burial alive"; E334.2.1, "Ghost of murdered person haunts burial spot." See note 170.

180. ISUFA. Collected in Gary, May 1968, from a 21-year-old male student. Motif E587.6, "Ghosts walk at full moon." This text aptly shows how difficult it is to classify legends since it deals with a legendary hero, explains a place name, and includes a supernatural motif. See note 170.

181. ISUFA. Collected in Brazil, June 1971, from a 28-year-old male bartender. Motifs F547.3.1, "Long penis"; K2231, "Treacherous mistress." See note 170.

182. ISUFA. Collected in Terre Haute, July 1971, from a 23-year-old male salesclerk. Motif F547.3.1, "Long penis." See note 170.

183. ISUFA. Collected in Terre Haute, June 1971, from a 24-year-old female factory worker. See notes 170 and 182.

184. IUFA. Collected in Lebanon from a 70-year-old male owner of a trash removal service. Date of collection not recorded. For an attempt to prove that Dillinger is still alive, see Jay Robert Nash and Ron Offin, *Dillinger: Dead or Alive?* (Chicago, 1970).

185. IUFA. Collected in Lebanon from a 70-year-old male owner of a trash removal service. Date of collection not recorded. See notes 170 and 184.
186. ISUFA. Collected in LaPorte, May 1970, from an anonymous middle-aged male informant. Motifs 560, "Cruel spouse," and K2213, "Treacherous wife." Cf. Type 312, "The Giant-killer and his Dog (Bluebeard)." See Janet Langlois, "Belle Gunness, Lady Bluebeard: Community Legend as Metaphor," *Journal of the Folklore Institute*, XV (May-Aug. 1978), 147–160; Lillian de la Torre, *The Truth about Belle Gunness* (New York, 1955).
187. ISUFA. Collected in West Terre Haute, May 1968, from a 22-year-old male student. This text includes familiar motifs in the Blue Hole legends: F713.2, "Bottomless lakes"; N513, "Treasure hidden under the water"; and G308.2, "Water-monster." See Ronald L. Baker, "Legends about Lakes Named 'Blue Hole'," *Indiana Names*, I (Fall 1970), 50. In 1971 scuba divers from the Vigo County Sheriff's Department found that Blue Hole is not bottomless. It is only about 22 feet deep.
188. ISUFA. Collected in Terre Haute, November 1969, from a male informant, age and occupation withheld. See note 187.
189. ISUFA. Collected in Terre Haute, December 1968, from a 20-year-old male student. Cf. Motif B874, "Giant fish." See note 187.
190. ISUFA. Collected in Terre Haute, December 1968, from a 76-year-old male president of a coal company. See note 187.
191. ISUFA. Collected in Terre Haute, April 1968, from a 19-year-old female student. Motif E414, "Drowned person cannot rest in peace." See note 187.
192. ISUFA. Collected in Seymour, August 1969, from a 60-year-old traveling salesman. This tale begins like a typical bottomless lake legend (Motif F713.2, "Bottomless lakes") but ends with what seems to be a tall tale motif (Motif X1301, "Lie: the great fish"). On March 27, 1913, a work train moving over the Blue Hole trestle west of Washington during high waters actually fell into one body of water named Blue Hole when the trestle collapsed. Since Blue Hole is a common name for lakes throughout Indiana, it seems that the incident was localized in several areas. See *The Washington Times-Herald*, October 3, 1966. Cf. note 187.
193. ISUFA. Collected in Seymour, April 1971, from an 80-year-old housewife. See note 192.
194. ISUFA. Collected in Paoli, June 1971, from a 78-year-old male owner of a lumber company. Motif E713.2, "Bottomless lakes." Cf. notes 187 and 192. Half-moon, or Halfmoon, is a descriptive name.

195. WPA. This tale comes from Rush County. Along the southern Atlantic seaboard, hoosier is a derogatory name referring to someone who is "conspicuously rural and usually at an economic or educational or social disadvantage." See Raven I. McDavid, Jr., "Word Magic, or 'Would You Want Your Daughter to Marry a Hoosier?'" in *Dialects in Culture*, ed. William A. Kretzschmar, Jr. (University, Alabama, 1979), pp. 254–257.

196. ISUFA. Collected in Terre Haute, May 1968, from a 21-year-old female student. See note 195.

197. ISUFA. Collected in May 1971 from a 20-year-old male student from Indianapolis. See note 195.

198. ISUFA. Collected in Jasper, December 1970, from a male informant, age and occupation withheld. See note 195.

199. ISUFA. Collected in Terre Haute, May 1968, from a 21-year-old female student. See note 195.

200. ISUFA. Collected in Logansport, August 1969, from a 23-year-old male student. See note 195.

201. ISUFA. Collected in Indianapolis, December 1971, from a 25-year-old male student. See note 195.

202. ISUFA. Collected in Montezuma, April 1970, from a 55-year-old male undertaker. See note 195.

203. ISUFA. Collected in Mt. Vernon, April 1973, from a 73-year-old male insurance agent. See note 195.

204. ISUFA. Collected in Brazil, June 1971, from a 64-year-old female retiree. Alum Cave, a ghost town, was located about a mile northwest of Coalmont. Founded by the New Pittsburgh Coal and Coke Company around 1887, it was named for a local cave which was called Alum Cave because water from a spring in the cave tasted like salty alum water (WPA).

205. ISUFA. Collected in Etna Green, August 1968, from a 70-year-old female banker. This place legend preserves an ancient motif, S261, "Foundation sacrifice."

206. ISUFA. Collected in Cannelburg, July 1969, from a 69-year-old male retiree.

207. ISUFA. Collected in May 1967 from a 20-year-old female student from Jamestown.

208. ISUFA. Collected in Cayuga, December 1967, from a male informant, age and occupation withheld.

209. ISUFA. Collected in Worthington, January 1969, from a 63-year-old male bank president. Devil place names in the United States do not always reflect belief in the Devil or a devil. Usually they are derogatory names suggesting rough, treacherous, impassable, or unproductive terrain.

210. ISUFA. Collected in Terre Haute, May 1970, from a 19-year-

old male student. Motifs E274, "Gallows ghost," and E421.1.2, "Ghost visible to horses alone."

211. ISUFA. Collected in Mishawaka, March 1970, from a 22-year-old male student. Elkhart was named for the Elkhart River. Elkhart is a literal translation of the Potawatomi name of the stream and is descriptive of an island resembling an elk's heart at the mouth of the river. Mishawaka also is a Potawatomi name, meaning "country of dead trees," descriptive of a tract of dead timber there.

212. ISUFA. Collected in Paoli, June 1971, from a 51-year-old female teacher. Cf. Motifs F91, "Door (gate) entrance to lower world"; D933, "Magic sink hole."

213. ISUFA. Collected in August 1969 from an 18-year-old female student from Versailles.

214. ISUFA. Collected in Seymour, August 1969, from a 22-year-old male student. Actually, three of the Reno brothers were hanged in New Albany, not in Seymour, on December 11, 1868. The fourth criminal brother, John Reno, died of old age. Three members of the Reno gang, however, were hanged by vigilantes at Hangman's Crossing on July 20, 1868. See note 165 and Jeffrey Schrink and Frances Schrink, "Hangman's Crossing," *Indiana Folklore*, XI: 1 (1978), 87–97.

215. WPA. This text is from Franklin County. According to George R. Stewart in *American Place Names* (New York, 1970), pp. 202–203, Hell was a common derogatory place name on the American frontier.

216. ISUFA. Collected in Hobart, May 1972, from a 21-year-old female student. Hobart, founded in 1849, was named for Hobart Earle, brother of the founder.

217. ISUFA. Collected in Farmersburg, August 1969, from a 33-year-old male student. Versions of this text appear in Thomas J. Wolfe, ed., *A History of Sullivan County, Indiana* (New York, 1909), I, 209; and *A Guide to the Hoosier State*, American Guide Series (New York, 1941), p. 489. Hymera probably is a classical place name. Founded in 648 B.C., Himera was an ancient city on the northern coast of Sicily. See Ronald L. Baker, "The Role of Folk Legends in Place-Name Research," *Journal of American Folklore*, 85 (October-December 1972), 369–370; and Ronald L. Baker, "Legends about the Naming of Hymera, Indiana," *Indiana Names*, IV (Fall 1973), 62–63.

218. ISUFA. Collected in Shelburn, May 1968, from a 21-year-old female student. See note 217.

219. ISUFA. Collected in Terre Haute, December 1968, from a 68-year-old housewife. Motif F800, "Extraordinary rocks and stones." Cf. Motif F721.4, "Underground treasure chambers."

220. ISUFA. Collected in Stinesville, December 1970, from a female informant, age and occupation withheld. See Richard Sweterlitsch, "Jack's Defeat and His Creek," *Indiana Folklore*, V: 1 (1972), 1–30.

221. ISUFA. Collected in Jasper, December 1970, from a male informant, age and occupation withheld. Although Jasper as a place name usually comes from a personal name, it is generally held that the name for the Hoosier city was selected from the Bible. Another account in the ISU Folklore Archives— collected in Jasper, May 1970, from a 24-year-old female hairdresser—runs: "Jasper was named when some ol' lady opened the Bible and put her finger on the word *jasper*. She was the oldest in the community, so she got the honor of naming the town." Cf. Motif D1311.14, "Divination from sacred books."

222. ISUFA. Collected in Kokomo, May 1971, from a 43-year-old female teller. Kokomo was named for a Miami Indian, Kokama, "The Diver."

223. ISUFA. Collected in April 1971 from a 65-year-old male retired teacher from Hope. Lick Skillet, or Lickskillet, was a derogatory unofficial name for several American communities.

224. ISUFA. Collected in July 1969 from a 20-year-old female student from Loogootee. Loogootee was founded in 1853 by Thomas Gootee. The name was coined from Lowe, the name of an engineer of the first train through town, and Gootee, the name of the founder.

225. ISUFA. Collected in Terre Haute, October 1969, from an 18-year-old female student. For various accounts of the naming of Mecca, see Robert M. Rennick, "The Folklore of Place-Naming in Indiana," *Indiana Folklore*, III: 1 (1970), 63–65.

226. ISUFA. Collected in Blanford, April 1968, from a 22-year-old male student. Motifs F531.1.1.6.3, "Giants with shaggy hair on their bodies," and D1840.3, "Magic invulnerability of ogres." For a discussion of this legend, see Ronald L. Baker, "'Monsterville': A Traditional Place-Name and Its Legends," *Names*, 20 (September 1972), 186–192. Cf. note 128.

227. ISUFA. Collected in Montezuma, April 1970, from a 55-year-old male undertaker. Montezuma, settled in 1821, was named for the Aztec emperor.

228. ISUFA. Collected in November 1969 from a 19-year-old female student from Seymour. Informal names often serve as a better index of culture than official names. Names like Nigger Hill, Nigger Hole, and Nigger Run sometimes preserve prejudices against blacks, for example. In variants of this legend,

though, the white informants generally are sympathetic toward the blacks allegedly hanged, for the injustice is emphasized. See Ronald L. Baker, "The Role of Folk Legends in Place-Name Research," *Journal of American Folklore*, 85 (October-December 1972), 372. Motifs E274, "Gallows ghost," and E402.1.1.3, "Ghost cries and screams."

229. ISUFA. Collected in Noblesville, December 1967, from a 58-year-old housewife. Founded in 1823, Noblesville apparently was named for the first U.S. Senator from Indiana, James Noble.

230. WPA. This is one of the few texts from the WPA Files with the name of the informant and the exact date of collection, February 15, 1936. The WPA collector notes that this account "is from the lips of the pioneers themselves" and cites specifically a Mrs. Newton, "a young matron during these early times," as the informant. Although the legend is commonly accepted, Orland probably is a transfer name.

231. ISUFA. Collected in Terre Haute, March 1967, from an 83-year-old housewife. Wyoming and New Mexico have communities called Pie Town, too.

232. ISUFA. Collected in Terre Haute, January 1972, from a 26-year-old female medical technician. This text is about Pinhook in Lawrence County, but at least six Hoosier communities have been called Pinhook. Although the name seems descriptive of twists in a road or bends in a stream, varied legends have arisen to explain the name. For a discussion of the several communities called Pinhook and legends about the naming of each, see Robert M. Rennick, "The Folklore of Place-Naming in Indiana," *Indiana Folklore*, III: 1 (1970), 79–81.

233. ISUFA. Collected in Paoli, November 1972, from an 82-year-old male newspaper editor. This Pumpkin Center is in Orange County, but there is another community with the same name in Washington County. George R. Stewart, in *American Place-Names* (New York, 1970), p. 390, cites only one Pumpkin Center, and it is in South Dakota. He suggests the name is "a humorous name for a small community, with the word used in the derogatory sense to denote a place excessively rural and isolated."

234. ISUFA. Collected in August 1968 from a 19-year-old male student from Dale. Santa Claus is one of the most celebrated place names in Indiana. When the community was founded in 1846, Santa Fe was the suggested name; however, there already was a Santa Fe in Indiana, so Santa Claus was a humorous substitute.

235. ISUFA. Collected in Freelandville, April 1972, from a 75-year-old housewife. According to George R. Stewart, *American Place-Names* (New York, 1970), p. 437, Shake Rag is widely used as a "rural derogatory," but the origin of the name is unknown.

236. ISUFA. Collected in Crawfordsville, April 1967, from a 20-year-old male student. Cf. Motif E421.3, "Luminous ghosts." This tale of a ghost haunting a parking spot is a typical adolescent legend.

237. ISUFA. Collected in Bloomington, May 1972, from a 72-year-old male retiree. Founded about 1840, Tampico probably was named for the Mexican seaport.

238. ISUFA. Collected in West Terre Haute, March 1972, from a 27-year-old male laborer. Tecumseh, a famous Shawnee chief, is commemorated in this Hoosier place name. Sometimes Tecumseh's name is translated "Shooting Star," but literally it means "going across" or "crossing over," which apparently refers to a meteor crossing the sky.

239. ISUFA. Collected in West Terre Haute, August 1969, from a 76-year-old housewife. This probably is a derogatory place name suggesting a small, rurally isolated community. Toad Hop is in Vigo County west of Terre Haute. Another version of the naming of Toad Hop is reported in Robert M. Rennick, "The Folklore of Place-Naming in Indiana," *Indiana Folklore*, III: 1 (1970), 53.

240. ISUFA. Collected in May 1969 from a 21-year-old female student from Jamestown. Thorntown is a translation of the name of an Indian village there. The Indian name was Kawiakiungi, "Place of Thorns."

241. ISUFA. Collected in Guilford, December 1968, from a 63-year-old male farmer. Cf. Motif F628.1.1.4, "Strong man kills bear."

242. ISUFA. Collected in Shelburn, May 1968, from a 21-year-old female secretary. A journalistic treatment of this very popular migratory legend (Motif E332.3.3.1, "The Vanishing Hitchhiker") is in the WPA Files from Johnson County. Although the WPA text is not traditional in style, it is interesting because it shows that the story was spread by mass media—radio and newspaper, in this case—even before the use of the legend in popular song, television drama, and short story. For discussion of "The Vanishing Hitchhiker" and related tales, see Richard K. Beardsely and Rosalie Hankey, "The Vanishing Hitchhiker," *California Folklore Quarterly*, 1 (1942), 305–335; Richard K. Beardsley and Rosalie Hankey, "A History of the

Vanishing Hitchhiker," *California Folklore Quarterly*, 2 (1943), 13–25; William B. Edgerton, "The Ghost in Search of Help for a Dying Man," *Journal of the Folklore Institute*, 5 (1968), 31–41; Louis C. Jones, "Hitchhiking Ghosts in New York," *California Folklore Quarterly*, 3 (1944), 284–292; Philip Brandt George, "The Ghost of Cline Avenue: 'La Llorna' in the Calumet Region," *Indiana Folklore*, V: 1 (1972), 56–91; Katharine Luomala, "Disintegration and Regeneration, the Hawaiian Phantom Hitchhiker Legend," *Fabula*, 13 (1972), 20–59; William A. Wilson, "The Vanishing Hitchhiker among the Mormons," *Indiana Folklore*, VIII: 1/2 (1975), 80–97; Lydia M. Fish, "Jesus on the Thruway: The Vanishing Hitchhiker Strikes Again," *Indiana Folklore*, IX: 1 (1976), 5–13. See note 39.

243. ISUFA. Collected in Sullivan, March 1972, from a 27-year-old male clerk. See Richard M. Dorson, *American Folklore*, (Chicago, 1959), pp. 250–251, for variants of this legend going back to 1944.

244. ISUFA. Collected in March 1970 from a 21-year-old female student from Dana. See note 243.

245. ISUFA. Collected in Terre Haute, November 1968, from a 22-year-old male student. See note 243.

246. ISUFA. Collected in Sullivan, January 1972, from a 64-year-old housewife. See note 243.

247. ISUFA. Collected in Dugger, November 1968, from a 54-year-old male insurance agent. See Carlos Drake, "The Killer in the Back Seat," *Indiana Folklore*, I: 1 (1968), 107–109; Xenia E. Cord, "Further Notes on 'The Assailant in the Back Seat,'" *Indiana Folklore*, II: 2 (1969), 47–54.

248. ISUFA. Collected in Terre Haute, March 1968, from a 20-year-old female student. See note 247.

249. ISUFA. Collected in Terre Haute, May 1970, from an 18-year-old male student. Jan Harold Brunvand, in "Urban Legends: Folklore for Today," *Psychology Today*, June 1980, p. 55, calls this tale "The Solid Cement Cadillac."

250. ISUFA. Collected in Fowler, December 1971, from a 20-year-old female student. See note 249.

251. ISUFA. Collected in Mooresville, December 1968, from a 17-year-old female student. Another Gravity Hill is located near South Bend (see text 252). At Lake Wales, Florida, a motorist can park his or her car at the bottom of "Spook Hill," shift to neutral and turn off the engine, and feel the car move up the hill, too. See Ronald L. Baker, "The Influence of Mass Culture on Modern Legends," *Southern Folklore Quarterly*, 40 (1976), 368–369.

252. ISUFA. Collected in South Bend, January 1969, from a 21-year-old male student. See note 251.
253. ISUFA. Collected in Brazil, May 1972, from a 21-year-old female student. This parking story has been one of the most popular modern legends. See Linda Dégh, "The Hook," *Indiana Folklore*, I: 1 (1968), 92–100; Kenneth A. Thigpen, Jr., "Adolescent Legends in Brown County: A Survey," *Indiana Folklore*, IV: 2 (1971), 183–186.
254. ISUFA. Collected in May 1968 from a 23-year-old male student from Merrillville. This parking legend is as popular as "Hook Man." See Linda Dégh, "The Boy Friend's Death," *Indiana Folklore*, I: 1 (1968), 101–106; Kenneth A. Thigpen, Jr., "Adolescent Legends in Brown County: A Survey," *Indiana Folklore*, IV: 2 (1971), 174–177.
255. ISUFA. Collected in November 1968 from a 20-year-old male student from Hammond. See note 254.
256. ISUFA. Collected in Terre Haute, July 1969, from a 19-year-old female student. Cf. Motif E425.1.4, "Revenant as woman carrying baby."
257. ISUFA. Collected in West Terre Haute, May 1968, from a 20-year-old female student. Familiar motifs of belief in life after death (Motif V311), reincarnation (Motif E600), and fear of live burial (Motif S123) are found in versions of this legend. See Ronald L. Baker, "The Phone in the Mausoleum: A Local Legend," *Midwestern Journal of Language and Folklore*, IV (Fall 1978), 70–76.
258. ISUFA. Collected in Terre Haute, July 1969, from a 64-year-old female retired telephone operator. See note 257.
259. ISUFA. Collected in May 1970 from a 20-year-old male student from Columbus. This is one of several modern legends about a baby-sitter. Another popular one is "The Hippie Baby-Sitter," sometimes called "The Grilled Baby," which tells of a sitter who gets high on drugs and roasts a baby instead of a turkey. For another version of "The Baby-Sitter and the Phone Call," see Sylvia Grider, "Dormitory Legend-Telling in Progress: Fall, 1971-Winter, 1973," *Indiana Folklore*, VI: 1 (1973), 6–7. For a version of "The Hippie Baby-Sitter," see Jan Harold Brunvand, "Urban Legends: Folklore for Today," *Psychology Today*, June 1980, p. 55.
260. ISUFA. Collected in Terre Haute, December 1967, from a 47-year-old housewife. Jan Harold Brunvand gives a version of this legend in "Urban Legends" Folklore for Today," *Psychology Today*, June 1980, p. 59. This legend was used in the movie "With Six you Get an Egg Roll." In Dan and Inez Mor-

ris, *The Weekend Camper* (Indianapolis and New York, 1973),
pp. ix–xii, the legend is reported as "A True Story."

261. ISUFA. Collected in August 1969 from a 21-year-old female
student from Rockville. This migratory legend is discussed by
Linda Dégh in "The Runaway Grandmother," *Indiana
Folklore*, I: 1 (1968), 68–77. Also see Charles Clay Doyle,
"Roaming Cannibals and Vanishing Corpses," *Indiana
Folklore*, XI: 2 (1978), 133–139.

262. ISUFA. Collected in December 1967 from a 21-year-old male
student from Clinton. This tale appears to be related to "The
Roommate's Death" (see note 278), although "The Licked
Hand" is not as popular as "The Roommate's Death" and lacks
the college setting.

263. ISUFA. Collected in December 1967 from a 22-year-old male
student from Brazil. For a discussion of the subtypes of this
legend, see William Hugh Jansen, "The Surpriser Surprised: A
Modern Legend," in *Readings in American Folklore*, ed. Jan
Harold Brunvand (New York, 1979), pp. 64–90.

264. ISUFA. Collected in November 1972 from a 20-year-old
female student from Rushville. A version of this text and other
modern legends are in George Carey, "Some Thoughts on the
Modern Legend," *Journal of the Folklore Society of Greater
Washington*, II (Winter 1970–71), 3–10. For related legends,
see Susan Domowitz, "Foreign Matter in Food: A Legend
Type," *Indiana Folklore*, XII: 1 (1979), 86–95.

265. ISUFA. Collected in September 1972 from an 18-year-old
female student from Tipton. See note 264.

266. ISUFA. Collected in December 1972 from a 20-year-old male
student from Clinton. See note 264.

267. ISUFA. Collected in October 1972 from a 20-year-old female
student from Rushville. See note 264.

268. ISUFA. Collected in West Terre Haute, May 1969, from a 22-
year-old female student. Cf. Susan Domowitz, "Foreign Matter
in Food: A Legend Type," *Indiana Folklore*, XII: 1 (1979),
86–95.

269. ISUFA. Collected in Lewis, November 1971, from a 61-year-
old male farmer. Cf. note 264.

270. ISUFA. Collected in November 1972 from a 20-year-old
female student from Covington. Cf. note 264.

271. ISUFA. Collected in Terre Haute, November 1971, from a 20-
year-old female student. See Xenia E. Cord, "Department
Store Snakes," *Indiana Folklore*, II: 1 (1969), 110–114.

272. ISUFA. Collected in Brazil, April 1970, from a 22-year-old
female student. For an analysis of this legend and its relation

to other forms of folklore, such as the ballad "Sir Hugh, or the Jew's Daughter" (Child 155), see Barre Toelken, *The Dynamics of Folklore* (Boston, 1979), pp. 176–179, 272–273.

273. ISUFA. Collected in Terre Haute, December 1971, from a 21-year-old female student. See note 272.

274. ISUFA. Collected in Terre Haute, February 1970, from a 47-year-old female teacher. See J. Russell Reaver, "Embalmed Alive: A Developing Urban Ghost Tale," *New York Folklore Quarterly*, VIII (Autumn 1952), 217–220.

275. ISUFA. Collected in Jasper, December 1970, from a female informant, age and occupation withheld. See note 274.

276. ISUFA. Collected in Hammond, December 1969, from a 20-year-old housewife. Motif N384.0.1.1, "The cadaver arm."

277. ISUFA. Collected in Kokomo, March 1969, from a 22-year-old enlisted man in the U.S. Air Force. See note 276.

278. ISUFA. Collected in May 1968 from a 20-year-old female student from Hammond. See Linda Dégh, "The Roommate's Death and Related Dormitory Stories in Formation," *Indiana Folklore*, II: 2 (1969), 55–74; Sylvia Grider, "Dormitory Legend-Telling in Progress: Fall, 1971-Winter, 1973," *Indiana Folklore*, VI: 1 (1973), 1–32.

279. ISUFA. Collected in Bloomington, March 1969, from a 21-year-old male student. See note 278.

280. ISUFA. Collected in Terre Haute, December 1970, from a 20-year-old female student. See note 278.

281. ISUFA. Collected in Terre Haute, December 1967, from a 19-year-old female student. Motif E402, "Mysterious ghostlike noises heard." Cf. James Gary Lecocq, "The Ghost of the Doctor and a Vacant Fraternity House," *Indiana Folklore*, VI: 2 (1973), 191–204, for texts of a noisy ghost on the Indiana University campus.

282. ISUFA. Collected in Terre Haute, April 1968, from a 21-year-old female student. See note 281.

283. ISUFA. Collected in Terre Haute, December 1970, from a 20-year-old female student. See note 281.

284. ISUFA. Collected in Terre Haute, August 1969, from a 20-year-old female student. Cf. text 285.

285. ISUFA. Collected in Terre Haute, May 1969, from a 21-year-old female student. Cf. text 284.

286. ISUFA. Collected in Bloomington, February 1970, from a 21-year-old female student. In the days of panty raids, the Bird Man became something of a local hero on the Indiana University campus.

287. ISUFA. Collected in Bloomington, February 1970, from a 22-year-old female student. See note 286.

288. ISUFA. Collected in Columbus, March 1970, from a 21-year-old male student. See note 286.
289. ISUFA. Collected in March 1969 from a 22-year-old female student from Princeton. This ubiquitous legend is mentioned by Jan Harold Brunvand in *The Study of American Folklore: An Introduction* (New York), p. 111, and in Appendix B of the same book by Barre Toelken, p. 277. For a version from Maryland, see George Carey, "Some Thoughts on the Modern Legend," *Journal of the Folklore Society of Greater Washington,*" II (Winter 1970–71), 8–9. For other versions from Indiana, see Kenneth Clarke, "The Fatal Hairdo and the Emperor's New Clothes Revisited," *Western Folklore*, XXII (1964), 249–252.
290. ISUFA. Collected in February 1969 from a 21-year-old female student from Kokomo. See note 289.
291. ISUFA. Collected in December 1968 from a 20-year-old female student from Evansville. See note 289.
292. ISUFA. Collected in Terre Haute, February 1969, from a 22-year-old female student. See note 289.
293. ISUFA. Collected in August 1969 from a 21-year-old female student from Clinton.
294. ISUFA. Collected in July 1969 from a 20-year-old female student from Clinton. For a version of this legend and discussion of other modern diet folklore, see Elizabeth Tucker, "The Seven-Day Wonder Diet: Magic and Ritual in Diet Folklore," *Indiana Folklore*, XI: 2 (1978), 141–150.
295. ISUFA. Collected in Terre Haute, January 1970, from a 16-year-old male student. Motifs E422.1.1, "Headless revenant," and E599.7, "Ghost carries lantern." For contemporary druglore, see Richard M. Dorson, *America in Legend: Folklore from the Colonial Period to the Present* (New York, 1973), pp. 260–310.
296. ISUFA. Collected in Sullivan, October 1968, from a 27-year-old male student. For a version of this legend that was reported in the *New York Times*, see Ronald L. Baker, "The Influence of Mass Culture on Modern Legends," *Southern Folklore Quarterly*, 40 (1976), 374–375. This legend also was used in the film "Smokey and the Bandit."
297. ISUFA. Collected in Linton, November 1969, from a housewife, age withheld.
298. ISUFA. Collected in April 1969 from a 21-year-old male student from South Bend. Richard M. Dorson collected versions of this tale in Gary in 1975–76.
299. ISUFA. Collected in Terre Haute, January 1972, from a 25-year-old male extension agent. See Virginia A.P. Lowe, "A

Brief Look at Some UFO Legends," *Indiana Folklore*, XII: 1 (1979), 67–85. Also see the selected bibliography on UFO's in the editorial note preceding Lowe's article on pp. 65–66.

300. ISUFA. Collected in Terre Haute, December 1967, from a 32-year-old female office manager. See note 299.

301. ISUFA. Collected in April 1968 from a 21-year-old male student from Indianapolis, See note 299.

302. ISUFA. Collected in November 1968 from a 20-year-old male student from Washington. See note 299.

303. ISUFA. Collected in March 1968 from a 21-year-old male student from Frankfort. See note 299.

304. ISUFA. Collected in Dugger, January 1972, from a 59-year-old housewife. See note 297.

305. ISUFA. Collected in April 1970 from a 20-year-old female student from Shoals. See note 299.